Equity and Inclusion in Physical Education and Sport

D0550537

The new statutory requirements for Physical Education (PE) in schools emphasise the importance of equity and inclusion and the responsibilities of teachers to provide programmes of study that incorporate pupils of both genders, all social backgrounds and ethnic groups, and those with special educational needs and disabilities.

Equity and Inclusion in PE and Sport examines the National Curriculum for PE (NCPE 2000) and looks at the range of social inclusion challenges faced by practitioners today. The book is structured around the key issues of social class, race and ethnicity, gender, sexuality, special needs, disability, and ability. These issues are discussed in relation to the principles of equity, equality of opportunity, pedagogy, curriculum planning and cultural awareness.

This text provides valuable advice for established professionals, newly qualified teachers, and trainees about how to meet equity and inclusion requirements. Examples of good practice are provided as well as ideas for how to implement an inclusive PE curriculum.

Sid Hayes is a former secondary school head of Physical Education. He is currently a senior lecturer in PE at the University of Brighton's Chelsea School.

Gary Stidder has over thirteen years of secondary school teaching experience in England and the USA. He is also presently a senior lecturer in PE at the University of Brighton.

Equity and Inclusion in Physical Education and Sport

Contemporary issues for teachers, trainees and practitioners

Edited by
Sid Hayes and Gary Stidder

Routledge
Taylor & Francis Group

LONDON AND NEW YORK

First published 2003 by Routledge
2 Park Square, Milton Park, Abingdon, Oxon OX14 4RN

Simultaneously published in the USA and Canada
by Routledge
270 Madison Ave, New York, NY 10016

Routledge is an imprint of the Taylor & Francis Group

Transferred to Digital Printing 2004

© 2003 Sid Hayes and Gary Stidder for selection and
editorial matter, individual chapters; the contributors

The right of Sid Hayes and Gary Stidder to be identified as the
Authors of this Work has been asserted by them in accordance
with the Copyright, Designs and Patents Act 1988

Typeset in Sabon by
Florence Production Ltd, Stoodleigh, Devon
Printed and bound in Great Britain by
TJI Digital, Padstow, Cornwall

British Library Cataloguing in Publication Data
A catalogue record for this book is available
from the British Library

Library of Congress Cataloging in Publication Data
A catalog record for this book has been requested

ISBN 0–415–28225–X (hbk)
ISBN 0–415–28226–8 (pbk)

Contents

'Picking Teams'

When we pick teams in the playground,
Whatever the game may be,
There's always somebody left till last
And usually it's me.

I stand there looking hopeful
And tapping myself on the chest,
But the captains pick the others first,
Starting, of course, with the best.

Maybe if teams were sometimes picked
Starting with the worst,
Once in his life a child like me
Could end up being first !!

A. Ahlberg (1983) *Please Mrs Butler*, Kestrel Books,
Harmondsworth: Penguin Books Ltd: 35.

Figures

Tables

Contributors

Dr Gill Clarke Senior lecturer in the Faculty of Educational Studies, University of Southampton. Extensive international research portfolio and publications in the area of PE, sport and sexual difference.

Sid Hayes Senior lecturer in PE at the University of Brighton. Former secondary school Head of Physical Education. Areas of academic interest include mentoring, ethnicity, teacher training and special educational needs.

Dr Marc Keech Senior lecturer in Sport and Leisure Studies at the University of Brighton who has an extensive research publication record. Sports Council member for the region of Sussex. Currently engaged in education, training and research with sports development practitioners and recently co-edited *Issues and Values in Sport and Leisure Cultures* (Aachen: Meyer and Meyer).

Saul Keyworth Former graduate from the Chelsea School, University of Brighton. Senior lecturer in dance studies at De Montford University, UK. Areas of academic interest include dance education and pedagogy.

Dr Gill Lines Senior lecturer at the University of Brighton. Former secondary school Head of PE. Course Leader in Leisure Studies degree and has numerous publications in the area of gender and media studies.

Ian McDonald Senior lecturer in the sociology of sport at the University of Brighton and has published widely in the areas of politics and policy in sport. Co-editor of *Race, Sport and British Society* (Routledge: Taylor & Francis).

Fiona Smith Senior lecturer and pathway co-ordinator for postgraduate dance at the University of Brighton and has a number of publications in dance education. Co-ordinator of the 'Kickstart' male dance team at Brighton University.

Gary Stidder   Senior lecturer in PE at the University of Brighton. Thirteen years of secondary school PE teaching experience in England and the USA. Former Assistant Head of a secondary school PE faculty. Areas of academic interest include gender issues in PE, accreditation, teacher training and mentoring.

Professor John Sugden   Professor in the Sociology of Sport and Deputy Head of the Chelsea School, University of Brighton. He has published widely in the political sociology of sport and has won national and international awards for his investigative research.

Andrew Theodoulides   Senior lecturer in PE and pathway co-ordinator for postgraduate PE at the University of Brighton. Former Head of PE at a London secondary school. Areas of academic interest include personal and social education and teacher training.

Philip Vickerman   Senior lecturer in the School of Physical Education, Sport and Dance at Liverpool John Moores University. Areas of academic interest include special education in PE and teacher training.

James Wallis   Senior lecturer in PE at the University of Brighton's Chelsea School. Former secondary school PE teacher and college lecturer. Areas of academic interest include sport psychology and curriculum development.

Alan Whetherly   Regional Development Manager for The English Federation of Disability Sport (South East) and former Paralympian.

Foreword

Everybody remembers something about their Physical Education (PE) lessons at school, and in the genre of the memoir the PE teacher is an unforgettable presence, for both those who loved their PE, and those who did all they could to get out of these lessons. The author Salman Rushdie, on BBC Radio 4's gentle confessional show *Desert Island Discs*, recalled how life as a precocious, black intellectual was difficult enough at one of England's most elite public schools. Being clever and difficult was tough enough. But even worse, he was bad at games.

No-one who ever saw the football lesson scene in the film *Kes* could forget the bullying, crude and selfish model of the games teacher who brushed aside scraggy boys in his personal fantasy of being the top football star of the day. At my own grammar school in the 1960s the PE lesson was simple. The best boys played a football game against each other. You might combine the best defence with the second best attack, or vice versa, in a mix of trialling and coaching. Those who didn't make it into either of these line-ups were tossed a worn-out casey (a leather football, flaking and battered), and dispatched to the swamp in the corner of the playing fields with the unforgettable command 'Remnants over there'. We were not permitted to play against the local secondary-modern school or technical high school and could not compete in the town's cup, whose final was played at Turf Moor, the ground of Burnley Football Club, league champions of the English football league and European trailblazers of the day.

Instead, we travelled around the county to other grammar schools, on round trips of up to 160 miles, in a comical parody of public school networking. In one game of a particularly competitive nature I conceded a free kick and the teacher-in-charge (who might be the physics teacher or the science master – the status of running the school side was often considered too precious to give to the lowly PE master) commented that it was 'the worst foul I've ever seen in schoolboy football'. He'd barked this, but then he smiled: 'Well done Tomlinson. That showed them.' So much for the character-building virtues of team sports and the school PE lesson.

One of the legendary PE teachers of my grammar school days was known for two things. Not the sophistication of his lesson plans. Not even his smile as he forced boys to heave themselves up the rope to the roof of the gym, thighs reddening on each tortuous pull. He was a minor celebrity, as son of the local Member of Parliament. And he was sunburnt every summer term, stripped down to his shorts for much of the day and lazing on the edge of the playing field. Mr Jones wouldn't have liked this book, encouraging as it does personal reflection about one's professional role, and a contextual awareness of the social, cultural and political influences that shape school-based Physical Education.

This valuable collection does several things, and trainees in Physical Education, as well as physical educationists in schools, colleges and universities have much to gain from its contents. On one level it is a professional manual, cataloguing the government educational policy of the day, or of pretty recent days. You'll learn here how Mr Jones and his colleagues could scarcely have survived in a contemporary professional world of accreditation, examination, and curriculum development and monitoring. And you'll be reminded how recurrently the Physical Education lesson has been claimed as a source of moralising – even the radical interventions proposed by some of the contributors to *Equity and Inclusion in Physical Education and Sport* are based upon a sense that work on the body has ideological repercussions way beyond the games field or the gym. At the heart of the book there is a plea for and exemplification of professional reflection, and an associated reflexivity that could transform practice.

Authors have been encouraged to excavate their own professional biographies, to break out of the personal passions (usually for sport in its most conventional sense) that drew them into the professional world of Physical Education, and to rethink what the very basis of the professional role might be. It is fascinating to read focused analyses of professional issues fuelled by such a degree of reflection, linked to debates about critical policy themes of the day such as the driving theme of the book, that elusive and all-embracing notion of social inclusion. And finally, this is a contribution to professional thinking and development that confirms the importance of evidence-based scholarship to the field. It champions the value of professionally rooted, modestly conceived but analytically focused, research for professional development.

Most authors have been members of or work in the Chelsea School at the University of Brighton. Since the end of the nineteenth century the Chelsea School has trained generations of physical educationists, and engaged in national and international debate about the values of the profession and the nature of its intensifying professionalisation. I feel both pleased and proud to have been asked to write the foreword for a book that reaffirms the place of Physical Education scholarship in the wider professional and research profile of the Chelsea School.

Professor Alan Tomlinson
Head of Chelsea School Research Centre, University of Brighton
February 2003

Acknowledgements

We would like to acknowledge the help, support, advice and encouragement provided by: Professor John Sugden, Professor Alan Tomlinson and in particular the contribution of Frances Powney whose continued expertise has been invaluable. We also wish to thank Paul McNaught-Davis, Head of Chelsea School, for his encouragement in pursuing this venture.

An edited book is dependent on its contributors and to this end we would like to thank all of the authors for their chapters.

Personally

Gary Stidder would like to thank close friends and family, especially Karen, for continuing to take an interest in the progress of the book. Also, to Eliot, Devin, Keegan and Daniel for providing the inspiration.

Sid Hayes would like to thank friends, family and colleagues, especially Steve Jackson, Mike Fury, Yvonne Jeffries – hopefully they know why. A special thank you, however, is reserved for my mother and father.

Abbreviations

AENA	All England Netball Association
AOTT	Adults other than teachers
AQA	Assessment and Qualifications Alliance
ASA	Amateur Swimming Association
BAALPE	British Association of Advisors and Lecturers in Physical Education
BELA	Basic Expedition Leader Award
BISI	Badminton Into Schools Initiative
BST	British Sports Trust
CCPR	Central Council for Physical Recreation
COA	Certificate of Achievement
CSLA	Community Sports Leader Award
DCMS	Department for Culture, Media and Sport
DES	Department of Education and Science
DfE	Department for Education
Dfe/WO	Department for Education/Welsh Office
DfEE	Department for Education and Employment
DfES	Department for Education and Skills
DNH	Department of National Heritage
EAL	English as an Additional Language
EBD	Emotional and Behavioural Difficulty
EFDS	English Federation of Disability Sport
EOC	Equal Opportunities Commission
ESAPLD	English Sports Association for People with Learning Disabilities
ETTA	English Table Tennis Association
FIFA	Fédération Internationale de Football Association
GCSE	General Certificate of Secondary Education
GNVQ	General and National Vocational Qualification
HEI	Higher Education Institution
HSLA	Higher Sports Leader Award
ICT	Information and communications technology
IDF	Israeli Defence Forces
ITT	Initial Teacher Training

JCGQ	Joint Council for General Qualifications
JSLA	Junior Sports Leader Award
KS	Key stage
LEA	Local Education Authority
LSA	Learning Support Assistant
MVP	Millenium Volunteers Programme
NC	National curriculum
NCPE	National Curriculum for Physical Education
NDTA	National Dance Teachers' Association
NGB	National Governing Body
NGBA	National Governing Body Award
OCR	Oxford, Cambridge and RSA Examinations
OFSTED	Office for Standards in Education
PAT	Policy Action Team
PDM	Partnership Development Manager
PE	Physical Education
PE(TE)	Physical Education (teacher education)
PEA UK	Physical Education Association UK
PEGP	Physical Education Gender Police
PLT	Primary Link Teacher
PSE	Personal and Social Education
QCA	Qualifications and Curriculum Authority
QTS	Qualified teacher status
RLSS	The Royal Life Saving Society
ROA	Record of achievement
SDO	Sports development officer
SEN	Special educational needs
SENDA	Special Educational Needs and Disability Act (2001)
SEU	Social Exclusion Unit
SLA	Sports Leader Award
SSC	Specialist Sports College
SSCo	School Sport Co-ordinator
TTA	Teacher Training Agency
WSPP	World Sport Peace Project
YST	Youth Sports Trust

I naturally grew to hate PE and games, generally, associating it with unpleasant, negative, and at times, humiliating experiences. Sport, games, PE – It's important. It's exercise. It can build confidence and character. It can be and should be fun. For me, and many others like me, it was an ordeal. Untold numbers of children in the past were never given a chance by PE teachers who only had eyes for the elite athletes in their charge. I would really like to believe that things are different now.

B. Asbury (2001) 'Why I Hated School PE',
PE and Sport Today 6: 52.

1 Social inclusion in Physical Education and sport

Themes and perspectives for practitioners

Sid Hayes and Gary Stidder

Social inclusion, in general terms, refers to processes through which individuals can be integrated into society and encompasses many aspects of government policy initiatives. Britton and Casebourne (2002) cite the Centre for Economic and Social Inclusion's definition of broader aspects of social inclusion, which refers to:

> the process by which efforts are made to ensure that everyone, regardless of their background, experiences and circumstances, can gain access to the services and facilities they need to achieve their own potential in life. To achieve inclusion, income and employment are necessary but not sufficient. An inclusive society is also characterised by a striving for reduced inequality, a balance between individuals' rights and duties and increased social cohesion.
>
> (Britton and Casebourne 2002: 14)

The Centre adds that, for inclusion to be achieved, a 'striving for reduced inequality' is essential. Physical Education (PE) and sport in schools have become an increasing focus for achieving the present UK government's objectives for social inclusion. Discussion relating to PE and sport has at times suggested that it may have the potential to improve educational achievement and health through increased opportunities for young people to participate in many competitive and non-competitive activities. It has also been associated with having the potential to increase employment opportunities, reduce crime and improve the physical environment. The establishment of Specialist Sports Colleges (SSc's) in the late 1990s undoubtedly accelerated the UK government's drive towards achieving social inclusion through PE and sport. Examples include government initiatives such as the School Sport Co-ordinator (SSCo) programme which saw the development of partnerships between Specialist Sports Colleges and local primary feeder schools. The Youth Sport Trust (2002) reported that disadvantaged and under-represented young people in PE and sport, such as pupils with disabilities, girls and those from ethnic minorities, were provided with increased access and opportunity to a range of activities in their local communities. PE and sport in this context aimed to have an impact on improving the self-esteem and confidence of young people and, therefore, raise standards across the school curriculum through increased levels of access and motivation.

Former UK Minister for Sport, Kate Hoey, outlined the political agenda of central government with regards to PE and sport in schools to the Physical Education Association UK (PEA UK). The focus on citizenship, leadership and social inclusion highlights how PE and sport programmes in schools could contribute to wider societal issues relating to opportunity, and undoubtedly raised the profile of school PE and sport, offering an opportunity for teachers to embrace aspects of equal opportunities:

> Sport can make a unique contribution to tackling social exclusion in society. We recognise that this is not something that sport can tackle alone but by working with other agencies sport can play a significant part ... We must work together to promote the provision of high quality physical education by qualified personnel for all ages, regardless of sex, race, religious or ethnic background or ability. We must promote the health and well being of the community through physical education. We must promote the education of teachers and those responsible for the delivery of physical education programmes in educational establishments and the community.
>
> (Hoey 2001: 23)

Although Hoey only held office for a relatively short period of time there has been no noticeable digression from the government regarding its approach towards PE and sport and it is with this in mind that this book tackles the critical interface between issues of equity, equality, and fairness relating to PE and sport.

The extent to which pupils experience equal opportunities in their schooling is a concern which cuts across all curriculum subjects. This is an issue that has generated much research and debate in the United Kingdom (Evans 1993, Clarke and Nutt 1999, Williams *et al.* 2000). The major themes in these debates are government legislation and related initiatives influencing equal opportunities in education. During the last thirty years there has been a number of legislative attempts to combat discrimination in public and educational contexts, aiming to create greater opportunities and increase provision for all pupils. The Sex Discrimination Act (1975), the Education Reform Act (1988) and the Special Educational

Needs And Disability Act (2001) are examples of significant statutes that have addressed the issue of equitable educational experience for pupils within the state-funded English schooling system.

The Education Reform Act (1988) revised and outlined the entitlement for all pupils in state education with the introduction of a National Curriculum that included PE as an integral part of the core curriculum. The National Curriculum for Physical Education (NCPE) was introduced for pupils aged 5–16 years in 1992 and was modified in 1995 (DfE 1995). It has since been revised for schools in England and became fully operational in September 2001. The revised NCPE (DfEE/QCA 1999) for England has attempted to address issues of social inclusion and provides guidance on how teachers can provide effective learning opportunities for all pupils. The statutory entitlement to learning for all pupils states that schools have a responsibility to provide a broad and balanced curriculum that meets the specific needs of individuals and groups of pupils. These new requirements have marked the third English NCPE in twelve years and suggest that teachers should ensure a more inclusive curriculum. The theme of social inclusion is embellished and underpinned by three key principles which should permeate throughout the learning and teaching process in schools. The document states that in order to develop a more inclusive curriculum educators should be:

A. Setting suitable learning challenges
B. Responding to pupils' diverse learning needs
C. Overcoming potential barriers to learning and assessment
(DfEE/QCA 1999: 28).

In this respect, OFSTED has stated that:

Educational inclusion is more than a concern about any one group of pupils ... Its scope is broad. It is about equal opportunities for all pupils, whatever their age, gender or ethnicity, attainment and background. It pays particular attention to the provision made for and the achievement of different groups of pupils within a school. Throughout this guidance, whenever we use the term different groups it could apply to any or all of the following:

– girls and boys;
– minority ethnic and faith groups, travellers, asylum seekers and refugees;
– pupils who need support to learn English as an additional language (EAL);
– pupils with special educational needs;

- gifted and talented children;
- children 'looked after' by the local authority;
- other children, such as sick children; young carers; those children from families under stress; pregnant school girls and teenage mothers; and any pupils who are at risk of disaffection and exclusion
(OFSTED 2001: 4)

Consequently, the current UK government's concern with social inclusion in many aspects of educational policy has generated much professional debate and exchange amongst teachers in terms of what the new policy directives will mean for their practice. The additions of both general and subject-related statements on inclusion within the revised NCPE (DfEE/QCA 1999) make many of these issues even more relevant to that practice. Exactly what a fully inclusive PE curriculum would look like is difficult to say and how teachers will face the challenges of meeting the needs and interests of pupils from such a wide range of backgrounds is not yet fully known. Robertson *et al.* (2000), however, have provided some guidance related to inclusive PE policy and suggest that teachers might consider principles adopted from Beveridge (1996) in which whole-school and department responsibilities are clearly defined. In this respect, teachers who establish a positive ethos and have high expectations of their pupils take into account the individual needs of the pupils within curriculum developments in partnership with both pupils and parents. To date there has been a number of research projects that have highlighted some of the germane issues to PE and sport. Benn (2000), for example, has discussed the issue of ethnicity and how PE teachers can respond to a number of cultural issues related to the Islamic faith, whilst the Youth Sport Trust (2000) has provided much-needed guidance in relation to girls' participation in PE. Other issues, however, such as homophobia, classism and ablism in PE and sport, discussed later in this book, remain largely unexplored.

The NCPE (DfEE/QCA 1999) acknowledges that established educational principles of equality, equity and social justice can and should be addressed in PE and school sport programmes. Additionally, inclusion has become a pedagogical 'buzz' word within social policy in general and education in particular, and is closely related to any such discussion. It is, however, necessary to emphasise at this point that there are difficulties associated with defining terms such as equality and equity, which are terms closely associated with fairness. Penney reminds us that:

Concerns to address equality, equity and/or inclusion can be associated with two things: difference and fairness or justice. Although these are matters of common concern, a key issue in understanding the distinctions between the various terms is the particular ways in which notions and justice are understood and approached in initiatives relating to the provision and development of physical education and sport.

(Penney 2002: 111)

As Penney goes on to suggest, clear definitions remain contestable, hence the frequency with which the terms are used interchangeably. Whilst other researchers (for example Talbot 1990, Evans *et al.* 1997, Clarke and Nutt 1999) have attempted to provide a clear definition of equity and equality, each of these also acknowledge the problems associated with clarifying such terms. Penney has, however, summarised the term equity and its association with Physical Education:

In short, equity is concerned with giving value to, and celebrating social and cultural differences of individuals and in society.

(Penney 2000: 60)

Equality, however, is defined as the:

State of being equal in some respect ... equality has usually been interpreted to mean equality between individuals or citizens within a number of contexts.

(Jary and Jary 1991: 198)

Whilst we are aware of the different meaning in certain contexts, we feel that it is also appropriate to highlight that there is a large degree of commonality between such terms and it is these common features relating to equal treatment, respect for difference, justice and fairness, that are of central importance to the topics in this publication. This is not to ignore the debate surrounding such concepts, as articulated by Penney (2002), but we feel it would be beyond the realms of this book to fully engage in this debate and would be more productive for the purpose of informing practitioners, that the commonality of the previously mentioned themes is the main focus. Central to this is the concept of inclusion, which underpins the contributions to this book, and it is necessary at this juncture to outline our working definition of this term.

Blunkett refers to inclusion as:

... a process not a fixed state. The term can be used to mean many things including the placement of pupils with SEN [special educational needs] in mainstream schools: the participation of all pupils in the curriculum and social life of mainstream schools: the participation of all pupils in learning which leads to the highest possible level of achievement; and the participation of young people in the full range of social experiences and opportunities once they have left school

(Blunkett 1998: 23)

Although such a statement is open to interpretation, it makes it clear that inclusion is a high priority on the Government's agenda in relation to pupils' experiences in schools. In this respect OFSTED has provided guidance to schools, which illustrates the broader concepts and understandings of educational inclusion:

> An educationally inclusive school is one in which the teaching and learning, achievements, attitudes and well being of every young person matter. Effective schools are inclusive schools. This shows, not only in the performance, but also in the ethos and willingness to offer new opportunities for pupils who may have experienced previous difficulties. This does not mean treating all pupils the same. Rather it involves taking account of pupils' varied life experiences and needs.
>
> (OFSTED 2001: 7)

The new statutory requirements for PE in primary, junior, and secondary schools have emphasised the importance of inclusion rather than exclusion and the responsibilities of teachers to provide programmes of study that incorporate pupils of both genders, all social backgrounds and ethnic groups, and those with special educational needs and disabilities. It is in this context, and with this professional commitment and motivation towards inclusion in mind, that this book examines a number of issues concerning PE and sport programmes, and pupils' experiences of them.

Much of the impetus for the book is derived from our personal experiences of PE and sport as pupils, trainees and teachers, but it is also a response to the evolving nature of contemporary professional practice. Equally, our vision for PE is based upon entitlement, equity, and fairness. As former PE teachers, we acknowledge that many of the experiences we provided to our pupils were often based upon the professional discretion of colleagues and ourselves without involving pupils (or parents) in the process. Similarly, these experiences were often based upon our own interests and those with whom we worked. In hindsight, this often resulted in a very prescriptive programme of activities usually with an overemphasis on team games. We have intimate knowledge of the influence that PE and sport can have on young people, and increasingly recognise the importance of listening to pupil voices with regards to inclusive policies and practices. We share in the opinions of other researchers (Groves and Laws 2000, Lines 1999, Cockburn 1999 for example) who have highlighted the need to engage with young people in order to identify and define their experiences of PE and sport, whether positive or negative. In the context of girls' experiences of PE Cockburn remarked:

> Whatever their level of disengagement I have always felt there is much to be learned from listening to girls' opinions and the reasons they

have for holding them, in our efforts to improve their participation and enthusiasm

(Cockburn 1999: 11)

Approaches such as this to curriculum innovation and change can enable those directly involved with the provision of these experiences to assess current practice and address the needs and interests of young people within contemporary education.

We recognise that for some pupil's school PE lessons can be a very negative experience and have long-lasting effects on their personal perceptions of sport and physical activity later in life. In keeping with the theme of inclusion, as editors we have drawn upon some anecdotal accounts regarding school PE and sport experiences in order to highlight the extent to which these impressions can have an impact upon future participation. We are aware that these stories could be interpreted superficially and we have no empirical evidence to support the claims that many of these writers have brought to the attention of the profession. There is research, however, that has shown how negative school PE experiences in key stage 3 can affect decisions related to curriculum choice in key stage 4 and whether girls would choose to study PE at GCSE examination level (Cockburn 2000). Other research (Wright 1996, 1999) has shown how single-sex boys' groups in PE have the potential to marginalise some boys and provide a breeding ground for homophobic, sexist bullies. Likewise, Wright has stated that:

many mature women speak of their school experiences and physical education with deep dislike as disabling experiences that left them feeling alienated from physical activity and their bodies

(Wright 1996: 77)

The personal accounts we have included merely serve to inform those within the PE profession of how PE can be potentially exclusionary for some pupils and these accounts precede, whenever possible, each chapter. From our experiences as teachers and trainers in PE we also recognise that many of these accounts are the exception rather the rule and that for every one of these types of experiences there are many more pupils with positive memories. The characterisation of male PE teachers such as Mr Sugden from the movie *Kes* and 'Dynamo Doug Digby' from the television series *The Grimleys* has arguably exacerbated many of the images that adults and young people may associate with PE and school sport. The intention is, therefore, to make others consider a more empathetic approach to learning and teaching.

As practitioners ourselves, we acknowledge that teachers in schools have the opportunity not only to deliver syllabus content but also to influence wider societal issues as indeed they have done in the past. We also accept that PE teachers and other professionals in the field require information, help, support, advice and encouragement as they plan and implement inclusive programmes in PE and sport. We also recognise the extent of the challenges that face the profession in an ever more demanding educational climate with respect to these issues, and suggest that an understanding of them may prove a crucial and distinctive aspect of the work of physical educators. The central theme of this book, therefore, revolves around inclusive practice in its numerous forms.

The three key principles for inclusion identified in the NCPE policy document are deemed essential in developing a more inclusive curriculum. The book critically evaluates these principles and the expectations and standards derived from them in the context of PE and questions the extent to which the revised NCPE (DfEE/QCA 1999) in England encompasses the wide range of challenges faced by PE teachers today in respect to social inclusion. Our intention is to address these issues analytically and provide practical advice and support for established professionals, newly qualified teachers, and trainees on implementing policies for social inclusion in PE and school sport. Examples of policy direction, and informed pedagogy, will provide PE specialists with ideas on how to implement an inclusive PE curriculum within the context of their professional practice.

Each chapter is based upon current educational studies related to social inclusion and challenges stereotypical views in PE and sport, which can contribute to exclusionary practice, whether arising from race, ethnicity, gender, social class, sexuality, ability or disability. For the purposes of the book we have agreed, in conjunction with our contributors, that the term 'social inclusion' will relate to the common features of equity, equality and fairness and how pedagogy, differentiation, curriculum planning and cultural awareness can influence such themes.

We have secured a cross-section of established authors who have employed a range of material, grounded in original research and other empirical studies, that addresses some of the latent issues in PE and sport that require professional debate. The collection of contributors includes individuals with expertise from across the disciplines of education and sociology, the large majority of whom are sport, sport policy or PE practitioners.

Each chapter has a common formula and highlights many of the 'isms' within PE and sport, providing considerations for addressing and challenging issues. Our authors have all contributed to the broader themes associated with inclusion with a shared understanding that the inter-relationship of the themes and issues is dependent on all of the component parts.

One of the key themes to permeate throughout each chapter is the need for critical self-reflection and each author, where appropriate, provides a short biographical account of his or her own PE and sport experiences as either a pupil, trainee, or teacher, in order to contextualise the particular contribution. To a certain extent this is a response to and recognition of the responsibilities teachers have in challenging practices that are discriminatory and the need for PE teachers to (re)examine what they teach, how they teach it and the means through which it is organised (Clarke and Nutt 1999). Other more extensive use of biographies and personal reflections has been used in the field of pedagogical research in order to highlight the daily demands faced by teachers and the practicalities of implementing new policy directives (Goodson 1992). This has also been used by researchers within PE and sport as a means of understanding the nature of professional practice in PE and sport as well as the context in which teachers work (Armour and Jones 1998). Our contributors have used their own personal recollections to assess the future direction that PE and sport might follow and aspire to help readers engage in critical reflections on their own learning and teaching. In addition, it is intended that this book will provide such assistance through practical orientation and strands in the material. This is supported, where appropriate, by key pedagogical issues highlighted at the end of each chapter in order to encourage readers to reflect critically upon their practice in respect to learning and teaching within the school environment.

In the first chapter we have outlined, analysed and evaluated the NCPE and the rationale for chapter selection. We briefly highlighted the introduction of key government landmark policies in relation to education, bringing to the fore changes in education since 1988, and have concluded with an exploration of the rhetoric and reality of inclusion within PE during the last decade.

In Chapters 2 and 3 Andrew Theodoulides continues the theme of social inclusion and draws upon his own personal experience as a secondary school PE teacher and Head of Department. In his first contribution Andrew Theodoulides discusses the development of strategies for inclusion within PE curriculum planning. He offers practical advice and solutions and takes into account schemes of work, lesson planning and how to differentiate for pupils' learning in PE through a range of NCPE activity areas. His second chapter outlines the contribution that PE/sport can make to the development of social justice by focusing on the teaching of social and moral issues within physical activity. This is addressed in three stages. First, the role of social and moral development within PE and its relationship with social justice are explored. It is argued that social justice is an inclusive term and provides a more embracing means of considering social and moral issues than the narrow way in which these are conceptualised within the national curriculum for PE. Second, common practices within PE are examined in order to challenge practitioners to think more critically about how PE can promote equality. It is claimed that by focusing on a concern for social justice, rather than social and moral development, PE staff are more likely to be effective in promoting the idea that 'other people matter'. This is viewed in the context of 'control and domination'. Finally, some practical suggestions for the way in which

PE teachers might effectively embrace the teaching of social justice will be put forward.

In Chapters 4 to 12 a range of contributors has addressed various issues specific to PE/sport and social inclusion such as special educational needs, gender, sexual orientation, race, social class, ability, disability and government policy and its implications for school PE and sport.

Philip Vickerman, Sid Hayes and Alan Whetherly have, in Chapter 4, pooled their resources and experience to discuss ways in which PE teachers can promote the learning of pupils with disabilities and additional learning needs, as well as providing practical advice on how to include pupils more effectively within the learning environment. This chapter uses existing literature and draws upon practical experience in order to highlight future strategies for PE teachers.

In Chapter 5 Gill Lines and Gary Stidder highlight why teaching styles and grouping strategies are particularly important in relation to PE and gender as they can potentially marginalise pupils and re-affirm assumptions regarding the abilities of boys and girls. Their chapter examines the effects of sex-segregated and integrated groups in PE and addresses the extent to which these have contributed towards a gender-divided PE curriculum, particularly in secondary school games teaching.

Gill Clarke's valuable contribution in Chapter 6 highlights the existence of heterosexism and homophobia in PE and sport, whose effects on pupils have, until very recently, been relatively undocumented. This chapter highlights specific issues related to the sexual orientation of pupils and the need to break the conspiracy of silence surrounding gay and lesbian issues in PE. It recognises the need for open dialogue related to prejudice and discrimination, and to acknowledge that PE and sport should be equally accessible to everyone. Conservative traditions of the PE profession are revealed and strategies offered for equitable participation within the secondary school environment that challenge and eliminate homophobia and heterosexism whilst promoting equity and social inclusion.

In Chapter 7 Saul Keyworth and Fiona Smith examine the teaching of dance to boys in secondary schools, which has traditionally been marginalised compared with other activities within the PE curriculum. Such marginalisation is often based on the assumption that boys and male teachers are uninterested and demotivated by this area of activity. Through an autobiographical approach they highlight the need to address a number of issues related to inclusive practice in dance, particularly for boys. They draw upon these personal experiences in order to show how the perpetuation of 'gendered' teaching in PE has contributed to the alienation of boys from artistic and aesthetic experiences in dance, and continues to do so. They conclude with a fictitious account of a school visit and provide hypothetical examples of how (male) PE teachers can challenge the homophobic label associated with teachers of dance through innovative approaches to dance education.

In Chapter 8 Gary Stidder and John Sugden discuss the use of sport as a means of addressing conflict resolution and peace. They highlight the main findings from their work in Israel and the occupied territories as an example of how sport can contribute to social inclusion within a divided society. They examine the need for teachers and coaches to differentiate their tasks in order to take into account cultural and religious differences. In the spirit of equal opportunities, this chapter provides suggestions that can enable all pupils to learn effectively, whilst recognising the diversity of backgrounds within the classroom setting, and the influence of the broader social context.

Ian McDonald and Sid Hayes provide, in Chapter 9, a challenge to key stereotypical assumptions related to participation in PE and sport, highlighting the pertinent issues in relation to 'race' and ethnicity. The teaching of PE and sport to pupils from different 'racial' and ethnic backgrounds is generally misunderstood and has often been based on stereotypical expectations. They reflect upon the need for teachers to understand how different racial, ethnic and religious affiliations impact upon the design and delivery of the PE curriculum within a multi-cultural society, highlighting the importance of teacher attitudes.

Ian McDonald's Chapter 10 investigates the relationship between social class and levels of educational achievement generally, as well as viewing the issue in the context of PE and the usage of the body as a defining indicator of class. He argues that, although class is discussed much more infrequently as a contributing factor in educational achievement, it remains statistically one of the key components in predicting performance in schools. He indicates that social inclusion appears to be high on the agenda of a number of organisations including the government, but points out that class is absent from such discussions. He also examines, historically, involvement in recreational and sporting activities in the UK, and how social class has influenced participation levels. This chapter considers how opportunity differentials associated with pupils from poorer backgrounds impact upon their capacity and motivation to participate fully in traditional forms of PE and sport.

In Chapter 11 Gary Stidder and James Wallis discuss accredited courses in PE and how they have continued to gain support amongst physical educationalists. This chapter discusses the opportunities teachers have in guiding all pupils towards nationally accredited courses in PE, such as examination courses and leadership awards, and considers the implications of this type of approach for teachers and for pupils aged 14–16.

Marc Keech brings together a number of inter-related issues in Chapter 12. The Labour Government's policy for sport, *A Sporting Future for All*, published in 2000, emphasised a commitment to sport in schools and went beyond the boundaries of the revised National Curriculum (DCMS 2000). The centrality of schools to the development of young people's sporting opportunities in the local community has meant that many schools have begun to reflect on how to extend their provision to link with a variety of local agencies. At the heart of recent changes of policy has been the emergence of Specialist Sports Colleges and the establishment of School Sports Co-ordinators, whilst the findings of the PAT (Policy Action Team) 10 report (DCMS 1999) affirmed sport as having significant potential to address social exclusion. This chapter evaluates these policy-based changes and offers examples of good practice from those responsible for policies which address social exclusion through PE and sport. School–community links are identified as the central mechanism for extending opportunities for participation for young people across the social spectrum and addressing the recent shifts in PE and sport policies.

The amalgamation of each of the areas covered, drawing on the analyses and insights of all the contributors, summarises how teachers can best address the issue of teaching PE to all pupils, regardless of social categorisation. We suggest a need to question the existing status quo, and to challenge, through reflective practice, resistance to change. Our readers will, undoubtedly, judge the extent to which we, and our contributing authors, have succeeded. This collection should prove essential reading for trainees and practitioners alike as the issues discussed can either unlock or close down the learning opportunities for many children within our schools.

References

Armour, K. and Jones, R. (1998) *Physical Education Teachers' Lives and Careers*, London: Falmer Press.

Benn, T. (2000) 'Towards Inclusion in Education and Physical Education', in A. Williams (ed.), *Primary School Physical Education*, London: Routledge: 118–35.

Beveridge, S. (1996) *Spotlight on Special Educational Needs: Learning Difficulties*, Stafford: NASEN.

Blunkett, D. (1998) *Meeting Special Educational Needs: A Programme of Action*, Suffolk: DfEE.

Britton, L. and Casebourne, J. (2002) *'Defining Social Inclusion'*, *Working Brief* 136, July 2002, available HTTPhttp://www.cesi.org.uk, accessed 20 August 2002.

Clarke, G. and Nutt, G. (1999) 'Physical Education', in D. Hill and M. Cole (eds), *Promoting Equality in Secondary Schools*, London: Cassell: 211–37.

Cockburn, C. (1999) 'The Trouble With Girls ... A Study of Teenage Girls' Magazines in Relation to Sport and PE', *British Journal of Physical Education* 30, 3: 11–15.

DCMS (Department for Culture, Media and Sport) (1999) *PAT 10 Report to the Social Exclusion Unit: The Contribution Arts and Sport can Make to Social Inclusion*, London: DCMS.

DCMS (Department for Culture, Media and Sport) (2000) *A Sporting Future for All: The Government's Plan for Sport*, London: HMSO.

DfE (Department for Education) (1995) *Physical Education in the National Curriculum*, London: HMSO.

DfEE/QCA (Department for Education and Employment/Qualifications and Curriculum Authority) (1999) *Physical Education: The National Curriculum for England*, London: HMSO.

Evans, J. (ed.) (1993) *Equality, Education and Physical Education*, London: Falmer Press.

Evans, J., Davies, B. and Penney, D. (1997) 'Making Progress? Sport Policy, Women and Innovation in Physical Education', *European Journal of Physical Education* 2, 1: 39–50.

Goodson, I. (ed.) (1992) *Studying Teachers' Lives*, London: Routledge.

Groves, S. and Laws, C. (2000) 'Children's Experiences of Physical Education', *European Journal of Physical Education* 5, 1: 19–27.

Hoey, K. (2001) 'The Prince Philip Lecture', *The British Journal of Teaching Physical Education* 32, 1: 20–3.

Jary, D. and Jary, J. (1991) *Collins Dictionary of Sociology*, Glasgow: Collins.

Lines, G. (1999) 'Setting the Challenge: Creating Partnerships: Young People, PE/Sport and the Media', *British Journal of Physical Education* 30, 2: 7–12.

OFSTED (Office for Standards in Education) (2001) *Evaluating Educational Inclusion: Guidance for Inspectors and Schools*, London: HMSO, online, available HTTP<http:// www.ofsted.gov.uk/public/docs00/inclusion.pdf> accessed 6 July 2002.

Penney, D. (2000) 'Physical Education . . . In What and Whose Interests?' in R. Jones and K. Armour, *Sociology of Sports: Theory and Practice*, Harlow: Pearson Education: 58–67.

Penney, D. (2002) 'Equality, Equity and Inclusion in Physical Education and School Sport', in A. Laker (ed.), *The Sociology of Sport and Physical Education*, London: Routledge: 110–28.

Robertson, C., Childs, C. and Marsden, E. (2000) 'Equality and the Inclusion of Pupils with Special Educational Needs in Physical Education', in S. Capel and S. Piotrowski (eds), *Issues in Physical Education*, London: Routledge: 47–63.

Talbot, M. (1990) 'Equal Opportunities and Physical Education', in N. Armstrong (ed.), *New Directions in Physical Education*, Leeds: Human Kinetics: 101–20.

Williams, A., Bedward, J. and Woodhouse, J. (2000) 'An Inclusive National Curriculum? The Experience of Adolescent Girls', *European Journal of Physical Education* 5, 1: 4–18.

Wright, J. (1996) 'The Construction of Complementarity in Physical Education: Working with Teachers', *Gender and Education* 8, 1: 61–79.

Wright, J. (1999) 'Changing Gendered Practices in Physical Education: Working with Teachers', *European Physical Education Review* 5, 3: 181–97.

Youth Sport Trust (2000) *Girls in Sport: Towards Girl-Friendly Physical Education, Final Report*, Loughborough: Institute of Youth Sport, Loughborough University.

Youth Sport Trust (2002) *Building a Brighter Future for Young People Through Sport: Annual Review 2001/2002*, Loughborough: Institute of Youth Sport, Loughborough University.

As I remember it, we only ever had one sympathetic PE teacher, and she was really the divinity mistress. Miss Jones would occasionally help out on the lacrosse field. Unlike Miss Froggatt, she never felt drawn to throw herself into the hurly-burly of the game, but hovered timidly on the side-lines, whistle poised and eskimo-snug in fur coat and scarf, whilst her charges shivered in skimpy shorts. But at least, if a girl fell heavily, or developed an asthmatic wheeze or a bad headache, Miss Jones would instantly slip a comforting arm around the afflicted one's shoulders and escort her to the sick room. Wonderful woman.

J. Green (2000) 'Why I Hated School PE',
PE and Sport Today 4: 56.

2 Curriculum planning for inclusion in Physical Education

Andrew Theodoulides

Debates about how to reduce barriers to participation in Physical Education (PE) has seen the issue of inclusion assume greater significance within PE circles throughout the 1990s and the early 2000s. As Evans and Davies (1993) suggest, promoting equality (and, therefore, inclusion) requires that the underlying structures that perpetuate inequality (exclusion) are challenged. Furthermore, as Penney comments:

> When addressing issues of equality, equity and inclusion we cannot restrict ourselves to the 'immediate' contexts of physical education and school sport. Rather, these contexts need to be recognised as being in a dynamic relationship with the wider social, cultural, political and economic contexts.
>
> (Penney 2002: 11)

Thus, the discussion about how to promote inclusive practices within PE functions in a variety of different arenas, and at a number of different levels. Consequently, alongside other strategies for promoting inclusive practices the underlying principles upon which the PE curriculum is planned can have a salient effect upon reducing barriers to participation. My intent in this chapter is to explore factors that underpin curriculum planning decisions, particularly in the light of the current National Curriculum for Physical Education (NCPE) requirements. The discussion will examine issues relating to the content and structure of the PE curriculum, that is what is taught (breadth of study) and how it is organised. At this point it is important to acknowledge the role of curriculum delivery. For example, the resources teachers have at their disposal, the learning and teaching strategies employed, the 'culture' of the gymnasium/playing fields, the ethos, values and traditions of the profession are just some of the factors that are fundamental to curriculum delivery, and so to creating an inclusive environment. Although mention will be given to some aspects of delivery within this chapter, this will not form a central part of the discussion. For some readers this may be a limiting factor, but matters relating to delivery have been well documented elsewhere in this book and, therefore, do not need reiterating here.

Curriculum planning – highlighting the scope for development

Arguably, decisions about what to include within the PE curriculum are taken predominantly on the grounds of three main factors, the requirements of the NCPE, the ideologies of PE staff, and the resources available. Depending upon one's position, the requirements of the NCPE may be seen in one of two ways. The prescriptive nature of the NCPE, which sets out clearly what departments must teach, may be seen as providing limited opportunities for widening pupils' access to a range of physical activities. On the other hand, the flexibility of the NCPE, that leaves curriculum planners free to choose what to teach once the minimum requirements of the orders have been met, can be seen as a further opportunity to develop inclusive practices. Whatever position one adopts, it is clear that the NCPE places (some) restrictions upon curriculum planners in that there is no blank canvas to work from. Thus, teachers' ideologies about the nature of PE then become crucial factors in how the PE curriculum is constructed, as it is these beliefs that determine which breadth of study areas are to be taught and how much time each area is allocated. In addition, resources (indoor and outdoor spaces, staffing, finance etc.) will impact upon curriculum planning decisions to the extent that the curriculum can only offer that which the resources can support. I have stated previously that I do not intend to discuss resource issues in detail, as these will be context-specific, but in exploring the possibilities within curriculum planning, there is always scope for flexibility. I am confident that given better resources most schools would be able to provide greater access to the PE curriculum, although there is no guarantee that this will happen due to professional ideologies and/or tradition. Perhaps what is more important is the extent to which teachers are committed to tackling inequalities and social exclusion. Arguably, it is easier to promote inclusive practices through positive action than it is to create new resources, particularly if these resources are dependent upon large-scale finance. A change in thinking does not require any financial obligation, simply a commitment to challenge one's assumptions and explore new ideas. The issues that are discussed here are not exhaustive but serve to show how, by considering matters of inclusion at the stage of curriculum planning, the PE curriculum might provide greater opportunities for pupils within school and ultimately within the wider community as well. An inclusive curriculum does not just happen, it needs to be planned for.

The starting point for exploring how to plan an inclusive PE curriculum ought to begin with an evaluation of the current curriculum framework. Thus, relevant questions might be: what does the current PE curriculum offer all pupils? How have matters relating to inclusion been considered in the planning stage? Questions of this nature provide a basis upon which curriculum planners can begin to consider how changes to their PE curriculum can have a positive impact upon widening pupils' access. Having recognised there are issues that need addressing it is then pertinent to ask: how can the curriculum offer more opportunities to a greater number of pupils? It is worth acknowledging here that no PE curriculum will ever be totally inclusive and there will always be some pupils whose needs are very difficult to meet. Furthermore, the extent to which curriculum planners aim to reduce barriers to participation is a constant balancing act in terms of the way in which the needs of some pupils are met in relation to those of others. There are no easy solutions. The discussion that follows seeks to highlight a number of relevant issues that might impact upon curriculum planning for inclusion.

Meeting the physical needs of *all* pupils

The entitlement of the NCPE (DfEE/QCA 1999) is premised on the notion that in meeting the minimum requirements of the orders, pupils will receive a broad and balanced PE curriculum. Thus, the different breadth of study areas each bring a unique learning experience to pupils which (in theory at least) will provide pupils with a range of experiences which enhance opportunities and widen access. As OFSTED (2002) points out, however, the reality is somewhat different. OFSTED alerts us to how the 'time allocated to team games is sometimes between three and five times that for gymnastics, dance and other aspects' of the PE curriculum[1] (OFSTED 2002: 4). Thus, we need to consider the implications this has for inclusion within PE. First of all, how does a curriculum that is dominated by games activities impact upon pupils' learning in other breadth of study areas? Is enough time given to other breadth of study areas for pupils to establish a good skill level? It seems not. OFSTED comments, 'Pupils' achievement is higher and more consistent in *major team games* than other elements of PE' (ibid.: 2, original emphasis). Thus, it appears the opportunities for pupils to access fully other areas of the PE curriculum are restricted by the amount of time they spend learning team games. In some schools, it may be that in meeting the requirements of the NCPE, the time allocated to some breadth of study areas amounts to little more than tokenism.

For those pupils who are not motivated by the traditional team games we need to consider why this might be. In the following chapter I explore how the idea of 'control and domination' serves to exclude some pupils from participating fully in PE and sport. In summary, I believe that the over-competitive nature of sport denies some pupils the opportunity for further involvement, as they do not identify with this way of participating. What implications does this have for curriculum planning? Are some sports likely to engender 'control and domination' more than others? If so, what is their place within the curriculum? What are the alternatives? For example, it may be that rather than teaching football, as Clarke and Nutt (1999) suggest, handball might provide a more viable alternative. Due to the non-contact nature of the game and it being more dependent upon skill than the criteria of size and strength that often prevail in contact sports, it might have the potential to widen access. Nevertheless, with the greatest percentage of curriculum time allocated to games and less time allocated to other breadth of study areas, curriculum planners need to consider if it is fair that those pupils who do not enjoy games activities spend less curriculum time learning those activities they do take pleasure in.

A further issue related to time allocation to breadth of study areas is the extent to which teachers attempt to cover a wide range of skills, knowledge and understanding in a relatively short period of time. In my work as a teacher educator I often receive feedback from trainee teachers who report teaching the same athletics lesson to year 7, year 8 and sometimes year 9 pupils because of the extent to which learning from previous years has not been retained. In an activity area that is often characterised by the teaching of one athletic event each week, we can see then one example of how progressing too quickly can preclude many pupils from access to the curriculum as they are not given the opportunity to consolidate their learning. This may be further exacerbated in areas of the curriculum that are organised into short-term units of work (OFSTED 1996), particularly if these are only 4–6 weeks in length. Furthermore, it is arguably those pupils who are quick and effective learners who are much more likely to be able to access the opportunities available when time is limited. Thus, pupils with special educational needs (SEN) face even greater difficulties. Even with the use of teaching strategies such as differentiation, different learning and teaching styles, this may not be enough to overcome the difficulties some pupils face due to a lack of time to reinforce their learning. Whitehead and Corbin (1997) identify how success is an important factor in pupils' motivation to continue participation in physical activity. Curriculum planning therefore ought to consider how time can be allocated efficiently to content so that pupils are given the best opportunity to access the PE curriculum.

One way of making a more efficient use of curriculum time has been to 'set' pupils, that is, pupils are grouped and taught according to their ability. The impact of grouping policy on inclusive practice within PE, however, is not unproblematical. The following section explores the extent to which how pupils are grouped impacts upon inclusive practices within PE.

The impact of grouping policy on inclusive practices

On initial reflection it might seem that 'setting' pupils provides greater access to the curriculum as pupils are taught with other pupils of a similar ability. Thus, the argument goes, the material that pupils are taught can be more readily adapted to their capacity to learn. Furthermore, because of the relatively 'equal' skill level of the pupils in each 'set', pupils are more likely to feel comfortable working with peers of similar ability. On the other hand, there are good reasons to suggest that this might be detrimental to inclusion. As Clarke and Nutt point out:

> Everyone should have the opportunity of working with others of varying levels of ability and aptitude so that they can learn to appreciate and value the different types of achievements and individual contributions that all can bring to the learning process.
>
> (Clarke and Nutt 1999: 220)

Thus, we can see that what might appear to be a positive strategy for inclusive practice within PE is not clear-cut.

The opportunity to work with 'others' is one that is not always readily available to pupils within PE. Like other contributors to this book (Lines and Stidder) I point to the lack of opportunity for girls and boys to work together because of the way in which the PE curriculum in many schools is taught in single-sex groups. The reasons for this have been well documented, in particular how boys tend to dominate in mixed PE settings (Evans 1989, Scraton 1993, Hardy *et al.* 1994). Thus, in order to provide greater access to the curriculum for girls, single-sex PE lessons are thought to be a more viable way of grouping pupils. We are left wondering, however, whether such policies reinforce gender stereotypes. Whatever answer we come to, the central question becomes: how can we structure our PE curriculum in order to try and break down gender stereotypes in PE? At first glance it appears that curriculum planners are in an unenviable position, in that whichever grouping policy is adopted (mixed or single-sex) there are likely to be negative effects. Clarke and Nutt (1999), however, suggest an alternative approach. In terms of curriculum planning they argue that games should include 'activities that are non-gender specific' (ibid.: 216) such as korfball and handball, and modified versions of popular games such as rugby and football, such as the Lloyds TSB Live Rugby Programme which has been designed for girls and boys of all abilities. Other games include the Swiss games of Tchoukball, which is a non-contact invasion game that can be easily played in mixed-sex teams.[2] What Clarke and Nutt are suggesting will require teachers to look critically at gender issues within PE in order to explore ways of reducing the barriers to participation. If this approach proves worthwhile, then it might be valuable to consider how this might be extended and carried forward into other breadth of study activity areas.

Once we begin to explore the impact grouping policy has on pupils' experiences within PE, it becomes clear that far from being merely an organisational matter in curriculum planning, how pupils are grouped also impacts upon the extent to which PE creates an inclusive environment for pupils' learning. Above I raised the matter of grouping policy with regard to gender, but a further issue would be the opportunity the curriculum provides for pupils to mix with fellow pupils from different 'social' groups. In a climate in which educational achievement is largely related to socio-economic status we can see how 'setting' might create barriers to inclusion through the formation of 'us' and 'them' groups that are determined by academic ability. This may be a particular concern in schools where grouping in PE is determined by whole-school grouping polices, that is, pupils come to PE in the groups in which they are set for other subjects (Maths, English, Science). Thus, curriculum planners are forced consider the constraints and opportunities whole-school grouping policy has for inclusion within PE.

Planning to meet the needs of pupils from ethnic groups

Pupil difference also manifests itself in other ways, one of which is in terms of ethnicity. Fleming (1991) reminds us how stereotypes about the interests of boys from different ethnic groups serve to reinforce perceptions about what is and is not appropriate physical activity for pupils from different ethnic groups. In particular, he points to the false perception that Asian boys do not like football but are more likely to enjoy cricket. Similarly, Hayes and Sugden (1999) remind us how stereotypical assumptions are still evident within the profession with regard to black pupils being perceived as 'natural' athletes, and how they are more 'suited' to certain sports, namely football, basketball, cricket and athletics. Research has also focused upon the experiences of girls from ethnic groups. Carroll and Hollinshead (1993) remind us of the difficulties faced by Muslim girls when it comes to balancing the requirements of adhering to religious beliefs and taking part in PE, and how anti-sexist policies of empowerment for women can be at odds with Muslim culture. Similarly, curriculum planners will need to balance the conflicts that might arise between attempts to reduce gender stereotypes through mixed PE and the expectations of pupils and parents from ethnic groups who express a preference for single-sex PE lessons (Benn, 2000).

Thus, when we explore matters relating to the experience of pupils from ethnic groups, it becomes clear that there is much for curriculum planners to ponder. So how might meeting the needs of pupils from ethnic groups impact upon aspects of curriculum planning? Carroll and Hollinshead (1993) point to the conflict Muslim pupils face when learning swimming during Ramadan in terms of the difficulties of not taking in water during this period of fasting. Thus, the timing of Ramadan is one consideration that curriculum planners ought to consider. A further issue identified by Carroll and Hollinshead is teachers' expectations of pupil effort during Ramadan. One solution they suggest is for ' less strenuous activities such as table-tennis' (ibid.: 164) to be taught at this time. Again, bearing in mind the demand most schools have on indoor spaces, this needs to be considered at the planning stage.

Benn (2000) highlights the potential difficulties that surround the place of dance in the PE curriculum for Muslim pupils, and in particular girls. She suggests that dance movements that have sexual undertones, or over-tones, might give rise to feelings of conflict as pupils attempt to balance the demands of being a pupil and those of the Muslim religion. Responding to concerns from some quarters of the Muslim community that partici-pation in dance is anti-Islamic, Benn comments, '[it] is not to suggest that dance is completely unproblematical for some Muslims. Increased sensi-tivity can lead to planning and teaching that avoids aspects that could be offensive, for example pop music and tight-fitting lycra leotards' (Benn 2000: 74). As Britain has become a more multicultural society teachers have had to be more aware and sensitive to cultural expectations. In some schools mixed PE may not be an option (Carrington and Leaman 1986). In other schools, however, it 'may be seen as quite acceptable provided that certain rules about clothing are upheld' (Williams 1996: 83). In order to understand the cultural expectations placed upon pupils and how this might impact upon the planning of the PE curriculum, discussion and consultation with members from ethnic groups can prove extremely valu-able. We can see then how a greater understanding of the dilemmas some pupils from ethnic groups face can assist in reducing the barriers to partic-ipation. Another way of providing a more meaningful experience for pupils would be to build upon pupils' preferences for physical activity. Thus, for pupils from ethnic groups this would provide further opportunities through which they could balance the tensions between school and cultural demands. It is to a discussion of how pupils' interests might be utilised by curriculum planners that the discussion now turns.

Widening access to the curriculum through pupils' interests

Pupils' interests have a rather ubiquitous position within PE as they are central to innovation and change within curriculum development. At the same time they also have a non-specific place within the planning of PE curriculum. Arguably, when planning the PE curriculum staff will consider what breadth of study areas they feel pupils would like to learn. And rightly so. Any curriculum that fails to captivate pupils' interests would be educationally less effective than one which pupils were enthusiastic about. However, a cautionary note needs to be acknowledged here. Are we guilty of making decisions based on stereotypical assumptions about what pupils enjoy?[3] Arguably, in choosing what is to be taught (and also what will not be taught) it has been highlighted above how decisions still appear to be determined to a large extent on the basis of what is 'traditional'. Thus, team games dominate the PE curriculum. Furthermore, it is all too easy to make assumptions that some games (football, rugby, cricket) are for boys and others (netball and hockey) are for girls. But can we assume that '*all* boys like football' and 'girls prefer gymnastics and dance to games activities'? Certainly football is popular amongst some boys, but for others it holds no attraction. Similarly some girls like gym and dance, but there may be others who would rather learn to play rugby. So what other alternatives are there for utilising pupils' interests in order to widen access to the PE curriculum?

One option might be to encourage more pupil choice within PE. Choice is often restricted to pupils in key stage 4, but why not introduce some choice at other key stages? Thus, pupils might be given the option in gymnastics of learning Olympic or rhythmic gymnastics. Similarly in games, pupils would be able to choose between tennis and badminton. Alternatively, pupil choice might be extended to giving pupils a greater input into which breadth of study areas form the PE curriculum. For example, pupils could be asked which activities they would like to learn in PE. Once the decision to give pupils a voice in what the PE curriculum offers has been made, the central issue then becomes the amount of pupil choice that is allowed. Are pupils free to choose at all times, or are there some compulsory elements to their PE, with choice options made available at certain times of the year? I acknowledge that this approach to curriculum planning may well pose organisational problems. As I stated above, resources (facilities, finance and staffing) will be amongst some factors that will determine the extent to which pupils' interests can be accommodated. Nevertheless, giving pupils a voice in the PE curriculum has the potential to widen pupil access. Thus, and this may be a further stumbling block, giving pupils a greater say in what the PE curriculum has to offer will require a change in ethos that sees some regulation of the curriculum shift from teachers to pupils.

Planning to meet pupils' 'extended' physical needs

It has been highlighted above that *all* pupils have physical needs that ought to be met through the PE curriculum. My aim here is to explore in more detail matters that relate to the inclusion of pupils with physical disabilities. In particular, I want to discuss the extent to which curriculum planners consider pupils with physical disabilities when deciding upon which activities to teach. I begin by considering the central question that often frames the debate in this area, that is to what extent the PE curriculum should be planned with the needs of one, two or even a few pupils with disabilities in mind. How far should curriculum planners go in attempting to meet the needs of pupils with disabilities at the 'expense' of other pupils? Initially, it might seem that this would not be fair, as the needs of all pupils should be given equal attention. Equality is not about treating everyone equally, but unequally, and there is a good case for considering the needs of some pupils first. For example, it might be pertinent to consider whether a pupil who is a wheelchair user would have greater access to the games curriculum when taking part in volleyball or tennis. To a large extent this may well depend upon the individual pupil(s) and what is feasible given the resources of the department. But a number of other pertinent matters arise. In choosing volleyball over tennis might this give teachers the opportunity to promote pupils' understanding of the needs of others and in particular some of the difficulties faced by wheelchair users? I point to the way in which volleyball could be adapted so that at times chairs could be introduced so *all* (even the able-bodied) pupils have to play seated. Alternatively, some players (in certain areas of the court) might play seated whilst others are able to move more freely and hence the rotation of players in volleyball means that pupils experience playing the game from a different perspective. We can see that by considering the extent to which some activities might be adapted, perhaps some sports have the potential to be more inclusive than others within the school context. Furthermore, in the example above, if the needs of able-bodied pupils can be met through either tennis or volleyball, then it becomes pertinent to consider the needs of pupils with disabilities first.

In terms of a two-way process of equal access to the curriculum it might also be worth exploring the possible advantages in opening up activities to able-bodied pupils that have hitherto been seen as specifically for disabled pupils. All too often we attach labels to the perceived appropriateness of different types of physical activity for different groups of pupils. It has been stated above how perceptions about the gendered nature of some sports reinforce stereotypes. So what is it about our thinking that makes us believe that some physical activities should only be available to specific groups of people? I am referring here to things such as hydrotherapy, boccia, or goal ball[4] that are sometimes seen as exclusively for pupils with physical disabilities. Might these be options available to able-bodied pupils? In addition to widening access, the benefit of this might also lie in the message it sends with regard to the labels we attach to different types of physical activity. For example, we would not want basketball, gymnastics, or orienteering to be seen as pursuits for able-bodied people. Similarly, it is also divisive to regard activities such as hydrotherapy, boccia, or goal ball as exclusively for people with disabilities. Thus, by opening up the range of physical activities offered to pupils the PE curriculum could have a wider role to play in reducing the discriminatory labels that are sometimes attached to some physical activities.

Having highlighted some issues that need addressing when planning for pupils' physical needs I now consider one further matter, that is the extent to which, if at all, the PE curriculum should attempt to promote able-bodied pupils' understanding of and empathy for pupils with physical difficulties. In the discussion above I raised the question of how curriculum planners might consider the needs of pupils with physical disabilities. Therefore, when a group includes one or more pupils with specific physical needs it is incumbent upon curriculum planners to consider how the needs of these pupils can be met. But what about if there are no pupils with specific physical needs? Should pupils still play volleyball sitting down, experience an adapted form of athletics, or play boccia? Whilst there may initially seem to be no reason to include these within PE, perhaps on further reflection it might be worthwhile. Let me give an example to illustrate. In schools such as Church of England or Roman Catholic schools where there are no pupils of, for instance, Jewish or Islamic faith, pupils are not precluded from learning about other religions in Religious Education. So it is with our experiences of adapted forms of physical activity. Just because a school has no pupils with disabilities it does not necessarily mean that adapted forms of physical activity are not a worthwhile learning experience. The value in learning to empathise and understand the daily challenges faced by people with disabilities might serve as a worthwhile learning activity in itself. As Clarke and Nutt (1999: 213) point out, however, if the PE curriculum is to include experiences that are considered to be outside of the 'normal' range of physical activities, 'care must be taken to avoid "tokenism".'

The significance of taking part in adapted forms of physical activity to which I have hinted above lies in the fact that at some stage in their lives, pupils are likely to meet people with disabilities. Rather than seeing people with disabilities as 'lacking' (Robertson *et al.* 2000) it is to be hoped that people will be accorded recognition for what they can achieve. In her autobiography, Tanni Grey-Thompson (2001), a Paralympic champion, highlights the lack of awareness within society about people with disabilities. She comments: 'Like most disabled people, I have come up against the "does-she-take-sugar?" syndrome on a few occasions. Because I'm in a chair some people assume I'm mentally subnormal and treat me like dirt' (ibid.: 100). Consequently, we can see how this awareness is sorely needed. For Grey-Thompson her success in sport has been achieved through her participation outside of the school context. For the majority of people the possibility of becoming an Olympic medal winner is not what spurs them on. Whatever one's motivation, however, it is generally recognised that continued participation will be built upon access to physical activity within both schooling and the wider community.

Promoting inclusive practices through the wider community programme

The relationship between what is taught within the PE curriculum and access to local amenities is an important consideration for curriculum planners. For many teachers, the nature of the PE curriculum is one that should offer pupils the opportunity to access one, maybe even more, sports or physical activities that engages pupils' enthusiasm in the hope of continued future participation. In terms of widening access, therefore, what pupils learn in school ought to bear some relationship to the opportunities available in the wider community. Thus, when planning the curriculum, consideration ought to be given to whether it is best use of curriculum time for pupils to learn outdoor and adventurous activities in an area where a lack of access to facilities might mean that pupils are unable to continue with this activity outside of school. Similarly, teaching squash, if pupils do not have access to courts, or athletic activities if there are no clubs nearby, might mean that curriculum time would be better allocated to another breadth of study activity.

The relationship between curriculum planning and facilities in the wider community also extends to the impact that financial considerations have upon inclusion within PE. Where option choices (generally in key stage 4 pupils) require pupils to pay for the hire of facilities and/or equipment, such practices might serve to restrict access for some pupils. I am referring here, for example, to the cost of hiring a squash court at the local sports centre, or paying to use the pool for a swimming option. In theory, schools are only allowed to ask for a voluntary donation in order to cover the cost of financing the use of off-site facilities. With alternative non-cost activities usually offered alongside the cost options, however, the practice of charging pupils for PE appears to be popular, particularly in key stage 4. Despite the benefits to those pupils who can afford to pay for these types of activities, this has obvious implications for those who cannot. It is difficult to claim to be inclusive when pupils are asked to pay for access to some aspects of the curriculum, as there are always likely to be pupils for whom the cost is prohibitive. Thus, schools will need to consider whether it is fair that some pupils are denied the opportunity to particular educational experiences. Alternatively, of course, to widen access, this cost could be met by the school/department either for all pupils, or at least for those who cannot afford it.

The discussion thus far has focused upon how planning for inclusive practices within curriculum time might be developed. With one aim of PE being to promote participation in physical activity outside of the curriculum, some acknowledgement needs to be given to how PE could widen pupils' access in this area. Developing community links and partnerships has always been an aim of PE departments, but this has received increased recognition more recently under government proposals (DNH

1995, DCMS 2000). Thus, developing links with local clubs and sports centres where pupils can go to take part in physical activity out of school is often seen as a major aim of PE departments. But how often are pupils given information about clubs to join, or where they can go to continue their physical activity but then fail to take up the opportunities available to them? Arguably, amongst the many factors that prevent pupils from joining clubs or groups outside of school may be their social and organisation skills and a lack of confidence. For some pupils phoning or writing a letter of introduction to a club, or simply turning up on a training evening might present no problem at all. For others, however, a lack of confidence or poor social skills might mean that joining a club or attending an evening session at the sports centre appears a daunting prospect. Thus, inclusive practices within PE might mean that pupils are given support in their attempts to participate out of school. For example, pupils might be taught how to write a letter of introduction, or a phone call is made to the club on their behalf. Alternatively, a member of staff might even meet the pupil(s) and take them to the club or sports centre and make the introduction personally. Whatever strategies are employed, the point to bear in mind is that inclusion within PE requires that pupils are given help and support in their efforts towards further participation. Perhaps a good starting point for this is the extra-curricular activities that are such a central part of the work of PE staff. It is to this that the discussion now turns.

Widening access through extra-curricular activities

In theory, extra-curricular activities provide an opportunity for PE staff to provide access to a wider range of physical activity opportunities. The reality, however, is somewhat different. Penney and Harris (1997) ask whether extra-curricular activities are simply 'More of the same for the more able?' Thus, they identify two issues that stand out as relevant here. These are the range of extra-curricular activities offered and the underlying philosophy as to who and what these activities are for. It appears that, like the school curriculum, extra-curricular activities in some schools are dominated by team games (Penney and Harris 1997, Green 2000). If this is so, then the opportunity to widen access is curtailed. Thus, it becomes incumbent upon PE staff to consider more critically what the extra-curricular programme will offer. As stated above, whilst team games appeal to some pupils, for others they hold little interest. The potential of extra-curricular activities to widen pupils' access to meaningful physical activity, however, is problematic. Hill (2001) points out the tensions between government policy and inclusive practices, and in particular how the need for schools to be seen as successful in the 'marketplace' serves to erect barriers for some pupils. This is evident within PE. Green (2000: 194) comments, 'This concern for the prestige of the school in the context of an educational market was particularly evident with regard to the constraints teachers felt themselves to be under vis-à-vis extra-curricular PE.' Thus, for many departments, the drive for success on the sports field manifests itself through the provision of team games activities for the able performers. If extra-curricular activities are to fulfil their potential to widen access, PE staff will need to develop strategies that enable them to balance the provision for competitive team sports with those that offer pupils other attractive alternatives.

Thus, it might be that in addition to team games, more provision for extra-curricular gym and dance is provided. Furthermore, non-mainstream activities such as cycling, step-aerobics, roller-blading or Kabaddi[5] might provide opportunities for other pupils to take part in extra-curricular PE.

In addition to what is offered, it is also important to consider when and for whom it is offered. Not all pupils are included or have access to activities that are provided outside of the curriculum, because of other commitments such as family responsibilities, or difficulties with transport after school. Furthermore, Penney and Harris (1997) comment upon the gendered nature of extra-curricular activities which sees some 'male' sports offered to boys by male teachers and 'female' sports offered to girls by female teachers. Some schools have sought to address inequalities by offering extra-curricular activities at different times of the day. However, as Penney (2002: 113) points out, 'Essentially the interest has been in extending access to particular opportunities. There has been little to indicate an appreciation that what different people recognise and value as "an opportunity" will vary.' An example of this is highlighted by Penney and Harris (1997) and Green (2000) who argue that, although many teachers profess that extra-curricular activities are 'open to everyone', they are essentially organised for, and thus attended by, those pupils who are team players and who want to be involved in competitive sport. Again we can see, then, how this overriding concern for competitive team sports serves to restrict the opportunities for other forms of participation that might promote inclusive practices within PE. Fleming (1991: 48) identifies how 'Sport, or more specifically football, plays an important part in the lifestyle of Asian street-kids, though they are seldom sufficiently motivated or committed to join and remain members of a sports club or team.' In addition to 'team' practices, what may be required, therefore, are other forms of taking part in PE and sport which engender 'inclusion, equity, involvement, enjoyment, social justice, caring, cooperation, movement and so forth' (Tinning 1997: 103).

Conclusion

As I have indicated throughout this chapter, curriculum planning for inclusion within PE is not unproblematic. It represents one of the biggest challenges facing PE staff. It is evident that there is a great deal of scope for the PE curriculum to offer pupils wider access to physical activity. Central to this, as I have attempted to show, is the extent to which the curriculum is planned to meet the needs of all pupils. It is also clear that much of the responsibility for this lies with those who plan the PE curriculum and the commitment staff have towards inclusive PE. As guardians of the PE curriculum, it is important that PE staff reflect upon what constitutes a worth while experience *for all pupils,* not just those who are competent performers, or like games activities. Given this, the notion of what constitutes a meaningful PE curriculum has remained largely unquestioned over the last few decades. Arguably, this has resulted in a static PE curriculum, one that is perpetuated on the basis of what is traditional. In order to overcome this, PE staff will need to reflect upon their own 'philosophy' with regard to what PE is about. Developing new ways of thinking about PE, however, is not easy, but this should not detract from the challenge to do so. If PE is to become more inclusive, then one requirement will be the need for curriculum planners to develop a more critical approach to what they teach, and also more importantly, *why* they teach it.

Reflective questions

1   Make a list of the different physical activities you think that pupils would choose if you gave them a totally free choice in PE. How does this match up with the PE curriculum and range of extra-curricular activities that is offered? What does this tell you about pupils' preferences for participation in physical activity? Consider how fair it is for those pupils who would like to learn more about physical activities that are not on the PE curriculum. What impact might this have on their future participation?

2   Do a time audit of the PE curriculum in your school (or one where you have taught) to determine the amount of time allocated to the different breadth of study activity areas. To what extent do team games activities dominate the PE curriculum? What reasons can you give for why this might be? How does this impact upon access to the curriculum for those pupils that do not enjoy team games?

3   Reflect upon what you know about pupil difference. Plan a PE curriculum framework that you consider to be inclusive. What activity areas will pupils learn? Why? How will you balance the wide-ranging needs that pupils have? Upon what basis will you allocate time to each of the different areas? Which extra-curricular activities would you run to widen pupils' access to physical activity?

Notes

1   For a more detailed discussion of the dominance of team games within the PE curriculum see Clarke and Nutt (1999) and Kirk (1992).

2   For further details of these games see Jones (2000) and French (2001) respectively.
3   A study by the Sports Council for Wales (1994) found that over one-third of pupils commented that there was at least one activity that was not offered as part of extra-curricular PE in which they would like to participate. Bearing in mind the way in which team games dominate the PE curriculum there are good reasons to assume the situation may be similar with regard to curriculum PE.
4   Boccia is a recognised team sport played by disabled athletes which can also be played by able-bodied players. It involves throwing a ball into a hoop. Goal ball is another sport played by disabled athletes.
5   Kabaddi is a tag game played between two opposing teams within a defined area and has Asian origins.

References

Benn, T. (2000) 'Valuing Cultural Diversity: The Challenge for Physical Education', in S. Capel and S. Piotrowski (eds), *Issues in Physical Education*, London: Routledge Falmer: 64–77.

Carrington, B. and Leaman, O. (1986) 'Equal Opportunities in Physical Education', in J. Evans (ed.), *Physical Education, Sport and Schooling: Studies in the Sociology of Physical Education*, London: Falmer Press: 215–26.

Carroll, B. and Hollinshead, G. (1993) 'Equal Opportunities: Race and Gender in Physical Education: A Case Study', in J. Evans and B. Davies (eds), *Equality, Education and Physical Education*, London: Falmer Press: 154–69.

Clarke, G. and Nutt, G. (1999) 'Physical Education', in D. Hill and M. Cole (eds), *Promoting Equality in Secondary Schools*, London: Cassell: 211–37.

DCMS (Department for Culture, Media and Sport) (2000) *A Sporting Future for All: The Government's Plan for Sport*, London: HMSO.

DfEE/QCA (Department for Education and Employment/Qualifications and Curriculum Authority) (1999) *Physical Education: The National Curriculum for England*, London: HMSO.

DNH (Department of National Heritage) (1995) *Sport: Raising the Game*, London: HMSO.

Evans, J. (1989) 'Swinging from the Crossbar: Equality and Opportunity in the Physical Education Curriculum', *British Journal of Physical Education* 20, 2: 84–7.

Evans, J. and Davies, B. (1993) 'Equality, Equity and Physical Education', in J. Evans and B. Davies (eds), *Equality, Education and Physical Education*, London: Falmer Press: 11–27.

Fleming, S. (1991) 'Sport, Schooling and Asian Male Youth Culture', in G. Jarvie (ed.), *Sport, Racism and Ethnicity*, London: Falmer Press: 30–57.

French, A. (2001) 'Focus on Tchoukball', *The British Journal of Teaching Physical Education* 32, 4: 10–11.

Green, K. (2000) 'Extra-curricular Physical Education in England and Wales: A Sociological Perspective on Sporting Bias', *European Journal of Physical Education* 5, 2: 179–207.

Grey-Thompson, T. (2001) *Seize the Day: The Story of a Heroine of our Time*, London: Hodder and Stoughton.

Hardy, C. E., Hardy, C. A. and Thorpe, R. (1994) 'Pupil Misbehaviour in Secondary Schools and Mixed-sex Physical Education Lessons', *British Journal of Physical Education* 25, 4: 7–11.

Hayes, S. and Sugden, J. (1999) 'Winning through 'Naturally' Still? An Analysis of the Perceptions held by Physical Education Teachers Towards the Performance of Black Pupils in School Sport and the Classroom', *Race, Ethnicity and Education* 2, 1: 93–107.

Hill, D. (2001) 'Global Capital, neo-Liberalism and Privatisation: The Growth of Educational Inequity', in D. Hill and M. Cole (eds), *Schooling and Equality: Fact, Concept and Policy*, London: Kogan Page: 35–54.

Jones, S. (2000) 'Lloyds TSB Live! Rugby', *The British Journal of Teaching Physical Education* 31, 3: 10–11.

Kirk, D. (1992) *Defining Physical Education: The Social Construction of a School Subject in Post-war Britain*, London: Falmer Press.

OFSTED (Office for Standards in Education) (1996) *Subjects and Standards: Issues for School Development arising from OFSTED Inspection Findings 1994–5: Key Stages 3 & 4 and Post-16*, London: HMSO.

OFSTED (Office for Standards in Education) (2002) *Secondary Subject Reports 2000/01: Physical Education*, London: HMSO.

Penney, D. (2002) 'Equality, Equity and Inclusion in Physical Education and Sport', in A. Laker (ed.), *The Sociology of Sport and Physical Education: An Introduction*, London: Routledge/Falmer: 110–28.

Penney, D. and Harris, J. (1997) 'Extra-curricular Physical Education: More of the Same for the more Able?' *Sport, Education and Society* 2, 1: 41–54.

Robertson, C., Childs, C. and Marsden, E. (2000) 'Equality and the Inclusion of Pupils with Special Educational Needs in Physical Education', in S. Capel and S. Piotrowski (eds), *Issues in Physical Education*, London: Routledge: 47–63.

Scraton, S. (1993) 'Equity, Coeducation and Physical Education in Secondary Schooling', in J. Evans and B. Davies (eds), *Equality, Education and Physical Education*, London: Falmer Press: 139–53.

Sports Council for Wales (1994) 'A Matter of Fun and Games: Children's Participation in Sport', in D. Penney and J. Harris (1997), 'Extra-curricular Physical Education: more of the same for the more able?', *Sport, Education and Society* 2, 1: 41–54.

Tinning, R. (1997) 'Performance and Participation Discourses in Human Movement: Towards a Socially Critical Physical Education', in J. M. Fernandez-Balboa (ed.), *Critical Postmodernism in Human Movement, Physical Education and Sport*, New York: SUNY: 99–119.

Whitehead, J. R. and Corbin, C. B. (1997) 'Self-Esteem in Children and Youth: The Role of Sport and Physical Education', in K. R. Fox (ed.), *The Physical Self: From Motivation to Well-being*, Champaign, Ill.: Human Kinetics: 175–203.

Williams, A. (1996) *Teaching Physical Education: A Guide for Mentors and Students*, London: David Fulton.

Even I wasn't bad at everything. I was a pretty fair swimmer and I had a reputation as a hard hitter with a softball bat – but softball, of course, was not a sport the school competed in. It was just given to duffers as something to do while the teachers coached their golden boys at cricket, tennis or athletics. To be given a chance to play tennis, you really had to be one of the elite. I never got the chance even to pick up a tennis racquet, much less find out whether I had an aptitude for it.

B. Asbury (2001) 'Why I Hated School PE',
PE and Sport Today 6: 52)

3 'Other People Matter'

Contesting control and domination in Physical Education and sport

Andrew Theodoulides

It would seem at first glance that Physical Education (PE) and sport could be inclusive. In essence the underlying philosophical, social and moral base upon which sport is premised provides competitors with an equal experience. For example, rules provide a means through which each competitor has an equal chance to participate. A referee or umpire stands in arbitration to ensure that no one has an unfair advantage. Furthermore, being meritocratic, the winner in a sporting contest should be the competitor or team who demonstrates the most skilful performance.[1] But upon closer scrutiny another side to sport emerges. Players bend and break the rules; sport has the propensity to lead to acts of aggression. In short, sport has its 'ugly side', and it is this aspect of sport that can be exclusionary for some pupils. This chapter looks beyond the way in which PE and sport discriminates against individuals from minority groups and focuses more generally on pupils who find some of the practices and values inherent within PE and sport inhibiting.

Specifically, I refer to a common belief that in order to be successful in a sporting context (a game, match or competition), participants are required to dominate their opponent, to 'manipulate' them in such a way so that they do not pose a threat to the ultimate goal of winning. This is achieved by regulating opponents' movements usually through exerting one's own physicality and psychological will upon the opposition. In one sense, it might be argued that this is what sport is all about, being the better competitor both physically and psychologically. But all too often players come to view their opponents as 'the enemy', as an obstacle that has to be overcome through whatever means possible. The focus of this chapter concerns the nature of participation that emphasises this as the natural and inevitable consequence of participation in PE and sport. I shall call this way of participating in PE and sport 'control and domination'. I will argue that 'control and domination' is characteristic of a 'performance discourse' (Tinning 1997: 102) that denies some pupils the opportunity to participate fully in the sporting contest and consequently that it serves to exclude some pupils from PE and sport. I will then suggest how, through the teaching of sportspersonship and fair play ideals, this might enable pupils to appreciate that 'other people matter'.

'Control and domination' within sport

In seeking to illustrate how the idea of 'control and domination' might serve to exclude some pupils from PE and sport, it is useful to explore some common ways in which we think about sport and sporting contests. Our understanding of what sport is about, how we view competition between two teams or players is a result of our upbringing (see Fernandez-Balboa 2000). Furthermore, we come to see sport as having certain inevitable and natural characteristics that lead us to accept unquestioningly the culture of sport. It is this naturalness that needs to be explored, because as Dodds (1993) points out, we may not always be aware of the effects our practices have on others.

Arguably at the very heart of the way in which society thinks about sport is the classical assumption that a sporting contest must have a winner and a loser. In this context the zero-sum gain of sport, that if A wins, then B loses, when viewed as the only outcome of taking part in sport can only serve to exclude all those who end up as Bs. Biddle (1997) points out how success in sport is a factor in continued participation. When winning assumes the mantle of success in sport, then inevitably a large number of pupils are doomed to failure. Let me state at this stage that I am not against sporting contests having a winner and a loser. Indeed, I am positively in favour of this as winning (and learning to lose) is an important part of any sport. It is an athlete's attempt to win that enables him/her to engage in sport. It allows a competitor to show what he/she can do, to utilise all his/her skills, to develop the skills that are weak and reinforce those that are strong, to rise to the challenge and to have fun. The important point to consider, however, is that winning is not the only aim, it is one of many. When the desire to win subsumes other goals then the resulting practice can be exclusionary for pupils who lose.

Having acknowledged how winning is sometimes seen as the ultimate goal of participation in sport, it is useful to pursue how, in the quest to win, the nature of the contest between two players can be exclusionary. Specifically, players often come to regard opponents as 'the enemy', an obstacle that has to be overcome. Fernandez-Balboa (2000) points out how sport can become 'us against them'. Furthermore, he states that this can give rise to feelings of 'apprehension, hatred and madness' towards opponents (Fernandez-Balboa 2000: 137). Drewe (1999) provides an example of this in her interviews with college athletes. She reports how, out of a sense of loyalty to the team, some athletes were prepared to break the rules and even injure an opponent. For many athletes, self-interest (either individual or team self-interest) is assumed to be a central part of participating in a sporting contest. Although all performers do not exhibit this approach to competition there does seem to be a developing body of literature that would support this.

Shields and Bredemeier (1995) emphasise how participation in sporting activities can lead to what they have called 'game reasoning', a form of 'bracketed morality' which is separate from everyday life. For Shields and Bredemeier 'bracketed morality' refers to the way in which players justify ways of behaving in sport that would be unacceptable in other contexts. Consequently, 'game reasoning' explains how players are more accepting of injurious and/or aggressive acts when they are part of a sporting experience than they are when this type of behaviour is propagated in situations outside of sport. Thus, the strategies and tactics players adopt in their quest to win can become a salient factor in determining the extent to which sport is inclusive. These strategies and tactics range from employing *only* skilful performance in order to outwit an opponent or team, to using a combination of skill *and* unfair and illegal practices. Frequently, deception of the referee and opponents through various forms of cheating and the use of aggression[2] is tolerated (to varying degrees). We should all recognise and abhor aggression within sport, such as when a player deliberately fouls an opponent, and make our condemnation known to the perpetrator. 'Lesser' acts, however, such as a player playing on after he/she (and his/her opponents) knows the ball has gone out of play might not draw as much criticism. Moreover, because of the way in which we are socialised into sport (see Stroot 2002) acts such as these might even pass without comment, as they could simply be seen as 'part of the game'. At the very least we ought to recognise that acts such as these are unsporting, but would we acknowledge them as exclusionary? There are two reasons why we might. First, when a player privileges his/her self-interest in pursuit of victory to the extent that he/she engages in acts such as over aggression, or cheating (for example), this violates the principle of fairness that is assumed to have been agreed upon when entering into the game (Leaman 1988). The perpetrator of the unfair and illegal act does not allow his/her opponent an equal opportunity to participate in the sporting contest. He/she is 'freeloading', accepting that an opponent will play fairly but not making the same commitment (Wigmore and Tuxill 1995). Consequently, what both players put into the game is uneven. Second, they serve to provide some pupils with a negative experience. As Penney (2002: 112) states, 'children are not equally positioned to participate in Physical Education and sport'. Consequently, those pupils who do not identify with this way of participating in sport might come to believe that they do not have what it takes in order to be successful in the sporting domain. Sport therefore becomes an unattractive pastime.

Not all practices that young athletes employ in pursuit of winning are examples of cheating, yet some might still serve to exclude certain pupils from sport. For example, consider the actions of an athlete who 'stares out' an opponent or competitor, or one who points out to a fellow swimmer how he/she is going to be placed well down the field. Acts such as these, like many others, are not neutral, they can be the attempts of one athlete to impose his/her power and authority over an opponent, a form of dominance. We might recognise these acts as gamesmanship, but they are not against the rules. Moreover, bowling a bouncer in cricket is also not against the rules, but is clearly intended to intimidate the batter. Again, we might recognise acts such as these as an inevitable part of sport, but do they exclude others? I think the answer is yes, for some children they do. Involvement in acts of cheating, gamesmanship and intimidation may well present some pupils with the view that this is a natural and inevitable part of sport. As Penney (2002) reminds us, exclusion is based upon assumptions that some people 'just haven't got it'. For those pupils who do not identify with this way of participating, then they might come to believe that PE and sport is not for them.

Having illustrated some common assumptions about the nature of sport and how this might serve to exclude some pupils, I now turn to the notion of 'control and domination'. 'Control and domination' as I use it here refers to a way of participating in sport that athletes employ in their desire to win. But, more importantly, it relates to a way of participating in sport (in which players use a range of strategies such as, but not limited to, those that I have outlined about) that serve to restrict the opportunity of an opponent to take part in a sporting context. Moreover, it is based upon features that are evident within professional models of sport, which are often characterised by a 'win at all costs' approach. If, as I have stated here, strategies aimed at 'control and domination' marginalise the experience of an opponent, or deny them the opportunity to take a full part in the sporting contest, then we can begin to see how sport played in this way is not inclusive.

Thus far in this discussion I have focused on sport. I turn now to consider PE. One objection to the line of reasoning I present here might be that the notion of 'control and domination' is a characteristic of sport and is unlikely to be reflected within a school context as there are marked distinctions between PE and sport.[3] The discussion that follows, however, seeks to highlight how the relationship between PE and sport is likely to perpetuate the notion of 'control and domination' within PE.

PE and school sport

Proponents of the view that PE and sport are different might argue that, because of the educative nature of PE, winning does not assume as high a priority, therefore it does not reflect the aspects of 'control and domination' that are characteristic of sport. There is some merit in this argument as PE and sport played within some schools is not as 'serious' as that played within the wider social context, but I am concerned to pursue the extent to which we might find aspects of 'control and domination' within PE and school sport. As Zine (2001: 239) reminds us, within any discourse there are 'often conflicting goals and interests vying with each other for limited spaces', which gives rise to competing discourses with some given more prominence than others (Penney and Evans, 1999).

To begin with, I point to the way in which the boundaries between PE and sport have been drawn closer together over the last decade. This has been particularly evident both within government publications (DNH, 1995; DCMS, 2000) and the wider PE literature (Siedentop, 1994). In many people's eyes, therefore, pupils' in particular, PE and school sport is seen to reflect wider connotations of sport and all that this entails. Indeed, as Fernandez-Balboa (2000) reminds us, PE cannot divorce itself from the influences of the wider societal context within which it sits. Links between PE and sport, therefore, appear strong.

A further reason as to why we might find practices linked to the notion of 'control and domination' within PE and school sport is to do with the process of socialisation. All PE teachers will have been, and perhaps still are, sports participants themselves, and, therefore, engender the values that they have learned through sport. PE teachers are therefore, products of their sporting experiences, they have been socialised into the game. Consequently, some practices might be so ingrained into teachers' consciousnes that they are unquestioningly natural. For example, take the pushing and shoving that goes on within football, that is seen by many as 'all part of the game'. Several years ago whilst on a Football Association coaching course, the instructor told the group of which I was a part that when marked tightly, to create space, an attacker should 'move away from the ball and then check back into the space created to receive the pass'. That seemed like good advice, but here is the catch. When checking back into the space the instructor told us that an attacker should 'just give the defender a little push to get him/her off balance'. For years I taught this to attackers, and could not understand why some pupils would get upset with opponents when others were pushing and shoving them off the ball. 'It's all part of the game', I would tell them, 'get used to it.' Sport is replete with examples such as this. As I have illustrated above, however, this way of playing sport is not inclusive.

The final reason I give for why 'control and domination' might be evident within PE and school sport relates to how traditionally elitism has become the dominant discourse (Tinning 1997, Penney 2002). If Tinning and Penney are correct, it seems reasonable to assume that one would also find values and ideals that are characteristic of participation in this manner, that is 'control and domination'. For Thomas (1993), the introduction of the Education Reform Act (DES 1988) meant that the focus on elitism within PE and school sport became a marketable asset for both PE departments and schools. Indeed, as I have argued elsewhere, in the era of 'open enrolment' and schools' 'marketability' the pressure on PE staff to produce winning teams is leading to the adoption of some practices from elite sport (Theodoulides 2002: 17). As one teacher confided to me:

> It's the league tables ... we're no longer in the situation of [simply 'playing the game'], we're all at such a level it's not good enough for us to turn around now and say, 'Well look we are one of the better schools, we will win 80 per cent of our games every year.' It's not like that. We've got to get every single edge we can, from hospitality of referees, by making sure we have someone to meet them and greet them [when they arrive]. But it might count for three points somewhere in the season. And specifically talking to the players and saying, 'Well the referee is on the right of the scrum, let's go left.' Why are we doing this? We're looking to maul as opposed to ruck, because if we maul the ball and they drag it down that's potentially three points. Now that's not a positive encouragement of the game, but it's gamesmanship because if you need three points you're going to maul the ball as opposed to ruck it because the opposition have got more chance of giving away a penalty. We teach that heavily.
>
> (Malcolm, Head of Games)

It seems clear, therefore, that, along with some of the practices that might be associated with elite sport, 'control and domination' has become a more salient part of pupils' experience of PE and sport. Furthermore, I have shown how PE and sport, when seen in terms of 'control and domination', has the potential to be a negative experience for many pupils. One frequently hears arguments in favour of PE and sport, however, which attempt to justify what I have argued here are exclusionary practices. For example, it might be argued that aggression is part of sport, indeed part of society, and sport is a good way for pupils to learn that they need to stand up for themselves and strive for what they want, to work hard for their success. This propagates 'the survival of the fittest'. Those pupils who are excluded are expected to find another physical activity to participate in where they will find success. Or worse still, they look for something outside of PE and sport to which they are more suited. It is these pupils who are excluded from participation because they do not identify with this notion of 'control and domination'. Yet it does not have to be like this, as this is only one way of viewing PE and sport (albeit a common one) and one that can be challenged. Yet, adopting a critical approach to PE and sport and 'undertaking the difficult task of confronting our biases and perceptions' that seem so natural and inevitable is not easy (Fernandez-Balboa 2000: 139). So what can PE teachers do about this? How can they get across to pupils that 'control and domination' do not have to be a natural and inevitable part of sport, and that if, as I have argued here, this serves to exclude some pupils from PE and sport, a more inclusive pedagogic strategy could be adopted?

Changing the nature of participation in PE and sport

Although 'control and domination' might be seen as a natural and inevitable part of playing sport it is not, it is only one way, albeit a popular one. Other alternatives can be sought which might prove more relevant to the current debate. In particular, Tinning (1997: 103) maintains that PE ought to focus more on 'participation discourses', which are 'about inclusion, equity, involvement, enjoyment, social justice, caring, co-operation, movement and so forth'. Thus, in order to focus on a more participatory form of taking part in PE and school sport, a useful strategy might be for staff involved in teaching PE and sport to pupils in schools to focus on other ways of participating in which players come to appreciate that 'other people matter'. What I am suggesting here is only one way of making PE and sport *more* inclusive for some pupils; it will not make PE and school sport *totally* inclusive for everyone. Dodds (1993: 31) draws our attention to how teachers should be proactive in 'recognising and being sensitive to equity issues in their own classes; developing specific strategies to interpret inequalities and address oppression'. I aim to conclude by exploring how, through a greater focus upon sportspersonship and fair play values, PE and school sport can be made a more positive experience for a greater number of pupils.

To begin with it is useful to consider that any commitment towards teaching an 'alternative' way of participating in sport requires teachers to show resolve in meeting their goals in this area. Often when 'new' initiatives are put forward they fail because, for a variety of reasons, teachers are resistant to change. As Ennis (1992) points out, teachers' values are central to the learning experience they provide pupils. Furthermore, Fernandez-Balboa (2000) states how making PE and sport more equitable requires physical educators to take a long, hard look at the practices in which they are engaged. In this context, this will require teachers to consider their own values about how players should compete in a sporting contest. This 'alternative' that I aim to explore is not new, but requires teachers to make a greater commitment to what is already part of the PE rationale. By focusing on the teaching of social and moral issues within PE and school sport, and, more specifically, notions of fair play and sportspersonship, this might help us to clarify to pupils how participating in PE and school sport can provide a positive experience for both the player and his/her opponent. But the development of sportspersonship and fair play does not occur automatically within PE and sport. Although the teaching of social and moral issues within PE is often believed to be a central part of the rationale for PE,[4] there is little empirical evidence to suggest that these aims are being met (Theodoulides and Armour, 2001). That does not presuppose, however, the possibility that they might not be met in the future. Fernandez-Balboa (1997: 123) has argued for changes in PE and sport in order to be more 'socially critical', to challenge 'the status quo and construct new avenues for integration and possibility' within sport.

Having acknowledged how 'control and domination' refers to a form of participation through which players aim to dominate an opponent it is useful now to explore how a greater commitment to teaching sportspersonship and fair play ideals might serve to make PE and school sport more inclusive. Shields (2001) alludes to the inadequate use of language within sport to refer to the different values that people hold with regard to what sport entails. He provides a distinction between two important concepts, what he calls competition and decompetition. This distinction is useful in that it presents a means of separating different ways of taking part in sport. Like 'control and domination', decompetition refers to the playing of sport in which players are involved in a battle, opponents are rivals, officials obstacles and rules there to be broken. But it is his notion of competition that is particularly useful. He writes, 'Competition reflects a metaphor of partnership. By this metaphor, each competitor is viewed as an enabler (in the positive sense) for the other; each requires the other to bring out the best in each' (ibid.: 3). Through this metaphor of partnership an opponent is no longer 'the enemy' but someone who players participate with in a co-operative activity. In this way of playing the game players become predisposed to consider their opponents and his/her experience of the sporting contest. It is the player who appreciates that other competitors have the right to participate in a swimming race without being subjected to derogatory comments about how they are going to be well beaten who makes taking part more inclusive in the school environment. Thus, pupils can come to learn that one can still set out to win, but do so in a manner that enables an opponent to gain a positive experience rather than one in which he/she is subjected to the potentially harmful effects of 'control and domination'. Furthermore, Shields continues, 'Competitors are fundamentally guided in their actions by the ideals of fairness and non-injurious play ... Upholding the ideals of fairness, non-injurious play and the spirit of competition – even when not required by the rules – is the core of sportspersonship' (ibid.: 4). So it is with regard to the ideals of sportspersonship and the social and moral basis upon which it is premised that we might find one opportunity to provide a more inclusive experience for many pupils within PE and school sport. Through an understanding of sportspersonship and fair play ideals pupils should come to realise that 'other people matter'.

When played in the spirit of competition as outlined above, sport has the potential to be more inclusive. In particular, the idea that PE and school sport requires a player to develop strategies aimed at 'control and domination' becomes less salient when players appreciate how their actions impact upon an opponent. So, for example, a player will come to realise that playing on after the ball has gone out of play is a selfish act, and one that has consequences for the other players involved. Thus, the player develops an appreciation of how what they do is part of the larger process of interaction between sporting competitors and how each player has a responsibility to those he/she competes with. Furthermore, as Feezell (1998) suggests, sportspersonship by winning through skilful means becomes a more valued outcome than winning through cheating. Feezell goes on to state that unsporting actions tend to 'arise from an excessive seriousness that negates the play-spirit because of an exaggerated emphasis on the value of victory' (ibid.: 158). Furthermore, in this light we can see how acts of intimidation also appear out of place within PE and school sport. For instance, the example given above of the bowler that bowls a bouncer to intimidate a batter becomes inappropriate when players are taking part in an activity that is non-serious and play-like. Played in this manner, sportspersonship and fair play ideals play down the notion that PE and school sport is congruent with self-interest in a way that encourages children to reflect upon the idea of how 'other people matter'. In addition, PE and school sport becomes more magnanimous and reflects further the values of equity, fairness and justice. It is this idea that 'other people matter' which can serve to make PE and sport more inclusive.

Conclusion

This chapter has shown how a popular way of viewing participation in PE and sport presupposes that competitors strive for 'control and domination.' Yet, as I have also stated, this is only one way of participating in sport and, whilst it is not indicative of all sporting contests, it might serve to exclude those pupils who fail to identify with this way of taking part in sporting activities. Thus, 'control and domination' is one example of the unconscious way in which PE and sport continues 'perpetuating that which is damaging and degrading' for some children (Fernandez-Balboa 2000: 135). A more inclusive approach to PE and school sport requires that both PE staff and pupils give greater attention to the way in which players participate within a sporting contest so as to consider the notion that 'other people matter'. In this way players are encouraged to consider what an opponent gains from his/her sporting experience. Consequently, this might provide a more positive experience for those pupils who find the aggressive and 'win at all costs' nature of PE and sport a negative experience. This, however, will require a more proactive approach from some teachers, as there is a general belief amongst teachers of PE that pupils learn sportspersonship and fair play simply by taking part in PE and sport. When we examine this more critically we become aware that, just as pupils might learn about sportspersonship and fair play, so they might come to see PE and sport in terms of 'control and domination'. With the introduction of citizenship onto the key stage 3 and key stage 4 curriculum in England in September 2002, there is an opportunity for PE and school sport to help 'Create a society where people matter more than things' (Archbishop Desmond Tutu, quoted in DfEE/QCA 1999b: 13). This may provide a good opportunity to review the way in which PE and school sport can contribute to a more equitable society within the framework of democratic rights.

Reflective questions

1   Consider your own sporting values. How do you view your opponent(s) within the context of a game or a match? What factors might impact upon the way in which you view the opposition?
2   Do all sports and physical activities give rise to forms of 'control and domination', or are they likely to occur in some sports more than others? What reasons would you give for this?
3   Reflect upon different ways in which 'control and domination' might manifest itself upon the manner in which pupils participate in PE and sport. List the type of behaviours that it might give rise to. Are all of these exclusionary? Give an example of how 'control and domination' can serve to exclude some pupils within the context of their PE lessons.
4   Pupils come to PE with their own idea vis-à-vis what sport is about. How might you challenge these ideas to get across to pupils that 'other people matter'? What learning and teaching strategies might you use?
5   Reflect upon the concept of citizenship. What does it mean to you? How might PE contribute to citizenship?

Notes

1   Skilful performance presupposes an accompanying level of fitness and psychological characteristics.
2   I believe that this is an impoverished way of viewing participation in sport, but it is one that nonetheless is commonly held. Drewe (1999) highlights the way in which some athletes reason about aggressive acts and cheating within sport and come to see it as 'all part of the game'.
3   I do not want to explore in detail alleged differences in definitions of PE and sport, although it is worth pointing out that I do not believe that any perceived differences are as great as sometimes professed. At this point I merely point out that this is an on-going debate within the PE profession.
4   See the NCPE (DfEE/QCA 1999a: 8) or the PEA UK (www.peauk.com/menu/html)

References

Biddle, S. J. H. (1997) 'Cognitive Theories of Motivation and the Physical Self', in K. R. Fox (ed.), *The Physical Self: From Motivation to Well-being*, Champaign, Ill.: Human Kinetics: 59–82.

DCMS (Department for Culture, Media and Sport) (2000) *A Sporting Future for All: The Government's Plan for Sport*, London: HMSO.

DES (Department for Education and Science) (1988) *The Education Reform Act*, London: HMSO.

DfEE/QCA (Department for Education and Employment/Qualifications and Curriculum Authority) (1999a) *Physical Education: The National Curriculum for England*, London: HMSO.

DfEE/QCA (Department for Education and Employment /Qualifications and Curriculum Authority) (1999b) *Citizenship: The National Curriculum for England*, London: HMSO.

DNH (Department of National Heritage) (1995) *Sport: Raising the Game*, London: HMSO.

Dodds, P. (1993) 'Removing the Ugly '-Isms' in Your Gym: Thoughts for Teachers on Equity', in J. Evans and B. Davies (eds), *Equality, Education and Physical Education*, London: Falmer Press: 28–39.

Drewe, S. B. (1999) 'Moral Reasoning in Sport: Implications for Physical Education', *Sport, Education and Society* 4, 2: 117–30.

Ennis, C. (1992) 'The Influence of Value Orientations in Curriculum Decision Making', *QUEST* 44: 317–29.

Feezell, R. M. (1998) 'Sportsmanship', in W.J. Morgan and K.V. Meier (eds), *Philosophic Inquiry in Sport*, Champaign, Ill.: Human Kinetics: 152–60.

Fernandez-Balboa, J. M. (1997) 'Teacher Education and Teacher Preparation in the Postmodern Era: Toward a Critical Pedagogy', in J. M. Fernandez-Balboa (ed.), *Critical Postmodernism in Human Movement, Physical Education and Sport*, New York: SUNY: 121–38.

Fernandez-Balboa, J. M. (2000) 'Discrimination: What Do We Know, and What Can We Do About It?' in R. L. Jones and K. M. Armour (eds), *Sociology of Sport: Theory and Practice*, Harlow: Longman: 134–44.

Leaman, O. (1988) 'Cheating and Fair Play in Sport', in W. J. Morgan and K. V. Meier (eds), *Philosophic Inquiry in Sport*, Champaign, Ill.: Human Kinetics: 193–97.

Penney, D. (2002) 'Equality, equity and inclusion in physical education and sport', in A. Laker (ed.) *The Sociology of Sport and Physical Education: An Introduction*, London: Routledge/Falmer: 110–28.

Penney, D. and Evans, J. (1999) *Politics, Policy and Practice in Physical Education*, London: E. and F. Spon.

Shields, D. L. (2001) 'Opponents or Enemies: Rethinking the Nature of Competition', *Paper Presented at the Mendelson Centre's Inaugural Conference: Sport Character and Culture: Promoting Social and Moral Development Through Sport*, University of Notre Dame, 11–14 May.

Shields, D. L. and Bredemeier, B. J. L. (1995) *Character Development and Physical Activity*, Champaign Ill.: Human Kinetics.

Siedentop, D. (1994) *Sport Education: Quality PE Through Positive Sporting Experiences*, Champaign, Ill.: Human Kinetics.

Stroot, S. A. (2002) 'Socialisation and Participation in Sport', in A. Laker (ed.), *The Sociology of Sport and Physical Education: An Introduction*, London: Routledge/Falmer: 129–47.

Tinning, R. (1997) 'Performance and Participation Discourses in Human Movement: Towards a Socially Critical Physical Education', in J. M. Fernandez-Balboa (ed.), *Critical Postmodernism in Human Movement, Physical Education and Sport*, New York: SUNY: 99–119.

Theodoulides, A. (2002) 'I Would never Personally tell Anyone to break the Rules, but you can Bend Them', *Paper Presented at The BERA 2002 Annual Conference*, University of Exeter, 12–14 September.

Theodoulides, A. and Armour, K. M. (2001) 'Personal, Social and Moral Development Through Team Games: Some Critical Questions', *European Physical Education Review* 7, 1: 5–23.

Thomas, S. (1993) 'Education Reform: Juggling the Concepts of Equality and Elitism', in J. Evans and B. Davies (eds), *Equality, Education and Physical Education*, London: Falmer Press: 105–24.

Wigmore, S. and Tuxill, C. (1995) 'A Consideration of the Concept of Fair Play', *European Physical Education Review* 1, 1: 67–73.

Zine, J. (2001) '"Negotiating Equity": The Dynamics of Minority Engagement in Constructing Inclusive Educational Policy', *Cambridge Journal of Education* 31, 2: 239–69.

On the sports field he was a track-suited tormentor with a whistle. It was this lack of enthusiasm, this covert bullying, that gradually wore me down. I was hopeless at sport, and because sport is played mostly in terms of winners and losers, members and non-members, I stayed hopeless. Wasn't it the job of the teacher to teach me how to be better at it? Or to find a way of sustaining my flagging enthusiasm, rather than leaving me to be figuratively and literally beaten down into the ground? Apparently not.

A. Miller (2002) *Tilting at Windmills: How I Tried to Stop Worrying and Love Sport*, London: Viking Books: 15.
Reproduced by permission of Penguin Books.

4 Special educational needs and National Curriculum Physical Education

Philip Vickerman, Sid Hayes and Alan Whetherly

> Through Education for All, it should be possible to enable all human beings – including the disabled – to develop their full potential, to contribute to society and, above all, to be enriched by their difference and not devalued. In our world constituted of differences of all kinds, it is not the disabled but society at large that needs special education in order for a society to become a genuine society for all.
>
> (Federico Mayor, cited in McConkey 2001: 10)

Background and context

The statement above sets demanding goals for all those involved in education and does, to an extent, reflect the present Labour Government's approach to the inclusion of pupils with special educational needs (SEN). The issues surrounding inclusive practice have risen up the political and statutory agenda to such an extent that more pupils than ever before are being educated within mainstream contexts. Statistical evidence from the Department for Education and Skills (DfES) shows, for example, year on year rises in the number of pupils with SEN being included within mainstream education (DfES: 2001). In 1993, 48 per cent of SEN pupils were taught in mainstream environments, rising to 57 per cent in 1997 and most recently 61 per cent completing their education in a mainstream school. In addition, this commitment to inclusion of pupils with SEN is further emphasised by the DfES which states, 'The education of pupils with special needs is a key challenge for the nation. It is vital to the creation of a fully inclusive society' (DfES 1998: 1).

This increased focus upon inclusion has recently seen legislation implemented through the Statutory Inclusion Statement in the most recent National Curriculum 1999 (NC), SEN and Disability Rights Act 2001, and the Revised Code of Practice 2001. In addition, the Teacher Training Agency (2002) revised standards for the award of Qualified Teacher Status and the Office for Standards in Education (OFSTED) Inspection Framework (OFSTED 2002) have enhanced their focus on the scrutiny, competence and implementation of inclusive Physical Education (PE) for pupils with SEN.

Thus, the commitment to inclusive PE for pupils with SEN is well evidenced, and PE teachers will need to embrace these issues within their learning and teaching practices in order to ensure that they maximise opportunities for all pupils to participate and perform. This chapter will consider how teachers can begin to address issues surrounding the inclusion of pupils with SEN, as defined by the 2001 Code of Practice, within mainstream PE contexts. It will examine both the philosophical and practical application of PE for pupils with SEN, whilst offering strategies to enhance the delivery of barrier-free inclusive activity. The chapter concludes with a summary of key features for teachers to address when planning and delivering inclusive PE for pupils with SEN.

Personal reflections

Philip Vickerman

The issue of inclusion for me has been one of the most rewarding aspects of teaching both PE and sport. Planning and delivering inclusive physical activity does pose many challenges for teachers, but central to any success is a positive, open mind and high expectations for pupils with SEN.

In the past, teacher training related to inclusive issues was rather patchy. Over time, however, and in part due to the increased numbers of pupils with SEN in mainstream schools, the training agenda has started to shift in a positive direction. This greater emphasis, supported through changes to the curriculum, is now beginning to focus much more clearly on the issues that teachers need to address in order to deliver good quality learning and teaching experiences to pupils with SEN. The personal motivation to write this chapter comes from work I have undertaken over recent years to train teachers and higher education institutions to reflect much more on this aspect of their work, and to recognise that the most important factor is gaining the confidence to look at your teaching from different perspectives in order to make your lessons accessible to the many rather than the few.

Sid Hayes

The issue of inclusion has been of interest ever since my teacher training days where it constituted a small but significant part of my B.Ed. course in Physical Education. It was in these informative stages of professional development where attempts within my pedagogical practice to be inclusive were hatched, with relatively limited success. The inclusion debate has remained high priority for me since then and has certainly remained consistently at the forefront of government discourse in education matters. The fact that it has remained high-profile suggests that the circumstances surrounding 'best' inclusive practices have yet to be resolved. The PE profession has without doubt moved on from past practices, in its patronising recognition of inclusion as about giving those pupils with additional learning needs the stopwatch to time the other pupils, to a genuinely more inclusive approach, allowing pupils, irrespective of circumstance, to engage in the curriculum. There are still some challenges ahead, however, and the motivation for contributing this chapter stems from work with trainees who still at times find it difficult to incorporate inclusive practices within their teaching, or to recognise the place of such principles in their professional rationale and mainstream practice.

Alan Whetherly

I have experienced first-hand both exclusion and inclusion in sporting activities. Being a visually impaired person who is keen to participate in sport I am aware of the benefits that sport can provide to people with disabilities. Apart from the obvious health benefits, it has given me social skills, self-confidence, self-esteem, opportunities for travel and the vehicle to show my ability rather than my disability. With increasing numbers of SEN children being integrated into mainstream education I hope that they will be able to access fully the PE curriculum. Disappointingly, the numbers of young disabled people participating in sport outside of school have dropped. I strongly believe that by creating a strong interest at school we have a chance to reduce the isolation that some young disabled people feel and to encourage possible future Paralympic champions to continue to participate in sport after they leave school.

Equality for pupils with SEN

In order for teachers to plan for inclusion within mainstream PE lessons it is important to first clarify that pupils with SEN have a fundamental right to an inclusive education, which is supported through legislation. In interpreting this legislation, however, PE teachers must recognise that in facilitating inclusion the critical success factors are an open mind, positive attitude and a readiness to review and modify existing learning and teaching strategies.

It is important to recognise that equality for pupils with SEN in PE is both socially and morally right in any modern society, and that schools offer pupils an ideal opportunity to learn mutual understanding and respect for difference and diversity. In considering the principles of equality, however, it is important to recognise that equality for pupils with SEN is not about treating all pupils in the same fashion. In contrast, in order for PE teachers to enable full access to the curriculum, they need to recognise individual pupils' needs, then plan accordingly for them. Dyson (1999) supports such a view and notes that equality of opportunity and inclusiveness should be concerned with celebrating difference, and creating systems in which pupils with SEN are treated equally, but differently, in order to meet their individual needs for accessibility and entitlement to all aspects of the PE curricula and extra-curricula programmes.

When planning for inclusion, Westwood (1997) supports the promotion of citizenship and the social model of disability within the curriculum as a means of shifting the emphasis away from pupils with the disability, and towards the roles that teachers and non-disabled peers can play (The 'social model' views disability in terms of the result of the interaction between people's physical, mental or sensory impairments and how the social environment impacts on them). For example, the concept of citizenship within the curriculum is based upon mutual understanding and respect for individual diversity. In support of this, the social model of disability recognises that often the greatest disabling factor is not the child with SEN, but the lack of flexibility and/or commitment to modify and adapt existing practices by schools and teachers. Inclusion for pupils with SEN should, therefore, be recognised as a process that is responsive and flexible to pupil needs, and moves beyond traditional concepts of integration and mainstreaming in which additional or separate practices are often bolted on to existing provision. Thus, inclusive PE for pupils with SEN is concerned with recognition of both the philosophical basis of inclusion as well as a commitment and desire to support its action through both policy implementation and a desire to change practice.

In order to implement change Farrell (2001) and Ainscow *et al.* (1999) advocate that PE teachers need to consider new ways of involving all pupils with SEN, and to draw on their skills of experimentation, reflection, and collaboration with external agencies.

The revised NCPE (QCA 1999) suggests that PE teachers should consider assessment in alternative activities, with flexible judgements and contexts in order to facilitate accessibility to the curriculum for pupils with SEN. In addition, as part of a systematic process, schools should audit their current practices and areas of expertise, and identify areas for further development. The Centre for Studies in Inclusive Education's (2000) *Index for Inclusion*, for example, is one such method in which schools can begin to review and evaluate the extent to which they are enabling pupils with SEN full access to the curriculum.

The NCPE and pupils with SEN

The NCPE goes on to state that 'teachers must take action' and 'ensure that their pupils are enabled to participate' (1999: 33), and be responsive to a diverse range of pupil needs in order to facilitate inclusive education. In meeting this requirement, therefore, PE teachers will need to review actively their learning and teaching approaches in order to ensure they meet the statutory requirements to facilitate entitlement and accessibility to inclusive activities for pupils with SEN.

In attempting to address the requirement of enabling pupils with SEN full access to the curriculum, Depauw and Doll-Tepper (2000) suggest that agencies such as Initial Teacher Training (ITT) providers, schools and PE teachers need to work in partnership to review and modify their current practices. In reviewing inclusive activity for pupils with SEN, however, it is vital that schools and teachers move beyond the level of merely getting on the inclusion bandwagon, paying lip-service to superficial changes such as policy statements but backed up by no real action in practice. In order for change to have a real impact, teachers need to acknowledge that the inclusion of pupils with SEN is part of a 'process model' in which principles of equal access are embedded throughout everything they do.

Thus, in order for schools and PE teachers to address the needs of pupils with SEN satisfactorily, Farrell argues that teachers must be willing to move beyond an acknowledgment of inclusion policies and be prepared 'to reconsider their structure, teaching approaches, pupil grouping and use of support.' (1998: 81).

In setting out to achieve such a socially inclusive PE context for pupils with SEN, however, Dyson notes some concern with the concept of disability now being 'at the heart of a new and privileged society' (1999: 2). According to Dyson, 'social inclusion' for pupils with SEN may be limited as it only pursues measures to remove difference that focus upon predicted equality, and are not necessarily outcome based.

Implementation of inclusive PE policies for pupils with SEN, therefore, may appear to be socially and morally right, but the danger is that the measurement of success will be seen through the expectation of statements written into school policies. The critical factors, however, need to be judged in terms of their impact and effects upon a child's quality of education and achievement, and not just in relation to a policy statement. (See Depauw and Doll-Tepper 2000, Dyson 2001, Farrell 2000, 2001 for further issues related to policy implementation and practice.)

Key guiding principles for pupils with SEN in PE

The 1992 National Curriculum for Physical Education (NCPE) identified four key principles in relation to equality that still hold true today as guiding principles that should be considered when including pupils with

SEN within mainstream PE. These are entitlement, accessibility, integration and integrity, and have acted as the corner stones upon which the most recent curriculum in PE has been built.

In relation to *entitlement*, for example, the premise is to acknowledge the fundamental right of pupils with SEN to be able to access the PE curriculum. This is of particular relevance with the emergence of the SEN and Disability Rights Act (2001) that gives pupils a right to inclusive activity, and the revised Code of Practice implemented in January 2002. The 2002 Code focused much more on the action of schools to implement and deliver inclusive PE through further delegation of centralised SEN budgets, which were re-directed directly into schools.

Thus teachers are expected to take action within the individual school context and modify and adapt existing practices in order to facilitate full entitlement to the NCPE for pupils with SEN. This shift in legislation recognises the philosophy of positive attitudes and open minds, and the commitment to a process that offers inclusive education, in which teachers overcome potential barriers through consultation and the adoption of flexible learning, teaching and assessment strategies.

In terms of the second principle, *accessibility*, it is the responsibility of teachers to make PE lessons accessible and relevant to the child with SEN. This recognises the social model of disability in which teachers should adjust their teaching in order to accommodate the needs of individual pupils rather than the child's disability being seen as the barrier to participation.

In examining the need to make PE lessons relevant and accessible it is important to recognise the view of Sugden and Talbot (1998) who advocate that 95 per cent of teaching pupils with SEN is merely an extension of existing mixed ability teaching. Teachers should, therefore, already have the necessary skills to facilitate inclusive PE, and will only occasionally require specialist advice and guidance. Thus the fundamental factor in a successful inclusive activity for pupils with SEN is a positive attitude and suitable differentiation within PE lessons. Whilst we recognise that there may be a few difficulties for practitioners to become more inclusive, we feel the profession is well placed to embrace inclusive practice in our subject area and, to a large extent, the process has begun. Evidence to support this is borne out of the responses to Ph.D. work presently being undertaken by one of the authors of this chapter (Vickerman, 2000). The work examines the training of PE teachers in relation to the inclusion of children with SEN. Twenty-four responses were received from ITT institutions and early findings indicate that the profession is moving in the right direction. For example, 87.5 per cent of all ITT PE providers support the notion of inclusive education as an integral aspect of their course programmes. In addition over 94 per cent of trainee PE teachers supported the notion of a child's right to an inclusive education.

The third principle of *integration* recognises the benefits of disabled and non-disabled pupils being educated together and the positive benefits that can be achieved for all pupils through such approaches. Although simply integrating pupils into one environment has limitations, it is a fundamental stepping stone towards inclusive practice, recognising difference but treating pupils appropriately as to their learning needs and allowing inclusive practice to develop. In addition, this begins to address the current UK government's citizenship agenda in which pupils are to be educated to have mutual understanding and respect for individual diversity as part of their involvement and participation within a socially inclusive society. In our view PE is an ideal vehicle for this to occur, with many activities involving teamwork and co-operation.

In relation to the final principle of *integrity*, PE teachers need to underpin their learning and teaching practice with a recognition that they value and believe in the adaptations and changes that are made to the activities they teach. Thus, as part of this personal commitment, they should ensure that inclusive PE for pupils with SEN is of equal worth, challenging, and in no way patronising or demeaning to the individual child concerned. In doing this PE teachers should adopt an approach where they set appropriate and challenging tasks to pupils who have an additional learning need whilst avoiding the 'cotton wool' approach which often assumes that these pupils cannot cope with some of the demands that a challenging curriculum may offer.

Extending and developing the key guiding principles

PE teachers, as part of their wider teaching philosophy and practices, should embrace the guiding principles discussed above if they are to make a genuine commitment to inclusive PE for pupils with SEN. In addition, as part of the revised NCPE, in conjunction with the four principles noted and commented upon above, teachers should spend time interpreting the inclusion statement and recognise the need to set suitable learning challenges, respond to pupils' diverse needs, and overcome potential barriers to learning and assessment for individuals and groups of pupils.

For example, in relation to *setting suitable learning challenges*, the QCA states, 'Teachers should aim to give every pupil the opportunity to experience success in learning and to achieve as high a standard as is possible' (1999: 28). It suggests that this can be achieved by teaching knowledge, skills and understanding of PE from earlier key stages, if appropriate, with the aim of ensuring those pupils with SEN achieve and progress.

It could be argued, therefore, that inclusion for pupils with SEN is about focusing upon earlier developmental expectations, or adopting a more flexible teaching approach to accommodate individuals' needs in terms of learning, teaching and assessment. Sugden and Talbot, for example, support this view through the principles of 'moving to learn' and 'learning to move'. They argue that:

> Physical Education has a distinctive role to play, because it is not simply about education of the physical but involves cognitive, social, language and moral development and responsibilities
>
> (Sugden and Talbot 1998: 22)

Thus, to facilitate inclusion, a shift away from the traditional outcome of PE (learning to move) in which skills are taught and learned, to a wider experience of PE (moving to learn) may be a means towards enabling access to inclusive PE. PE teachers, therefore, need to consider their learning outcomes carefully in order to ensure that all pupils with SEN have the opportunity to demonstrate a wide variety of movement learning experiences.

In relation to *responding to pupils' diverse learning needs* the NCPE states, 'When planning teachers should set high expectations and provide opportunities for all pupils to achieve including ... pupils with disabilities and special educational needs' (1999: 29). This section suggests that lessons should be planned to ensure full and effective access, and that teachers need to be aware of equal opportunity legislation.

This begins to answer some of Dyson's (1999) concerns that the curriculum needs to focus on how outcomes can be differentiated and measured for each child, rather than focusing upon philosophical definitions of equality. A key feature of this would be based upon the social model of disability (previously mentioned) and a commitment to change the activity to fit the child rather than the other way round (Vickerman 1997).

In terms of *overcoming potential barriers to learning and assessment for individuals and groups of pupils* the NCPE (2000) states that 'a minority of pupils will have particular learning and assessment requirements which go beyond the provisions described earlier (sections one and two) and if not addressed could create barriers to participation' (DfEE/QCA 1999: 30). In addition, the document states that this is usually as a consequence of a child's disability or SEN.

The curriculum suggests, therefore, that in order to create access, greater differentiation on the part of teachers and the use of external agencies or specialist equipment will begin to enable inclusion to occur. This statement is fundamental in ensuring that teachers recognise their full responsibility for creating accessible lessons that cater for all pupils' needs, whilst recognising the need to work through a multi-agency approach to deliver inclusive activities. For example, this may necessitate teachers having different expectations of some pupils with SEN or the modification of the assessment in such a way that a child has the opportunity to demonstrate the development of their skills.

Inclusion and emotional and behavioural difficulty (EBD) pupils

As pointed out, we feel that schools and the PE profession are well placed to take on board the processes required for developing an effective inclusion strategy for pupils with a variety of learning difficulties. Developing inclusive practices for pupils who regularly demonstrate behaviour difficulties, however, poses a somewhat different set of issues for the teacher. As OFSTED states in its report outlining Local Educational Authority (LEA) strategy for the inclusion of pupils with special needs:

> It is in relation to these pupils that the tension between the needs of the individual pupil and the needs of the organisation (or, less pejoratively, the collective needs of all the pupils in the school) becomes most acute . . . The child with behavioural problems poses a different set of issues for inclusion than those set by pupils with learning difficulties or physical or sensory impairment.
>
> (OFSTED 2002: 15)

The reasons for such behaviour may be due to a complex number of circumstances, which may have their roots either within or outside the school environment, and these are well-documented (Martin and Hayes 1998, Cohen and Cohen 1987). It is not the purpose of this chapter to re-examine these causes but to consider how these pupils can be a part of a school-wide inclusive strategy. As we have pointed out, it is reasonable to assume that challenges posed by pupils with behavioural difficulties are somewhat different from those challenges posed by pupils with other learning needs. We do, however, feel it is correct and necessary to view these pupils as part of any overall inclusive strategy whilst also accepting that they constitute a different set of demands and occupy a distinctive, separate part of the whole inclusive spectrum. Behavioural problems are a key challenge facing a number of schools and this has been highlighted by OFSTED in its annual report on schools in 2001, where it is stated that 'The extent of unsatisfactory behaviour, is, as last year, a cause for concern' (OFSTED 2001).

It is prudent and realistic to suggest that the teaching profession should address issues of inclusive practice in stages as part of a previously mentioned process. It may be that, presently, issues of behaviour management within schools need to be tackled at a managerial level before we can expect PE teachers and teachers in general to embrace inclusive processes for pupils with major behavioural difficulties within their daily teaching regimes, as well as other inclusive processes that are already being developed. In some schools this is clearly happening, in others, there is still some way to go (OFSTED 2001). If managerial guidance and structure occurs then it should be possible for all teachers, including PE practitioners, to move forwards in achieving long-term inclusive practices for all pupil needs, including EBD pupils, as part of an overall inclusive school strategy. If behavioural issues are not addressed initially at a senior managerial level in the school, however, then face-to-face conflicts that practitioners regularly come across may continue to be dealt with in a haphazard way outside of an overall inclusive philosophy.

Practical examples of inclusive PE for pupils with SEN

When planning inclusive PE for pupils with SEN, it is important to start from the premise of full inclusion within the activity, and, where this may not be possible, to consider adaptation and/or modification of learning and teaching strategies or activities.

The central success factor for teachers is to consult initially, where appropriate with the child with SEN and relevant professionals as part of a multi-disciplinary approach. This enables the pupil and teachers to consider, at the planning stage, any differentiation that may be required. This further supports the principle of equality and the social model approach that acknowledges individual diversity. It also responds accordingly to the needs of pupils with SEN by modifying or adapting activities as appropriate.

An example of this could be in games activities such as hockey, where pupils may initially require lighter, larger or different coloured balls in order to access the activity. Adaptations to rules may need to be considered, such as allowing a player with movement restrictions five seconds to receive and play the ball. In addition, if utilising such a strategy, it is vital that all members of the group understand the need for such an adaptation in order that they can play to this rule during a game.

In dance, activities can be adapted through consultation with the disabled and non-disabled pupils, as part of the requirements of the curriculum to work co-operatively. For example a pupil in a wheelchair can use the chair as an extension of their body to move around a particular area. If group tasks are to be performed, then the group can work together on themes for inclusion in which the movement patterns of the pupils with SEN can be incorporated into the overall group piece being performed.

Another example of inclusive participation in athletic activities with physically disabled pupils may involve one push of their wheelchair, rather than a jump into the sandpit, or reducing distances to run or travel. In addition, if there are pupils with visual impairments teachers can organise activities such as a 100-metre race in which a guide stands at the finish line and shouts out the lane number they are in, or a guide runs alongside them for support.

Opportunities for pupils with disabilities outside of the curriculum

The structure of disability sport

Although the central focus of this chapter relates to core curriculum matters in PE, it is necessary to briefly highlight how pupils may access activity outside of curriculum time through extra-curricular activities or within the community. There are a number of organisations and initiatives aimed at providing activity for pupils who have additional learning needs, and PE departments may wish to develop partnership links with such organisations to serve the needs of the pupils' post-curriculum time.

The structure of disability sport is evolving. In 1997 Sport England's Task Force on the future of disability sport recommended the mainstreaming of disability sport into the work of governing bodies of sport. There was a clear recognition, however, that this was not going to occur in the short term and that a considerable amount of work was going to have to be undertaken to achieve this objective.

The English Federation of Disability Sport (EFDS) was established in 1997 in order to achieve this. Its aims are to expand sporting opportunities for people with disabilities and increase the numbers actively involved in sport. It also aims to ensure that people with disabilities are included in sporting opportunities. There are nine EFDS regions where teachers can access information about local and national opportunities.

In 2002 seven National Disability Sports Organisations were in membership of EFDS. Each of these organisations provided sporting opportunities for a specific impairment group:

- British Amputee & Les Autres Sports Association
- British Blind Sport
- British Deaf Sports Council
- British Wheelchair Sports Foundation
- Cerebral Palsy Sport (CP Sport)
- Disability Sport England
- English Sports Association for People with Learning Disabilities (ESAPLD)

Finding local opportunities

There are two key pathways that can be followed outside school-based provision – disability-specific sports club or mainstream sports club. Most local authorities will have a sports/leisure development officer who will know where local sports clubs meet and how accessible they are to disabled people. Some local authorities produce directories of sports clubs that provide opportunities for disabled people. Sports development officers (SDOs) can also provide an invaluable link between the school PE department and the local sports community.

Governing bodies of sport have also taken an inclusive approach. Initiatives such as the Amateur Swimming Association (ASA) Swim 21 programme have ensured that disabled swimmers can access local swimming groups. EFDS' Ability Counts Programme has worked with the Football Association to ensure that professional clubs include young disabled people in their community programmes and local sports disability groups provide a good way of bridging the link between school and the community. In some cases it may be more appropriate to play sport in this setting, for example wheelchair basketball or visually impaired cricket.

Development work in disability sport is concentrating on providing people with disabilities with a choice. Clearly there is still a considerable way to go before we reach total inclusion and mainstreaming of disability sport. It is easy to be critical but it should be recognised that inclusion is a reality and not just a possibility. For example, the Manchester 2002 Commonwealth Games were a positive example of athletes with disabilities competing at the same venue as mainstream competitors. Although this has been attempted during numerous sporting events previously, the 2002 Commonwealth Games interspersed events for athletes with disabilities into the main programme and they were not simply tagged on at the end. New initiatives such as the introduction of Youth Sports Trust TOP Sportsability Programme has added a new dimension into the area of inclusive PE provision. The equipment produced has been aimed specifically at special schools or mainstream schools with units for pupils with SEN. Although this equipment is aimed at young people with SEN, young people of all abilities can join in playing by the same rules as their disabled peers. Five separate games were included in the equipment bag issued by the Youth Sports Trust which can be used to help those pupils with severe disabilities. These games are known as Boccia (a bowls-type game), table cricket, table hockey, Polybat (an adapted version of table tennis), and goalball, a game played by visually impaired people. Four of these games have pathways for young people to go on and progress from recreational level through to National, International and Paralympic competition, the exception being table hockey.

The tabletop games (although designed primarily to be played on a table tennis table) have the versatility to be played at most tables. Polybat was designed for those young disabled people with control and co-ordination difficulties. The development of a glove bat has ensured that those pupils who find it hard to grip a bat can handle the Polybat and so participate successfully. Another game that can be used for this equipment is table skittles, using plastic cups if skittles are not available. Goalball is a three-a-side game developed for visually impaired people; sighted players can join in as everyone wears adapted goggles. This is an example of reverse inclusion where sighted people can be included in a disability-specific game. It is important to consider how these activities can be developed further. One possibility could be an inter-school Sportsability competition or perhaps establishing a lunchtime or after-school club. Although these activities may go some way to addressing activity levels for people with disabilities, research undertaken by Sport England (2000) has highlighted some interesting differences in sports participation between people with disabilities and their non-disabled peers:

- Over a quarter of young disabled people had not taken part in sport more than ten times in the past year, compared with 6 per cent of non-disabled young people.
- Just over 56 per cent of young people with a disability had taken part in sport outside of school compared with 87 per cent for the non-disabled population.
- 37 per cent of young people with a disability had taken part in sport during their lunch break compared with 67 per cent of the overall population of young people.

Opportunities are being created for young disabled people to participate either recreationally or competitively in sport. It is knowing, however, where and how to access the network of provision available at both local and/or national level. The situation could be improved through better-informed partnerships between school PE departments and disability organisations, both nationally and regionally, and this could be a developing role within a PE department's structure.

Summary: Facilitating inclusive PE for pupils with SEN

Inclusive PE is a key issue for the government, schools and teachers to address in the coming years. The philosophical basis of inclusive PE for pupils with SEN is both socially and morally sound, and is supported through legislation and the development of new practices in teacher education.

The role of schools and teachers, however, is central to the success or otherwise of the government's agenda for inclusion. In order to achieve this, teachers need to adopt a clear and consistent framework in relation to PE for pupils with SEN. A necessary framework for inclusion should encompass a combination of philosophy, process and practice, which draws together a number of key points for consideration when planning and delivering PE to pupils with SEN.

Vickerman (2002) encourages PE teachers to recognise and spend time analysing, planning and implementing their delivery through the consideration of a series of interrelated factors. The first being to recognise and embrace the philosophy behind inclusion discussed within this chapter as a basic and fundamental human right, which is supported by professionals in society through statutory and non-statutory guidance such as the SEN and Disability Rights Act 2001, the revised Code of Practice and the revised curriculum for PE 1999.

In order to facilitate this process schools and teachers must embrace a purposeful approach to fulfilling the requirements of inclusive PE. Thus, time should be spent examining philosophical standpoints and a clear recognition of the rationale and arguments behind inclusive education. In order to achieve this teachers will need to be proactive in the development and implementation of inclusive PE and consult actively as a whole school, with fellow teachers and pupils with SEN, in order to produce a collaborative approach to their delivery within the school.

Inclusive PE for pupils with SEN requires a recognition and commitment to modify and adapt existing learning and teaching styles in order to facilitate full access and entitlement to the curriculum, and an obligation to undertake this through a social model of disability. The development of inclusive PE for pupils with SEN must, therefore, be recognised as a process that evolves, emerges and changes over time and, as such, will need regular review by all the key stakeholders.

In summary, PE teachers and schools must ensure that inclusion is reflected within policy documentation, as a means of monitoring, reviewing and evaluating delivery. The critical factor, however, is the need to move policy through into the pedagogical practices of PE teachers. Whilst philosophies and processes are vital for schools and teachers, they must ultimately measure their success in terms of effective inclusive practice, which is embedded within a 'person centred' approach to the education of pupils with SEN. Let us hope that managers in schools allow sufficient time and resources to colleagues to engage fully in this process.

To highlight the contribution that PE can make to pupil development we would like to offer the following testimony. This statement was offered to a colleague undertaking doctoral research as yet unpublished (the pupil's name has been altered):

> My name is Joe. I am now 17 years old. I have Down's syndrome and cystic fibrosis. I have been in mainstream education since I was 5. At school I took and passed five GCSEs, including Physical Education. I was really pleased with my achievements, especially the C in PE. Football, basketball and rounders were my favourite sports. I could not do rugby because my Down's means that my neck could have been injured in a scrum. I did things like cross-country but it was sometimes difficult. Cystic fibrosis affects my lungs and can make me tired. In the school sports days I always did the tug of war for my house. My two helpers supported me in all my lessons. I would not have done the GCSE PE without them. My teachers and friends always helped me. My PE teacher also helped me to understand the work. Sometimes I could help others in my class. For example, I helped dyslexic friends to spell because I am good at spelling and have a good memory. The staff, my friends and my family helped me to raise money for my favourite charity, Demelza House. I did a sponsored swim and raised £1,177. After this I was asked to join the Kent swimming squad and I still go to the swimming club (with my sister Emma). I would like to thank all the teachers, LSAs and students who helped me.

Reflective questions

1 Is there an identified departmental ethos regarding inclusive practice written in the PE handbook?
2 What part does the PE department play in the overall school policy for inclusive practice?
3 What strategies do teachers use within the PE department to include all pupils in the curriculum and what are the problems encountered?
4 What equipment/training does the school PE department need to be more inclusive?
5 Does the PE department have any links with agencies that may help to provide inclusive opportunities for SEN pupils?
6 What is your vision for an inclusive PE curriculum in the year 2010 and how might this be achieved?

References

Ainscow, M., Farrell, D., Tweedle, D. and Malkin, G. (1999) *Effective Practice in Inclusion and in Special and Mainstream Schools Working Together*, London: HMSO.

Cavanagh, J. (1999) *Royal National Institute for the Blind Visability magazine* 27, autumn, RNIB.

Centre for Studies in Inclusive Education (2000) *Index for Inclusion*, available HTTP:<http://www.inclusion.uwe.ac.uk> accessed 17 August 2002.

Cohen, L. and Cohen, A. (1987) *Disruptive Behaviour: A Source Book for Teachers*, London: Harper Education.

Depauw, K. and Doll-Tepper, G. (2000) 'Toward Progression Inclusion and Acceptance: Myth or Reality? The Inclusion Debate and Bandwagon Discourse', *Adapted Physical Activity Quarterly* 17: 135–43.

DfEE/QCA (Department for Education and Employment/Qualifications and Curriculum Authority) (2000) *Physical Education and the National Curriculum*, London: HMSO.

DfES (Department for Education and Skills) (2001) *Statistics of Education: Special Educational Needs in England January 2001*, Circular 12/01, London: HMSO.

DfE/WO (Department for Education/Welsh Office) (1992) *Physical Education for Ages 5 to 16: Final Report of the National Curriculum Physical Education Working Group*, London: HMSO.

Dyson, A. (1999) *Examining Issues of Inclusion*, unpublished paper, Department of Education, University of Newcastle.

Dyson, A. (2001) 'Special Needs in the Twenty-First Century: Where We've Been and Where We're Going', *British Journal of Special Education* 28, 1: 24–9.

Farrell, M. (1998) *The Special Education Handbook*, London: David Fulton Publishers.

Farrell, P. (2000) 'The Impact of Research on Developments in Inclusive Education', *International Journal of Inclusive Education*, April: 153–64.

Farrell, P. (2001) 'Special Education in the Last Twenty Years: Have Things Really Got Better?', *British Journal of Special Education* 28, 1: 3–9.

McConkey, R. (2001) *Understanding and Responding to Pupils' Needs in Inclusive Classrooms*, UNESCO, France, online, available HTTP<http://www.unesco.org> accessed 17 August 2002.

Martin, H. and Hayes, S. (1998) 'Overcoming Obstacles: Approaches to Dealing with Problem Pupils', *British Journal of Special Education* 25, 3: 135–9.

OFSTED (Office for Standards in Education) (2001) *The Annual Report of Her Majesty's Chief Inspector of Schools*, available HTTP<http://www.ofsted.gov. uk> accessed 17 August 2002.

OFSTED (Office for Standards in Education) (2002) *LEA Strategy for the Inclusion of Pupils with Special Educational Needs*, Crown Copyright, HMI 737, London, online, available HTTP<http://www.ofsted.gov.uk> accessed 15 August 2002.

QCA (Qualifications Curriculum Authority) (1999) *The National Curriculum for England: Physical Education Key Stages 1–4*, London: QCA.

Sport England (2000) *Sport England Research into Young People with a Disability and their Participation in Sport*, available HTTP <http://www.sportengland. org.uk> accessed 30 August 2002.

Sugden, D. and Talbot, M. (1998) *Physical Education for Pupils with Special Needs in Mainstream Education*, Leeds: Carnegie National Sports Development Centre.

Teacher Training Agency (2001) *National Standards for Qualified Teacher Status*, London: Teacher Training Agency.

Teacher Training Agency OFSTED (Office for Standards in Education) (2001) *Inspection Arrangements for Initial Teacher Training 2002/2003 Onwards – Consultation*, London: Teacher Training Agency.

Vickerman, P. (1997) 'Knowing your Pupils and Planning for Different Needs', in S. Capel (ed.), *Learning to Teach Physical Education in the Secondary School*, London: Routledge.

Vickerman, P. (2000) *Training Physical Education Teachers to Include Children with Special Educational Needs within Mainstream Settings*, unpublished Ph.D. thesis, University of Leeds.

Vickerman, P. (2002) 'Perspectives on the Training of Physical Education Teachers for the Inclusion of Pupils with Special Educational Needs – Is there an Official Line View?' *Bulletin of Physical Education* 38, 2: 79–98.

Westwood, P. (1997) *Common Sense Methods for Pupils with Special Needs*, London: Routledge Press.

I hated games. I hated having to go out in the freezing cold, having to run around a wet muddy pitch, having my shins cracked by the girls' hockey sticks. I hated hockey. They put me in goal, which meant I often had to stand around for long periods getting even colder – we were a good side. So I started to let the goals in until they let me play for real. But I was useless at team games. I wanted to keep the ball to myself and they hated that – despite all the goals I scored. Netball was just as bad. I'm only 5'4" now and they put me in goal defence. Have you seen the size of those girls who play goal attack? They are huge – and they have spring-loaded legs. I let in too many goals. I hated netball.

D. Parkin (2001) 'Why I Hated School PE',
PE and Sport Today 7: 56.

5 Reflections on the mixed- and single-sex PE debate

Gill Lines and Gary Stidder

Introduction

The role of schools as agencies in the social construction of gender has been well researched and the secondary school curriculum, in general, is known to perpetuate gender-stereotyped behaviour (Wrigley 1992, Rudduck 1994, Abraham 1995, Shaw 1995, Darling and Glendinning 1996). Physical Education (PE) is one aspect of the secondary school curriculum where content and grouping arrangements can contribute to stereotypical expectations and assumptions about gender appropriate role-play. This can, and does, influence pupils' overall perceptions of sex differences and accentuates a broader, hidden, 'gendered' curriculum (Bain 1990, Kirk 1992a; Nutt and Clarke 2002; Ronholt 2002). Particular attention in this chapter is given to ways in which the PE curriculum, especially games, was and is constructed around gender distinctions. It critiques contemporary approaches that act to sustain notions of gender difference and perpetuate resistance to change across the primary and secondary school experience with particular reference to pupil grouping practices, staffing strategies, activity choices, and teacher, trainee and pupil perceptions.

Mixed- and single-sex PE during the past thirty years has been an issue of critical pedagogical debate amongst the PE profession both in the UK and overseas (MacDonald 1989, Humberstone 1990, Browne 1992, Scraton 1992, Treanor *et al.* 1998, O'Sullivan *et al.* 2002). This is not a new debate nor peculiar to PE within educational discussions. In England, school league tables and examination results have highlighted gender differentials in performance across coeducational and single-sex schools (OFSTED/EOC 1996; Gillborn and Mirza 2000). In some coeducational schools there have been moves to segregate girls and boys within and across subjects in order to optimise learning and increase academic performance (Syal and Trump 1996, Cassidy 1997, Fairhurst, 1999). For example, it has been shown that girls benefit from single-sex teaching in English, Science and Maths (Weiner 1986) whilst boys benefit in Modern Foreign Languages (Whyld 1983) and certain aspects of Music education

(Green 1997). The introduction of examination courses in PE for pupils has also contributed to wider educational debates related to gender performance, achievement and optimal grouping policies (Carroll 1995, Stidder 2001a, Stidder 2001b).

The gender divisions that exist within school PE and sports programmes are manifested in the wider social context of sport. Feminist approaches to sports sociology in the latter part of the twentieth century have highlighted the ways in which gender inequalities are prevalent in the world of sport (Hargreaves, 1994, Clarke and Humberstone 1997, Scraton and Flintoff 2002). In response to increasing literature addressing women's issues in sport, a wider debate around gender power relations and men, masculinity and sport has arisen (Messner and Sabo 1990, McKay *et al.* 2000). Insights into these discussions, in order to deconstruct the naturalised and biological rhetoric of gender distinctions in sport, are essential for PE teachers. Ways in which boys and girls, male and female teachers react and respond in PE situations are interwoven with dominant sporting and gender ideologies.

The media, too, reinforce gender distinctions in sport through selected representations (Creedon 1994, Rowe 1999, Boyle and Haynes 2000). The media under-representation of females in a number of sports, especially traditional male team sports such as soccer, rugby and cricket (Duncan and Hasbrook 2002, Humberstone 2002), could reflect the relatively low participation rates of girls in team sports in England compared with boys (OFSTED/EOC 1996, Sport England 2000). Scraton (1984: 17) argues that sex-stereotyped attitudes and gender-divided team games are part of a broader social agenda reinforced by the schooling process where 'Girls soon learn that hockey, lacrosse and netball are not worthy of more than a token annual coverage in the press or on TV'.

Yet the media role in shaping the attitudes of young people towards participation in physical activity is relatively unexplored (Cockburn 1999; Lines 1999; Lines 2000; Children International website www.children.org; Amateur Athletics Association of Los Angeles website www.aafla.org). Clearly the marginalised status given to women's team sports, even at international level, and the general invisibility of female sport stars as role models (Lines, 2001), can impact on girls' perceptions of the place of games in their lives. Similarly, school attempts to introduce mixed games are faced with the relatively low status and profile attached to mixed sporting activities in the wider sport culture.

Historically, PE in British secondary schools has been characterised by very different principles, objectives and codes of practice for girls as compared to boys (McIntosh *et al.* 1957, David Smith 1974, Kirk 1992b, Wright 1996). It has traditionally promoted organised team games and drill for boys and more appropriate 'feminine' activities for girls (Hargreaves 1994). Much of this can be attributed to the single-sex teacher training institutions and the development of separate programmes of PE during the early part of the twentieth century (Fletcher 1984).

Many of the team games provided exclusively for boys emphasised the notion of 'character-building' through which desired masculine qualities could be expressed (Parker 1996). As Fletcher (1984: 11) indicates, whilst boys' games developed as a means of constructing manliness so girls 'learnt to be a lady', partaking in more gentle forms of exercise. David Smith (1974: 27) endorses how games for girls 'rarely attained the status of isolated splendour that they achieved in boy's schools'.

Whilst there were opportunities during the 1950s to address these issues through the introduction of a comprehensive, coeducational system the reorganisation of secondary schooling failed to challenge the established content, organisation and gender differentiated practices in PE (Evans 1990). Consequently, PE at the secondary level, in England, has traditionally taken the form of single-sex groups and different activities for boys and girls often based on perceptions of biological sex differences rather than recognition of the complex processes of gender construction in determining the relationship between males and females. Recognising shifting and divergent versions of masculinity and femininity (Penney and Evans 2002), neither girls nor boys can be categorised into one homogenous group and gender issues in PE and sport can be equally predetermined by other factors which contributors to this book articulate.

Research has shown that physical activities play an important part in the social process of gender construction (Wright 1996). Whilst boys and girls have historically received a common curriculum in many of the other core subjects, they have characteristically taken part in different team games in PE lessons both at primary and secondary school, often as a direct result of gender stereotyping by PE teachers (Leaman 1984, Graydon 1987). Much of the decision-making, in terms of PE curriculum content and organisation, is made by PE teachers on behalf of pupils without involving them in the process (Williams *et al.* 2000). This may, therefore, be attributed to the limited understanding and narrowly defined perceptions of gender and physical activities amongst some teachers.

Evans and Davies (2002: 30) identify key points in relation to ways in which certain voices and priorities are 'privileged over others'. MacDonald (2002: 171) with reference to developing critical pedagogic practice urges teachers to 'listen to learners' voices' whilst Williams and Bedward (2001: 64) argue that inclusive practices will only fully be realised if teachers embrace 'ways in which female students position themselves in relation to gender and culture'. Research has tended to focus more on issues for girls in PE but it is clear that boys, too, have varying responses to and outcomes from their experiences.

The needs and concerns of young people may be conflicting with notions of 'sameness' across the genders. For they may hold very gender stereotypical assumptions about sports activities and their acceptable role in the world of sport. Similarly, Heads of PE might prioritise their own interests above the young people they are teaching, or simply not be aware of the gender issues and concerns that their pupils experience within the PE environment. Many of these issues often reflect inconsistencies between the views of pupils and teachers (Williams and Bedward 2001), highlighting the need to listen to pupils voices and engage with teachers.

Personal reflections

As former pupils, trainees and teachers we experienced many of the policies and practices related to the segregation and integration of boys and girls within the context of our own PE lessons. In many respects, our different experiences have led us to re-examine our own positioning, and through reflective evaluation reappraise our own professional opinions. During our secondary schooling, even across the divide of a coeducational comprehensive and an all-girls grammar school, it was evident that PE was different for boys and girls. We both took part in single-sex PE classes, participated in 'acceptable' forms of physical activity, wore different PE uniforms and were never taught by teachers of our opposite sex. In hindsight, these experiences, whilst positively encouraging us into the PE profession, rarely fostered understanding of sports participation and co-operation with our opposite sex and, it could be argued, reinforced the gendered construction of PE in the schools that we attended.

As trainee and qualified teachers in the mid 1970s and 1980s, we found that PE in secondary schools reflected key educational debates of the time related to equality, social conditioning and sex stereotyping of pupils (Sherlock 1977, Graydon 1980, Leaman 1984, Evans 1986, Turvey and Laws 1988). As a result, many of our teaching experiences were increasingly with coeducational classes and often involved teaching activities neither of us had previously learnt. This inevitably challenged our professional competencies and personal philosophies. Whilst shifts to mixed-sex groupings were perceived to be the solution to equity issues, such moves often lacked clear rationales, justifications, strategies and evidence for their success. As teachers and subject leaders, curriculum grouping policies within our own educational establishments ensured that we both experienced teaching combinations of mixed- and single-sex classes across different year groups and different physical activities.

Additionally, teaching experience in the United States of America at the beginning of the 1990s provided an insight into the perceived potential benefits that coeducational PE could provide pupils in ensuring equality of opportunity and access to all aspects of the PE curriculum, particularly for girls. It highlighted the impact of federal legislation such as Title IX,[1] and the mandatory requirement to provide PE on a coeducational basis, on the daily practices of many PE teachers in the US. It also reinforced the need to differentiate in both the planning and teaching of lessons with respect to gender.

Throughout this time little research evidence in PE was available to justify ways that most enhanced pupils' learning in different gendered groupings. Yet changing trends during the 1990s meant we both reverted back to predominantly teaching PE in schools to classes of same-sex pupils. The extent to which teachers like ourselves responded to educational research and debate, curricular organisational demands, their own professional reflections and bias or pupil reactions, remains unclear and research is clearly needed to support common sense assumptions about grouping policies in PE. As the Department for Education and Skills suggest:

> It is not easy to assess the impact of single-sex groupings on achievement. The experimental period in schools may be short and it takes time before the potential benefits of single-sex groupings are discernible in academic performance.
>
> (DfES 2002, online)

The impetus for this chapter has arisen as a result of our own experiences and reflections on contemporary practices. It raises critical questions concerning the revised National Curriculum for PE (NCPE) (DfEE/QCA 1999) in England and the statutory statement for social inclusion with respect to gender and grouping policy in PE. It is intended to encourage other teachers and trainees to think reflectively about gender and develop their own vision for innovation. It proposes ideas for ways in which reflective teachers could address ways of challenging gender stereotypes, 'celebrating gender differences' (Penney and Evans 2002: 16–17), implementing new approaches to games and listening to pupil voices. In many ways it supports the guidance provided by OFSTED (1996: 37) through which curriculum leaders in PE develop 'the creation of a shared vision amongst teachers of the subject and policies to ensure consistency of practice within the department'. In addition, it revisits some of the early guidance from the National Curriculum working party group (DES 1991: 63), supporting its vision for 'fostering awareness and sensitivity of issues of femininity, masculinity and sexuality'.

Gender, games and the National Curriculum for PE

The British Education Reform Act 1988 and the NCPE 1991 attempted to address gender equity issues but failed to produce many positive educational outcomes (Scraton 1992, Talbot 1993a). Recommendations rather than requirements within the documentation, and continued flexibility in activity choice, provided opportunities to sustain rather than challenge gender difference and British government initiatives such as 'Raising the Game'

(DNH 1995) encouraged schools to promote traditional team games without addressing the need to de-stereotype the PE curriculum. Contemporary PE in England, therefore, remains the most gender-segregated subject on the secondary school curriculum (Green and Scraton 1998), dominated and influenced by an over-emphasis on traditional, competitive team games (Penney 2002a). These are often gender-specific in nature (Williams and Bedward 2001) and frequently have sex-differentiated patterns of staffing (Harris and Penney 2002).

The current NCPE in England (DfEE/QCA 1999) has outlined what pupils should be taught in schools and the expected outcomes of pupil performance. This endorses an activity-focused curriculum that includes games, dance, gymnastics, swimming, outdoor and adventurous activities and athletics. It also includes guidance on how teachers can provide effective learning opportunities for all pupils. With regards to gender the statutory entitlement to learning for all pupils suggests that teachers should ensure:

> that boys and girls are able to participate in the *same* curriculum ... take account of the *interests* and *concerns* of boys and girls by using a *range* of activities ... [and] avoid *gender stereotyping* when organising pupils into groups and assigning them to activities
> (DfEE/QCA 1999: 30, our emphasis)

Moreover, the NCPE statement for inclusion recommends that teachers create effective learning environments in which 'stereotypical views are challenged and pupils learn to appreciate and view positively differences in others, whether arising from race, gender, ability or disability' (DfEE/QCA 1999: 29). These requirements have marked the third English NCPE since the Education Reform Act 1988. Whilst this purports to be fully inclusive, gender socialisation and sex role stereotyping in PE still remain marginalised issues on the agendas of government policy makers and key personnel. In this context, it is possible that the policies and practices within English secondary schools may not be addressing the needs and interests of pupils in contemporary PE or embracing the (UK) National Curriculum policy for social inclusion. For example, girls and boys may have the opportunity to experience the *same* curriculum but the provision of different activities does not necessarily mean an *inclusive* programme or learning experience. If the interests and concerns of boys and girls are to be taken into account through a range of activities, then the provision of separate and different activities could be considered as questionable practice in meeting the UK government's educational aims and intentions for social inclusion.

It is known that some secondary school PE teachers in England are doing little to challenge gender stereotyping in PE and hold attitudes that are either out-dated or gender biased (Waddington *et al.* 1998). This may be reflected in the provision of different and often separate activities, particularly games, within the formal PE curriculum. For example, invasion games such as netball are commonly taught in single-sex groups to girls by female teachers whilst football and rugby are often taught to boys by men and therefore may be indicative of their own school PE experiences as pupils themselves. These reinforce stereotypical gender assumptions about the suitability of particular team games for boys and girls and contribute towards the reproduction of traditionally sex-differentiated activity programmes. Cockburn (2001) also suggests that girls are often assumed to be more suited to netball, for example, simply because they are girls and not because they are necessarily better than boys.

UK inspection evidence (OFSTED 1998) has shown that as much as 70 per cent of available time for PE in secondary schools is taken up by games, leaving very little time for the teaching of other National Curriculum activity areas. In addition, Waddington *et al.* (1998) found PE teachers rank games as the most important activity within the NCPE and felt most competent to teach this aspect of PE. Furthermore, Penney (2002a, 2002b) has observed that the most recent revision to the NCPE has done little to encourage teachers to consider a curriculum that is free from the domination of 'traditional' team games and sex-differentiated patterns of provision, typically staffed by male or female teachers respectively. Consequently, the lack of clear guidance in this respect allows these forms of provision to be maintained and has thus raised questions as to whether this can be justified on educational grounds and whether parity and access to the PE curriculum is truly gender-inclusive for girls and boys (Penney 2002a: 113).

Gender difference and resistance to change

Schools have the potential to subtly reinforce notions of gender through organisation, management and teaching methods (Hargreaves 1994). The use of sex as a rationale for grouping arrangement, the allocation of male and female staff to same-sex classes, and the sex-differentiated games offered to boys and girls, can and does perpetuate stereotypical ideas of gender and influence pupils' perceptions of gender-appropriate behaviour.

Contemporary research has highlighted issues specific to inclusion, gender and PE yet Flintoff and Scraton (2001) have shown there is little difference between the findings of the late 1990s compared with the previous twenty years. Traditional forms of pedagogy and practice within secondary school PE programmes have resisted innovation and change (Williams and Bedward 2001) and some PE teachers have remained both hostile and defensive to anything other than conventional forms of PE (Youth Sport Trust 2000). Consequently, mixed-sex PE continues to be adversely affected by an inappropriate curriculum and limited pedagogical developments, resulting in little or no attitudinal change amongst practitioners in the classroom.

Whether schools and PE departments decide to adopt mixed and/or single-sex teaching there are significant social and cultural features that impact on the relative success of the initiative and form resistance to change. As Talbot (1993b: 39) suggests, the 'claim for equal treatment ignores the power and persuasiveness of gender in forming and reifying expectations'.

Games activities and curriculum policies

Nutt and Clarke (2002: 150) have commented that the choice of activities offered to pupils within the secondary school PE curriculum reinforces a hidden curriculum in which 'powerful messages are conveyed about what is acceptable practice and behaviour for girls (and boys) within the domain of Physical Education'.

Research has shown how single-sex PE and the provision of different team games for boys and girls reinforces ideologies that male physical skill and activities are not only more important but have more status and credibility and therefore 'pupils learn that male athletic prowess is to be admired whilst female participation and success should be questioned' (Scraton 1984: 18). For example, boys taking part in football and girls taking part in netball during lesson time is arguably part of a hidden curriculum in which stereotypical gender roles are learnt and can have a significant influence on what pupils think about existing power relations (Bain 1990).

Whilst much has been made of the 'gender gap' between boys' and girls' literacy and educational attainment, hitherto there has been less attention paid to the disadvantages experienced by girls and boys in relation to the provision of PE. Other research suggests that many girls in England have historically been deprived of the opportunity to participate in the dominant games of football, rugby and cricket on the grounds that they were born female (Harris 1993) whilst boys' participation in netball and rounders has often been restricted. Some schools have, therefore, provided privileged (competitive team game) experiences for boys in contrast to girls, where for the boys success, satisfaction and self-esteem are often the direct outcomes of such experiences (Williams and Woodhouse 1996).

The rationale for this has often been based on the notion that some forms of activity are unsuitable for girls, as they are unable to cope with the more competitive nature of games played by boys (Scraton 1984). As a result, the fixed ideas many teachers and pupils have about the appropriateness and status of particular team games and physical activities for boys and girls (Wigmore 1996), can impact upon the policies and practices related to the organisation of teaching and learning in PE. In a discussion of three recent surveys of young people's involvement in sport it was found that some schools provided fewer opportunities for girls and boys to take part in non-stereotypical activities in curriculum time and after school clubs and consequently 'school sport was not interrupting the reproduction of gender differences' (Roberts 1996: 55).

It has been shown that during the formative years of primary schooling boys and girls are socialised and educated to behave differently (Delamont 1990, Jordan 1995). The provision of separate team games within the junior school PE curriculum also contributes to the socialising process which reaffirms very clear messages concerning sexual identity and physical activity (Scraton 1984).

McManus and Armstrong (1996) have also shown how the teaching of different team games in the primary and junior school can enforce gender-specific role-play from an early age. Likewise, Shropshire *et al.* (1997) found that in thirty-two primary schools surveyed in North-West England there was no evidence to suggest that schools were challenging stereotypes of masculine and feminine behaviour in relation to physical activities. Consequently, by the time they leave junior school girls and boys have already started to play feminine-appropriate and masculine-appropriate team games, often in sex-segregated classes, and arrive at secondary school with eleven years of socialisation into dominant gendered practices behind them (Waddington *et al.* 1998, Youth Sport Trust 2000).

Pupil responses and teacher perceptions

During the 1980s the rationale for mixed-sex PE was regarded as an innovation that would challenge sex role stereotyping and the social conditioning of pupils. In some circumstances this was a direct response to pragmatic and economic constraints imposed by falling school rolls, staff shortages and timetabling implications (Talbot 1993a). In contrast, many believed that integrating girls and boys into coeducational classes would break down gender barriers and overcome stereotypical patterns of participation (Lopez 1985); allow staff to share their expertise amongst all pupils (Knox 1985); provide a natural progression from junior school (Rosen 1987); increase curriculum choice (Skillington 1989) and support the comprehensive ethos within the education system (O'Brien 1987).

Such decisions were considered to be naive, however, as mixed-sex PE failed to address cultural differences (Carrington and Leaman 1986) and did little to increase girls' participation, skill development and self-esteem within lessons (Turvey and Laws 1988, Hardy *et al.* 1994, Scraton 1992, Talbot 1996). Whilst the introduction of mixed-sex PE was seen to have particular implications for girls, only recently have researchers begun to focus their attention on the effects of grouping policies on male pupils. For example, Wright (1996) has suggested, that the presence of girls within mixed PE lessons can alleviate the fears and anxieties experienced by some boys in single-sex groups which are often suffered in silence. This is one way that mixed-sex PE can oppose practices and attitudes that promote and condone physical aggression, bullying and the associated pain and discomfort in single-sex boys' groups.

In secondary schools, UK inspection evidence (OFSTED 1998) has shown that where PE departments have moved to single-sex teaching at key stage 3,[2] the effect on standards has been positive. Yet, the effects this may have on gender co-operation and inclusive practices are less clearly articulated. According to Evans *et al.* (1987), one of the direct implications of single-sex PE in mixed-sex schools is that it can promote the development of two distinct subcultures between male and female teachers. This can often result in conflict and tension within departments as a result of different beliefs about how and what to teach. Moreover, single-sex PE has the potential to reaffirm the maintenance of separate teachers within gender-divided departments, often with separate heads of department, each offering sex-appropriate activities (Bloot and Browne 1994, Green and Scraton 1998).

In this context, classroom organisation of PE can contribute to the sex-differentiated activity programmes and, therefore, restrict opportunities for girls and boys as single-sex groupings in PE are the preferred method of organising pupils' learning (Stidder and Hayes 2002). Typically, men tend to teach classes of boys and women tend to teach classes of girls and this in turn may have a stereotyping effect in terms of the activities that are offered, the way they are taught and the expectations that teachers have of their pupils. Consequently, non-stereotypical activities remain marginalised within English secondary schools by other more traditional segregated team games and related activities.

It must be acknowledged, however, that many teachers have reservations about mixed-sex PE and have expressed distinct preferences for teaching same-sex classes (Scraton 1992, Stidder 2002b). In this context, male and female teachers have identified different reasons for their preferences, ranging from discipline and classroom management difficulties to anxieties associated with physical contact and, highlighting the need for further research with secondary school PE teachers.

Preliminary findings from research in one case study school where boys and girls have been taught PE in mixed-sex groups throughout the school since it opened in 1995 suggest that girls aged 14–16 have a positive attitude towards PE.[3] For example, very few girls (16 per cent) expressed a dislike of PE after having experienced three years of mixed-sex teaching. Whilst 61 per cent of girls admitted that they had tried to avoid taking part in PE lessons at some point during their time at school, this was mainly due to certain mixed team games such as football and rugby. In this context, OFSTED reported that:

mixed gender games teaching in Key Stage 3 is less successful than single gender classes. Boys' skill levels in games suffer in these circumstances and, as motivation wanes, in-discipline and poor behaviour results.

(OFSTED 1996b: 22)

The negative effects of mixed-sex games teaching upon boys' achievements and learning, and the subsequent misbehaviour that occurs, suggests that in particular circumstances single-sex groups might be most appropriate. It is known that male pupils receive far more reprimands in mixed-sex PE classes compared with girls and are more likely to be excluded from lessons (Hardy *et al.* 1994). Similarly, the disproportionate amount of time that PE teachers spend with boys in mixed-sex groups is the result of ensuring that male bravado does not result in injury (Leaman 1984). Moreover, the pressures on female adolescents to conform to particular notions of femininity and the opportunities for boys to 'show off' in mixed-sex PE classes can be exacerbated and, therefore, justify the move towards single-sex classes (Olafson 2002). In certain team game activities girls may need more time to improve techniques and skills before they feel comfortable and competent in participating within a mixed-sex group, whilst some boys may require greater exposure and practice in traditional female games before they feel equally confident.

To an extent, the differences between boys' and girls' technical and physical skills, noted by Scraton (1992), is a reflection of the greater opportunities afforded to boys outside of school that provides them with a significant advantage over girls within a mixed-sex setting. Other research (Milosevic 1996) has shown that girls are less committed to mixed-sex PE compared with boys and that, due to incompatible levels of skills, the subject is perceived more positively by pupils when organised in single-sex groups.

At the case study school, 85 per cent of the girls surveyed (n = 103) favoured the school's policy for mixed-sex PE. Whilst issues related to modesty, public displays of the body, physical appearance, developing sexuality and the onset of puberty are significant and contributory factors associated with the views of adolescent girls in mixed-sex PE lessons (Stidder 2000a, Stidder 2000a) the main issues for girls at the case study school were mostly associated with strong feelings against demonstrating during lesson time and the limited choice of activities provided. This would suggest that sensitive teaching and approaches to pedagogy as well as curriculum content and design are more important factors for teachers to consider than the groups in which they work. For example, many girls highlighted lacrosse, roller-blading, swimming, fitness training and yoga as possible alternatives to the more traditional prescribed activities.

The negative feelings about PE amongst adolescent girls are multiple and complex but traditional activities and lack of choice have been identified as significant determinants associated with this negativity. For example, Olafson has stated,

> The official curriculum of physical education appears to be a major influence in the construction of resistance. In other words, negative perceptions regarding physical education are associated with the activities and their instruction.
>
> (Olafson 2002: 69)

In addition, research by Flintoff and Scraton (2001) has shown that the choice of activities within PE programmes at schools is a major source of discontentment amongst some 15-year-old girls and regarded as out of date and irrelevant to the needs and interests of young women today, reflecting other research that has highlighted the negative experiences and dislike of school PE amongst many mature women (Wright 1996).

Whilst it is claimed that most girls are disaffected and put off physical activity by an over-emphasis on competitive team sports (McManus and Armstrong 1996) it is also known that traditional stereotyped feminine team sports can also demotivate and disaffect some girls (Williams and Bedward 1999). Likewise, restricted access to traditional female games may have had a similar effect on the attitudes of some boys with regards to participation and perceptions. For example, boys have limited opportunities to play netball before the age of 11 and even fewer opportunities to develop the skills and techniques of the game after this age. The All England Netball Association (AENA 1999) has recognised that men and boys do not have the same skills training and coaching opportunities as their female counterparts and are now actively trying to include more males into the game.

In addition, it has been argued that whilst girls have gained greater access to traditional 'boys'' activities there has not been an equivalent move to provide greater access for boys into traditional 'girls'' activities as many of the male games played at school have greater cultural status and value. The perpetuation of a traditional gender-differentiated PE curriculum in English secondary schools, often a direct outcome of single-sex groupings, can therefore have a limiting effect in encouraging pupils to participate in new team games.

Curriculum innovation and change, therefore, related to gender inclusive strategies and rationales in PE must be based upon policies and practices that optimise teaching and learning and takes into account the needs and interests of boys and girls. Within an education system driven by market forces (Penney and Evans 1999) this will require a shared understanding and agreement between both the consumers (i.e. pupils) and the providers (i.e. schools, teachers, policy makers) in order to be truly inclusive. As Denison has stated,

> More decisive and contemporary interventions based on what researchers know about girls, boys and sport are desperately needed. Until such programmes are designed and implemented, there is little hope that PE will change with the times and begin to serve anyone's needs
>
> (Denison 2002: 17)

Staffing policies

Teacher recruitment, too, exemplifies ways in which school employers and PE professionals can perpetuate a divided curriculum through the use of 'gendered' vocabulary as a basis to attract potential applicants. The link between advertising and recruitment policies with respect to gender differentiation and curriculum access for boys and girls has become a recent, topical issue (see Evans and Penney 2002, Stidder 2002a for further discussion of these issues). In this respect, schools advertising for teachers of 'girls' PE' and teachers of 'boys' PE' often exacerbate gender stereotyping in PE.

The inclusion of 'gendered' terms within the texts of advertisements raises a number of related questions with regards to curriculum content, professional practice and organisation of pupils' learning. It may also suggest that the organisation of pupils' learning in PE according to gender is still a salient factor for teachers at certain stages of secondary school education. In this context, biological and organisational issues within schools may be symptomatic of the constraints faced by teachers when considering innovation and change within PE and may also reveal much broader social issues underpinning the gendered construction of PE.

Staffing policies can also reinforce gender expectations and experiences for trainee teachers. Some trainees complete their teacher training with limited experience of teaching mixed-sex and opposite-sex classes and therefore have minimal teaching experience of non-stereotypical team games and activities (Hayes and Stidder 1999, Stidder and Hayes 2002). As Flintoff (1998: 308) points out, 'The fact that some trainees had only taught same-sex [PE] groups is itself an equal opportunity issue.'

A vision for gender inclusion

Like other contributors to this book (Theodoulides 2003) our vision for a gender-inclusive PE curriculum is based on a strong belief that 'other people matter' in a curriculum that gives pupils, parents and teachers a voice. As we have suggested elsewhere in this chapter, PE has the potential to celebrate differences between boys and girls and in this respect we believe that gender equity in PE is about diversity and inclusion. We share ideas that have advocated opportunities for self-reflection; challenging and questioning how gender is constructed in and through PE, sport, and the media (Wright 1999: 194). Likewise, our philosophy is one that encourages and celebrates a curriculum that offers 'greater flexibility and choice prior to key stage 4, set in a learning context which recognises multiple definitions of physical and leisure activity' (Williams and Bedward 2001: 64).

We recognise that a wholesale move to either mixed or single-sex PE will not necessarily provide more inclusive experiences for pupils but teachers should be aware of and prepared to confront existing practices that are either gender-exclusive or act to reinforce gender divisions within the PE curriculum. For example, simply providing mixed-sex groups in PE will have little or no positive effects on learning unless there are attempts to address and adapt policies and teaching strategies that counteract stereotypical practices, behaviours, structures, signals and language. Figure 5.1 (pages 80 and 81), amalgamates some ideas based on our on-going research, and draws together suggestions of other researchers to illustrate examples of these.

Reflective practice: Integrating critical theory and research

Innovation and change in gendered practices in PE are in the final analysis dependent on reflective practitioners. To be reflective, teachers are required to read beyond the rationales for gender division on the grounds of biological differences and seriously question why girls or boys should be denied access to a range of physical experiences across both mixed- and single-sex groupings.

First, they must acknowledge the difficulties of widening access and shifting between mixed- and single-sex groups. They must identify their own lack of experience in teaching some non-stereotypical activities and respond to this through in-service training. They must seek to question their own expectations of pupils of the opposite sex (see Hutchinson 1995, who refers to the 'self-fulfilling prophecy cycle'). Initially, the utilisation of staff expertise and the pooling of departmental strengths may address the issue of access to the PE curriculum and ensure a much broader experience for pupils. In the long term, PE teachers and teacher educators should consider innovative approaches to pedagogy, increase curriculum choice for girls and boys, and find ways of challenging the demarcation of physical activities when they are based on gender.

Breaking traditional gender barriers will, however, require more than just increased opportunities for boys and girls to participate in non-stereotypical activities. It will involve an attitudinal change amongst PE professionals and a greater emphasis on trainee preparation at university level and during school-based placements. Clearly, this has implications for current practice but sensitive in-service training courses such as those reported by Wright (1999) could help to address many of the issues highlighted earlier in this chapter.

Critical theory can help professionals to critique and justify gender practices for 'it radically questions taken for granted assumptions and familiar beliefs and challenges many conventional practices, ideas and ideals' (Gibson 1984: 2). Further enforcing the significance of integrating theory and practice, Curtner-Smith (2002: 47) argues for the role of the teacher as a critical, interpretative researcher 'documenting privilege, repression and the dominance of one group over others. In addition they try to create change which leads to greater social justice'.

PE can encourage girls and boys to challenge definitions of gender and accept new images and boundaries. In this respect, PE teachers should promote the status of traditional 'female sports' and non-stereotypical mixed games in order to challenge the hegemonic dominance of male team games. Raising the status of new sports and enhancing awareness of successful sport stars crossing the gender divide in activities is crucial for the success of new practices. Posters and videos of men's netball teams, women competing in traditionally male-dominated games and various mixed events will all provide visual images and role models to reinforce the potential of such gender co-operation and change.

Offering different, and sometimes new, experiences would also provide much needed variety to the PE curriculum and ensure parity in the provision of all physical activities, particularly team games, for girls and boys. Traditional team games are so much a part of established gender division that it is inevitable that stereotypical patterns are difficult to break in mixed-sex groupings. Games such as Korfball offer potential to equalise the gender experience (see the website www.korfball.org.nz). Dot Ibe, a PE teacher, argues that:

> It's an exercise in co-educational co-operation ... it helps to develop mutual respect and self esteem, because the rules create an equality within the game which unites the boys and girls on a level playing field.

> (*Daily Telegraph*, 2000: 42)

Other examples may include teaching traditional team games in mixed-sex groups without the need to incorporate any form of physical contact. 'Tag rugby', for example, can address the requirements of the NCPE programme of study for games. All pupils can develop their understanding of the skills, techniques and principles associated with this particular activity and alleviate many of the anxieties that pupils, including boys, sometimes feel with these forms of contact sports. Likewise, sensitive teaching of activities such as netball, football and basketball, either in mixed- or single-sex groups, can achieve the same desired effect.

Teaching practices

- In mixed-sex PE be sensitive when asking boys and girls to demonstrate.

- Provide opportunities for boys and girls to work together within groups using problem solving and team-building activities.

- In mixed-sex and single-sex schools use female and male examples as role models in a range of non-stereotypical activities.

- Involve boys and girls equally in principal roles.

- In mixed-sex and single sex schools introduce boys and girls to a different range of games activities other than traditional gender-stereotyped games based on their interests.

- Share the teaching of all activities, including those traditionally considered to be 'boys' and 'girls' activities, among female and male teachers.

- In mixed-sex schools female and male teachers should teach a range of mixed-sex, opposite-sex and same-sex PE classes.

Teaching behaviours

- In mixed-sex PE classes provide equal amounts of time and attention to boys and girls.

- In mixed-sex PE classes do not allow boys to dominate in games situations.

- Challenge forms of discriminatory behaviour such as ridicule and harassment (verbal and physical).

- In mixed-sex PE classes be aware of including boys and girls equally in question and answer sessions.

- Do not allocate indoor facilities exclusively to girls or expect boys to go outside for their PE lesson during inclement weather.

Figure 5.1 Gender-inclusive strategies within PE (continued p. 81)

Source: Adapted and modified template taken from Scraton 1992, Harris 1993, Hutchinson 1995, Flintoff 1996a and b, Wright 1999).

Clearly a range of striking and fielding games and net or divided court games also offer potential for mixed-sex teaching and teams. Examples of this may include softball, volleyball, badminton and tennis. Too often, however, the innovations in lesson time are not supported by opportunities to develop these activities beyond the normal school day and inevitably young people must question their potential value. Mixed-sex activities in lessons, therefore, should be supported by similar opportunities in extra-curricular time and through school clubs and teams. Planned research identifying and monitoring both boys' and girls' responses to mixed- and single-sex groupings is essential if effective PE experiences realising gender equity are to be identified and fostered.

Teaching structures

- Avoid gendered terms such as 'Head of Girls' PE' or 'Head of Boys' PE'.
- Avoid vocabulary within job advertisements such as 'boys' PE', 'girls' PE', 'boys' activities', 'girls' activities'.
- Within job advertisements avoid reference to specific activities such as netball or football.
- Encourage more appointments of male PE teachers in all-girls schools and female PE teachers in all-boys schools.
- Female trainee PE teachers should have more opportunity of gaining school-based experience in all-boys' schools and vice-versa.
- Provide teaching experiences to male and female trainees with respect to same-sex, opposite-sex and mixed-sex teaching groups.

Teacher signals

- Display posters of male and female athletes in non-stereotypical activities.
- Choose appropriate and comfortable kit that does not create unnecessary distinctions between boys and girls.
- Use GCSE PE textbooks and other related learning resources (videos etc.) that do not promote gender stereotypes in sport and physical activity.

Teacher language

Avoid the use of gendered terms or phrases: man to man (one to one); batsman (batter); sportsman (sports person); man of the match (player of the match); my *sister* can do better than that; boys don't like dance; rugby will sort the men out from the boys; girls need more time than boys to get changed.

Figure 5.1 concluded

In conclusion, our challenge to the PE profession is to consider new strategies for learning and to re-evaluate approaches to gender policy, practice and pedagogy. This will require teachers and trainees to acquire and take seriously an awareness of the effects of gender in education and PE. Schools and training institutions will need to reflect upon their own contribution and responsibility in developing well-trained individuals who are confident to teach all aspects of the PE curriculum in a range of different contexts. In this respect, teachers must be prepared to confront existing prejudices and myths concerning boys' and girls' involvement in male and female constructed activities. This, in turn, can help teachers to develop gender-equitable programmes of PE for both sexes through equal access and opportunity to all aspects of the PE curriculum. Mixed- and single-sex groupings have the potential to celebrate as well as challenge gender difference. Acknowledging the diverse needs and interests of young people could result in a wider provision of activities available to both boys and girls, with groupings in each activity offering pupil choice across mixed- or single-sex classes.

Reflective questions

Consider the following questions within the context of gender and inclusive practices:

1   Compare the educational benefits of mixed- and single-sex PE classes.
2   Do you consider the consistent use of single-sex PE classes and same-sex staffing arrangements to be questionable professional practice?
3   Can advertising and recruiting for PE staff on the basis of sex be justified within the context of equal opportunities?
4   How does the teacher training process perpetuate or challenge the development of gender stereotypes in PE?
5   What is your vision for gender-inclusive PE in the year 2010 and what might this curriculum look like?

Notes

1   Title IX of the American Education Amendments passed in 1972 was the first federal law that prohibited sex discrimination within American educational institutions and aimed to provide equal opportunities for boys and girls in all aspects of education. Title IX states 'No person shall, on the basis of sex, be denied the benefits of, or be subjected to discrimination under any education program or activity receiving Federal financial assistance.' One of the direct implications for PE in many US middle and high schools was a legal requirement to re-structure the provision of curriculum PE from sex-segregated classes to mixed-sex groups in an attempt to provide a gender equitable programme of study for boys and girls.
2   Key stage 3 refers to pupils aged 11–14 in the British education system.
3   The unpublished data discussed in this section of the chapter were gathered in 2002 and are part of an on-going Ph.D. study that is comparing and contrasting education policy and its impact on girls' PE in England and the United States of America.

References

Abraham, J. (1995) *Divide and School: Gender and Class Dynamics in Comprehensive Education*, London: Falmer Press.
AENA (All England Netball Association) (1999) 'Focus on Netball', *British Journal of Teaching Physical Education* 30, 4: 10–11.
Bain, L. (1990) 'A Critical Analysis of the Hidden Curriculum in Physical Education', in D. Kirk and R. Tinning (eds), *Physical Education Curriculum and Culture: Critical Issues in the Contemporary Crisis*, London: Falmer Press: 23–42.

Bloot, R. and Browne, J. (1994) 'Factors Contributing to the Lack of Female Leadership in School Physical Education', *Journal of Teaching Physical Education* 14: 34–59, Human Kinetic Publishers, Inc.

Boyle, R. and Haynes, R. (2000) *Power Play: Sport, the Media and Popular Culture*, Harlow: Pearson Education Ltd.

Browne, J. (1992) 'Coed or not Coed? That is the Question', *ACHPER National Journal* 136: 20–3.

Cassidy, S. (1997) 'A Singular Success', *The Times Educational Supplement* 2, 28: 16, November.

Carrington, B. and Leaman, O. (1986) 'Equal Opportunities and Physical Education', in J. Evans (ed.), *Physical Education, Sport and Schooling – Studies in the Sociology of Physical Education*, Lewes: Falmer Press: 215–24.

Carroll, R. (1995) 'Examinations in Physical Education and Sport: Gender Differences and Influences on Subject Choice', in L. Lawrence , E. Murdoch and S. Parker (eds), *Professional and Developmental Issues in Leisure, Sport and Education*, Brighton: LSA Publications: 59–71.

Clarke, G. and Humberstone, B. (eds) (1997) *Researching Women and Sport*, Basingstoke: Macmillan Press.

Cockburn, C. (1999) 'The Trouble with Girls ... A Study of Teenage Girls' Magazines in Relation to Sport and PE', *British Journal of Physical Education* 30, 3: 11–15, Autumn.

Cockburn, C. (2001) 'Year 9 Girls and Physical Education: A Survey of Pupil Perceptions', *Bulletin of Physical Education* 37, 1: 5–24.

Creedon, P. (ed.) (1994) *Women, Media and Sport: Challenging Gender Values*, London: Sage Publications Inc.

Curtner-Smith, M. (2002) 'Methodological Issues in Research', in A. Laker (ed), *The Sociology of Sport and Physical Education: An Introductory Reader*, London: Routledge: 36–57.

Daily Telegraph (2000) 'Screen Test for Korfball: Television Role would help Mixed Team Game', 29 December: 42.

Darling, J. and Glendinning, A. (1996) *Gender Matters in Schools: Pupils and Teachers*, London: Cassell.

David Smith, W. (1974) *Stretching Their Bodies: The History of Physical Education*, Newton Abbot: David & Charles.

Delamont, S. (1990) *Sex Roles and the School*, Second Edition, London: Routledge.

Denison, J. (2002) 'Not so Jolly Hockey Sticks', *The Times Higher Educational Supplement*, 19 July: 16–17.

DES (Department of Education and Science) (1991) *National Curriculum: Physical Education Working Group Interim Report*, London: DES and Welsh Office.

DfEE/QCA (Department for Education and Employment/Qualifications and Curriculum Authority) (1999) *Physical Education: The National Curriculum for England*, London: HMSO.

DfES (Department for Education and Skills) (2002) Online. Available HTTP <http://www.standards.dfee.gov.uk/genderandachievement/data> accessed 26 March 2002.

DNH (Department of National Heritage) (1995) *Raising the Game*, London: DNH.

Duncan, M. and Hasbrook, C. (2002) 'Denial of Power in Televised Women's Sports', in S. Scraton and A. Flintoff (eds), *Gender and Sport: A Reader*, London: Routledge: 83–93.

Evans, J. (ed.) (1986) *Physical Education, Sport and Schooling: Studies in the Sociology of Physical Education*, Lewes: Falmer Press.

Evans, J. (1990) 'Ability, Position and Privilege in School Physical Education', in D. Kirk and R. Tinning (eds), *Physical Education, Curriculum and Culture: Critical Issues in Contemporary Crisis*, London: Falmer Press: 139–67.

Evans, J. and Davies, B. (2002) 'Theoretical background', in A. Laker (ed.), *The Sociology of Sport and Physical Education: An Introductory Reader*, London: Routledge: 15–35.

Evans, J., Lopez, S., Duncan, M. and Evans, M. (1987) 'Some Thoughts on the Political and Pedagogical Implications of Mixed-sex Grouping in the Physical Education Curriculum', *British Educational Research Journal* 13, 1: 59–71.

Evans, J. and Penney, D. (2002) 'Introduction', in D. Penney (ed.), *Gender and Physical Education: Contemporary Issues and Future Directions*, London: Routledge: 3–12.

Fairhurst, J. (1999) 'Is Single-sex Teaching the Best Way to Boost Results?', *Teachers: Education for the Future*, 6: 10–11, December, DfEE.

Fletcher, S. (1984) *Women First: The Female Tradition in Physical Education 1880–1980*, London: Athlone Press.

Flintoff, A. (1996a) 'Anti-Sexist Practice in Secondary Physical Education', *British Journal of Physical Education* 27, 1: 24–31.

Flintoff, A. (1996b) 'We Have No Problems with Equal Opportunities Here . . . We've Got Mixed Changing Rooms', *British Journal of Physical Education* 27, 1: 21–3.

Flintoff, A. (1998) 'Sexism and Homophobia in Physical Education: The Challenge for Teacher Educators', in K. Green and K. Hardman (eds), *Physical Education: A Reader*, Aachen: Meyer and Meyer: 291–313.

Flintoff, A. and Scraton, S. (2001) 'Stepping into Active Leisure? Women's Perceptions of Active Lifestyles and their Experiences of School Physical Education', *Sport, Education and Society* 6, 1: 5–21.

Gibson, R. (1984) *Critical Theory and Education*, London: Hodder and Stoughton.

Gillborn, D. and Mirza, H. (2000) *'Educational Inequality: Mapping Race, Class and Gender – A Synthesis of Research Evidence'*, London: HMSO/OFSTED publications, available HTTP <http://www.ofsted.gov.uk/public/docs00/inequality.pdf.

Graydon, J. (1980) 'Dispelling the Myth of Female Fragility', *British Journal of Physical Education* 11, 4: 105–6.

Graydon, J. (1987) 'Genderwatch! Physical Education', in K. Myers, *Genderwatch: Self-assessment Schedules for use in Schools*, London: SCDC Publications.

Green, K. and Scraton, S. (1998) 'Gender, Coeducation and Secondary Physical Education: A Brief Review', in K. Green and K. Hardman (eds), *Physical Education: A Reader*, Aachen: Meyer and Meyer: 272–89.

Green, L. (1997) *Music, Education and Gender*, Cambridge: Cambridge University Press.

Hardy, C. A., Hardy, C. E. and Thorpe, R. (1994) 'Pupil Misbehaviour in Secondary Schools and Mixed-Sex Physical Education Lessons', *British Journal of Physical Education* 15, 3: 7–11.

Hargreaves, J. (1994) *Sporting Females: Critical Issues in the History and Sociology of Womens' Sports*, London: Routledge.

Harris, J. (1993) 'Challenging Sexism and Gender Bias in Physical Education', *Bulletin of Physical Education* 29, 2: 29–37.

Harris, J. and Penney, D. (2002) 'Gender, Health and Physical Education' in D. Penney (ed.), *Gender and Physical Education: Contemporary Issues and Future Directions*, London: Routledge: 123–45.

Hayes, S. and Stidder, G. (1999) 'A Survey of Physical Education Trainees' Experiences on School Placements in the South-East of England 1994–1998', *British Journal of Physical Education* 30, 1: 28–32.

Humberstone, B. (1990) 'Warriors or Wimps? Creating Alternative Forms of Physical Education', in M. Messner and D. Sabo (eds), *Sport, Men, and the Gender Order*, Champaign, Ill.: Human Kinetics: 201–10.

Humberstone, B. (2002) 'Femininity, Masculinity and Difference: What's Wrong with a Sarong?', in A. Laker (ed.), *The Sociology of Sport and Physical Education: An Introductory Reader*, London: Routledge: 58–78.

Hutchinson, G. (1995) 'Gender-Fair Teaching in PE', *Journal of PE, Recreation and Dance* 66, 1: 42.

Jordan, E. (1995) 'Fighting Boys and Fantasy Play: The Construction of Masculinity in the Early Years of School', *Gender and Education* 7, 1: 69–86.

Kirk, D. (1992a) 'Physical Education, Discourse and Ideology: Bringing the Hidden Curriculum into View', *Quest* 44: 35–56.

Kirk, D. (1992b) *Defining Physical Education: The Social Construction of a School Subject in Postwar Britain*, Studies in Curriculum History Series: 18, London: Falmer Press.

Knox, T. (1985) 'Mixed Physical Education', *Bulletin of Physical Education* 21, 3: 33–5.

Leaman, O. (1984) *Sit on the Sidelines and Watch the Boys Play: Sex Differentiation in Physical Education*, York: Longman, Schools Council Publications.

Lines, G. (1999) 'Setting the Challenge: Creating Partnerships: Young People, PE, Sport and the Media', *British Journal of Physical Education* 30, 2: 7–12.

Lines, G. (2000) 'Media Sport Audiences: Young People and the Summer of Sport '96: Revisiting Frameworks for Analysis', *Media, Culture and Society* 22: 669–80.

Lines, G. (2001) 'Villains, Fools or Heroes? Sport Stars as Role Models for Young People', *Leisure Studies* 20: 285–303.

Lopez, S. (1985) 'Mixed-Sex Groups in PE: Some Problems and Possibilities', *Bulletin of Physical Education* 17, 1: 19–22.

MacDonald, D. (1989) 'Australian Policy on Mixed-Sex Physical Education', *British Journal of Physical Education* Autumn: 129–31.

MacDonald, D. (2002) 'Critical Pedagogy: What Might it Look Like and Why Does it Matter?' in A. Laker (ed.), *The Sociology of Sport and Physical Education: An Introductory Reader*, London: Routledge: 167–89.

McIntosh, P., Dixon, J., Munrow, A. and Willetts, R. (1957) *Landmarks in the History of Physical Education*, London: Routledge and Kegan Paul.

McKay, J., Messner, M. and Sabo, D. (eds) (2000) *Masculinities, Gender Relations and Sport*, London: Sage.

McManus, A. and Armstrong, N. (1996) 'The Physical Inactivity of Girls – A School Issue?', *British Journal of Physical Education* 27, 1: 34–5.

Messner, M. and Sabo, D. (eds) (1990) *Sport, Men and the Gender Order*, Champaign, Ill.: Human Kinetics.

Milosevic, L. (1996) 'Pupils' Experience of PE Questionnaire Results', *British Journal of Physical Education* 27, 1: 16–20.

Nutt, G. and Clarke, G. (2002) 'The Hidden Curriculum and the Changing Nature of Teachers' Work', in A. Laker (ed.), *The Sociology of Sport and Physical Education: An Introductory Reader*, London: Routledge: 148–66.

O'Brien, D. (1987) 'Equal Opportunities in Physical Education', *British Journal of Physical Education* 17, 4: 152–3.

OFSTED (Office for Standards in Education) (1996) *Subjects and Standards: Issues for School Development Arising from OFSTED Inspection Findings 1994–5. Key Stages 3 & 4 and Post 16, A report from Her Majesty's Chief Inspector of Schools*, London: HMSO.

OFSTED (Office for Standards in Education) (OFSTED) (1998) *Secondary Education 1993–1997: A Review of Secondary Schools in England*, London: HMSO.

OFSTED/EOC (Office for Standards in Education/Equal Opportunities Commission) (1996) *The Gender Divide: Performance Differences Between Boys and Girls at School*, London: HMSO.

Olafson, L. (2002) 'I Hate Phys. Ed: Adolescent Girls Talk about Physical Education', *The Physical Educator* 59, 2: 67–74, Spring.

O'Sullivan, M., Bush, K. and Gehring, M. (2002) 'Gender Equity and Physical Education: A USA perspective', in D. Penney (ed.), *Gender and Physical Education: Contemporary Issues and Future Directions*, London: Routledge: 163–89.

Parker, A. (1996) 'The Construction of Masculinity within Boys' Physical Education', *Gender and Education* 8, 2: 147–57.

Penney, D. (2002a) 'Equality, Equity and Inclusion in Physical Education', in A. Laker (ed.), *The Sociology of Sport and Physical Education: An Introductory Reader*, London: Routledge: 110–28.

Penney, D. (ed.) (2002b) *Gender and Physical Education: Contemporary Issues and Future Directions*, London: Routledge.

Penney, D. and Evans, J. (1999) *Politics, Policy and Practice in Physical Education*, London: E & FN Spon/Routledge.

Penney, D. and Evans, J. (2002) 'Talking Gender', in D. Penney (ed.), *Gender and Physical Education: Contemporary Issues and Future Directions*, London: Routledge: 13–23.

Roberts, K. (1996) 'Young People, School Sport and Government Policies', *Sport, Education and Society* 1, 1: 47–59.

Ronholt, H. (2002) ' "It's only the Sissies..." Analysis of Teaching and Learning Processes in Physical Education: A Contribution to the Hidden Curriculum', *Sport, Education and Society* 7, 1: 25–36.

Rosen, D. (1987) 'An Outsider's View', *British Journal of Physical Education* 17, 4: 152.

Rowe, D. (1999) *Sport, Culture and the Media: The Unruly Trinity*, Buckingham: Open University Press.

Rudduck, J. (1994) *Developing a Gender Policy in Secondary Schools*, Buckingham: Open University Press.

Scraton, S. (1984) *Losing Ground: The Implications for Girls of Mixed Physical Education*, Buckingham: Open University Press.

Scraton, S. (1992) *Shaping up to Womanhood: Gender and Girls' Physical Education*, Buckingham: Open University Press.

Scraton, S. and Flintoff, A. (2002) *Gender and Sport: A Reader*, London: Routledge.

Shaw, J. (1995) *Education, Gender and Anxiety*, London: Taylor and Francis.

Sherlock, J. (1977) 'A Feminist View of Coeducational Physical Education', *Scottish Journal of Physical Education* 5, 2: 21–2.

Shropshire, J., Carroll, R. and Yim, S. (1997) 'Primary School Children's Attitudes to Physical Education: Gender Differences', *European Journal of Physical Education* 2, 1: 23–38.

Skillington, D. (1989) 'Mixed Physical Education Teaching – Guidelines for the Introduction of the Subject on a Coeducational Basis in Secondary Schools', *British Journal of Physical Education* 19, 3: 130–1.

Sport England (2000) *Young People and Sport National Survey 1999*, London.

Stidder, G. (2000a) 'Does Sex Matter? Pupil Perceptions of Physical Education in Mixed and single sex Secondary Schools', *British Journal of Teaching Physical Education* 31, 3: 40–4.

Stidder, G. (2000b) 'Does Sex Matter? Pupil Perceptions of Physical Education in Mixed and single sex Secondary Schools (Part Two)', *British Journal of Teaching Physical Education* 31, 4: 46–8.

Stidder, G. (2001a) 'Who's for Exams?', *British Journal of Teaching Physical Education* 32, 3: 46–8.

Stidder, G. (2001b) 'Who's for Exams? (Part Two)', *British Journal of Teaching Physical Education* 32, 4: 38–40

Stidder, G. (2002a) 'The Recruitment of Secondary School Physical Education Teachers in England: A Gendered Perspective?' *European Physical Education Review* 8, 3: 253–73.

Stidder, G. (2002b) 'Gender, Pedagogy and Social Inclusion: Teacher Perceptions of Mixed and single sex Physical Education in English Secondary Schools', *Bulletin of Physical Education* 38, 1: 3–18.

Stidder, G. and Hayes, S. (2002) 'A Survey of Physical Education Trainees' Experiences on School Placements in the South-East of England (1997–2001)', *British Journal of Teaching Physical Education* 33, 1: 43–8.

Syal, R. and Trump, S. (1996) 'Single sex Classes Raise Boys' Grades', *The Sunday Times*, 25 August.

Talbot, M. (1993a), 'A Gendered Physical Education: Equality and Sexism', in J. Evans (ed.), *Equality, Education and Physical Education*, London: Falmer Press: 74–89.

Talbot, M. (1993b) 'Physical Education and the National Curriculum: Some Political Issues', in G. McFee and A. Tomlinson (eds), *Education, Sport and Leisure: Connections and Controversies*, Eastbourne: Chelsea School Research Centre, University of Brighton: 34–64.

Talbot, M. (1996) 'Gender and National Curriculum Physical Education', *British Journal of Physical Education* 27, 1: 5–7.

Theodoulides, A (2003) 'Other People Matter: Contesting Control and Domination in Physical Education and Sport', in S. Hayes and G. Stidder (eds), *Equality and Inclusion in Physical Education and Sport: Contemporary issues for teachers, trainees and practitioners*, London: Routledge.

Treanor, L., Graber, K., Housner, L. and Weigard, R. (1998) 'Middle School Students' Perceptions of Coeducational and Same Sex Classes', *Journal of Teaching Physical Education* 18, 1: 43–56.

Turvey, J. and Laws, C. (1988) 'Are Girls Losing Out? The Effects of Mixed-Sex Grouping on Girls' Performance in Physical Education', *British Journal of Physical Education* 19, 6: 253–5.

Waddington, I., Malcolm, D. and Cobb, J. (1998) 'Gender Stereotyping and Physical Education', *European Physical Education Review* 4, 1: 34–46.

Weiner, G. (1986) *Just a Bunch of Girls: Feminist Approaches to Schooling*, Milton Keynes: Open University Press.

Whyld, J. (ed.) (1983) *Sexism in the Secondary School*, London: Harper Row.

Wigmore, S. (1996) 'Well It Just Is, Isn't It? An Examination of the Masculine Hegemony of Sport', *Bulletin of Physical Education* 32, 1:14–22.

Williams, A. and Bedward, J. (1999) 'A More Inclusive Curriculum Framework (QCA): Making Physical Education Relevant to Adolescent Girls', *British Journal of Physical Education* 30, 3: 6–10.

Williams, A. and Bedward, J. (2001) 'Gender, Culture and the Generation Gap: Student and Teacher Perceptions of Aspects of National Curriculum Physical Education', *Sport, Education and Society* 6, 1: 53–66.

Williams, A., Bedward, J. and Woodhouse, J. (2000) 'An Inclusive National Curriculum? The Experience of Adolescent Girls', *European Journal of Physical Education* 5, 1: 4–18.

Williams, A. and Woodhouse, J. (1996) 'Delivering the Discourse – Urban Adolescents' Perceptions of Physical Education', *Sport, Education and Society* 1, 2: 201–13.

Wright, J. (1996) 'The Construction of Complementarity in Physical Education', *Gender and Education* 8, 1: 61–79.

Wright, J. (1999) 'Changing Gendered Practices in Physical Education: Working with Teachers', *European Physical Education Review* 5, 3: 181–97.

Wrigley, J. (ed.) (1992) *Education and Gender Equality*, London: Falmer Press.

Youth Sport Trust, (2000), *Towards Girl-Friendly Physical Education: Girls in Sport Partnership Project Final Report*, Loughborough: Institute of Youth Support.

Websites

Amateur Athletics Association of Los Angeles: www.aafla.org

Children International: www.children.now

New Zealand Korfball Association: www.korfball.org.nz

No wonder I always hated sport. But sport started it ... it was sport that made me realise I was not like other boys. I was fantastically, record-breakingly not good at games. If there was a race to run, a ball to throw or a length to swim, I would be last, last, last. Baby, I was born to lose. Children can be so cruel, but they were nothing compared to the teachers ... They'd use the queer smear on boys from a frighteningly early age. Teachers would inform us losers that we were 'cissies', 'gay' or 'women'. Medicine balls were smashed in your face if you weren't paying attention. One teacher used to regularly heckle me on the football field with the cry: 'Hit it with your handbag Mr Smith!'

R. Smith (2002) 'Hit it with Your Handbag Mr Smith!',
Gay Times, June 2002: 41.

6   There's nothing queer about difference

Challenging heterosexism and homophobia in Physical Education

Gill Clarke

Introduction

This chapter explores the social construction and manifestations of heterosexism and homophobia within Physical Education (PE) and the impact
this has in particular on pupils. By doing so the conservative traditions
of the PE profession are revealed insofar as their pedagogical practices
and expectations contribute to and reinforce stereotyped ideologies of
masculinity and femininity. It is these narrow definitions which have led
many within the subject to fear the display of any emotional or physical
characteristics which do not fit these hegemonic images. In connection
with this the chapter illustrates how these prejudiced behaviours operate
on multiple levels, that is, the personal; interpersonal; institutional; cultural
or societal. Throughout the chapter strategies are offered to challenge and
eliminate homophobia and heterosexism whilst promoting equity and
social inclusion so that all may achieve their full potential within PE.

A brief autobiographical note and rationale

The impetus for the research which this chapter largely draws upon comes
from reflecting upon my own experiences of teaching PE for seven years
in secondary schools and partly from the lack of research into the lives
of lesbian PE teachers. It seemed to me at the time I commenced my
research into the lives of lesbian PE trainees and teachers that virtually
nothing was known about lesbian PE teachers' lives in England (Clarke
1996). The limited research that had been published related only to lesbian
PE teachers in North America (Griffin 1991; Woods 1992) and had failed
to address directly the impact of compulsory heterosexuality on lesbian
teachers' lives (see Rich 1981). A very small number of English studies
were to follow the lead of the previously mentioned researchers (see Sparkes

1994; Squires and Sparkes 1996). These studies were significant in that they brought issues around lesbian PE teachers' lives into the public domain; however, it was apparent that there was still much to find out and understand about lesbian women's (and gay men's[1]) lives and how heterosexism and homophobia impact on all within the 'gymnasium'.

Given my own experiences as a lesbian teacher both within secondary schools and higher education institutions I was anxious to use my own teaching and sporting experiences to help understand and interpret why lesbian PE teachers largely felt the need to conceal their real sexual identities within schools. These experiences and insights were as I have argued elsewhere both a strength and a resource rather than a threat to the integrity of the research endeavour (see Clarke 1998a).

Heterosexism and homophobia: Defining practice in Physical Education

Earlier chapters within this collection have pointed to the gendered, racialised and ableist nature of PE in schools. These traditional practices and associated stereotyped beliefs have contributed to the marginalisation and subjugation of those pupils and teachers who might be deemed different to what it is to be a 'normal' girl/boy, female/male. This process of othering needs to be located and understood within the confines of homophobia and (compulsory) heterosexuality (Rich 1981; Clarke 1998b). I use the concept of 'Other' like Kumashiro (2002: 26) to 'refer to those groups that are traditionally marginalized from society, i.e., that are *other than* the norm, such as students of color, students from under- or unemployed families, students who are female, or male but not stereotypically "masculine"'.

Discussions about heterosexism have until recently been absent from debates within PE (Clarke 1998b; Sykes 1998). Indeed, it is largely outside of this arena that the task of deconstructing heterosexuality as both an institution and practice has been conducted (Butler 1990; Jeffreys 1990; Wilkinson and Kitzinger 1993). Heterosexism refers to attitudes and institutional and cultural arrangements predicated on the belief that heterosexuality 'is the only normal and acceptable sexual orientation' (Griffin and Harro 1997: 146).

Sears's (1997: 16) conceptualisation of homophobia is helpful, in defining it as 'prejudice, discrimination, harassment, or acts of violence against sexual minorities, including lesbians, gay men, bisexuals, and transgendered persons, evidenced in a deep-seated fear or hatred of those who love or sexually desire those of the same sex'. Within England and Wales these fears and prejudices are shored up by the continued existence of Section 28 of the Local Government Act passed in 1988 by the Conservative Government under the then Prime Minister Margaret Thatcher. It stated:

(1) A local authority shall not –

(a) intentionally promote homosexuality or publish material with the intention of promoting homosexuality;

(b) promote the teaching in any maintained school of the acceptability of homosexuality as a pretended family relationship.

(2) Nothing in subsection (1) above shall be taken to prohibit the doing of anything for the purpose of treating or preventing the spread of disease.

(Smith 1994: 183)

This repressive legislation has been widely misunderstood, and as Johnson and Epstein point out:

It is very widely thought, even among teachers, that the section prohibits or renders very imprudent, the teaching of anything about homosexuality. Against this, it is crucial to stress that the Section did not apply to schools themselves, only to Local Authorities, a fact confirmed in later rulings. There is nothing in it that prevents teachers teaching about homosexuality, a fact confirmed in government circulars . . .

(Johnson and Epstein 2000: 29)

How this relates to PE and issues of (in)equity and inclusion in schools is discussed later in the chapter in the sections 'Towards a theory of homophobic and heterosexist oppression' and 'Manifestations of heterosexism and homophobia'. Suffice for now to say that schools in general, and PE departments in particular, are sites for social and moral regulation wherein gender and gender roles are produced against a dominant heterosexuality and a marginalised, often vilified, homosexuality. These gender roles are constructed along narrow, highly demarcated lines which are exemplified through stereotyped expectations about what it is to be male or female.

I turn now to examine how these restrictive conceptions of masculinity and femininity negatively impact on all in PE.

Playing the masculine and feminine game or not . . .

PE is about schooling bodies (and minds) into socially sanctioned and publicly approved ways of being. For boys, to be 'real' men revolves around the display of particular forms of hegemonic masculinity. These equate with sporting success; indeed, to fail or even dislike PE and sport is often to render the sexual identity of the self open to question and ridicule, factors I return to later in this chapter.

Playing the physical game successfully becomes for boys a signifier of a 'normal' masculine identity, that is one that is not queer. Rather, it is an identity that is exalted as strong, competitive, skilful and aggressive. Nevertheless, 'the nature of hegemonic masculinity is precarious, and ... need[s] to be continually defended and maintained' (Swain 2000: 104). Accordingly, those who fail to maintain this hegemonic masculinity are often subject to heterosexist and homophobic abuse. If sporting performances are viewed in such narrow ways it is no wonder that many boys (and male teachers) fail to engage with the more aesthetic and creative aspects of the subject, and in particular dance (Keyworth 2001), aspects too, that have been associated with the female tradition (Fletcher 1984).

For girls to be successful in Physical Education is to be caught in a double bind since successful working on the body and the concomitant social power (Gilroy 1997) also means they run the risk of vilification by their peers and others. The tensions here relate to the fact that the criteria for a successful physical performance are those deemed to be masculine and thus incompatible with the holding of a stereotypical feminine heterosexual identity; in other words if a girl is successful she must be playing like a man. Again it is unsurprising that girls drop out from physical activities and especially those that require the visible display of strength and aggression. Further, where girls/women are successful they are likely to have the pejorative label 'lesbian' attached to them. Consequently, girls/women (and boys/men) are likely to employ strategies to protect and project their feminine/masculine identity, hence, we see respectively hyperfemininity and hypermasculinity regularly being performed within and through the domain of the physical (Connell 1995). Those girls who seek to resist the gender regime often face alienation from the people around them and those important to them such as friends, boys, carers and neighbours (Cockburn and Clarke 2002). The following section seeks to explain and offer a framework for understanding how this cycle of oppression operates so successfully and why resistance is so hard won.

Towards a theory of homophobic and heterosexist oppression

Whilst for the purpose of this chapter I am focusing on homophobic and heterosexist oppression I want to acknowledge the multiplicity and situatedness of oppression and to question the actual adequacy of oppression as a term. Thus, I am inclined like Ramazanoglu (1989) to use the term 'oppression' as a relatively loose concept that can be qualified in different situations. Further, I recognise the danger of seeing those who are oppressed as just passive victims (in this case, teachers and pupils) without agency. Phelan's work is useful on this question, since she explains that:

Oppression is a word with many contexts and shades ... The problems and issues involved in the category of oppression are manifold.
When does another impose on me? What sort of power must be
involved to make this imposition oppressive? How are we to correct
this situation: is it a matter for political action, or a matter for education and social discussion? Are there perhaps many places to deal
with aspects of this problem?

(Phelan 1989: 15–16)

These are key questions which have escaped some of the research that
has focused on the oppression of lesbians and gay men within the educational system. Notwithstanding the complexities of teaching and learning,
these are also key questions for physical educationalists to address vis-à-
vis pedagogical practices within their subject area.

In seeking a more complete understanding of why homophobia and
heterosexism continue to oppress all in PE regardless of their sexual identity it is helpful to ask: who benefits? Who is empowered? Who is shackled
by it? (Messner and Sabo 1994).

This chapter has already demonstrated how male hegemony is reinforced in and through PE, insofar as identities that don't fit this hierarchical
model are deemed deviant and stigmatised. Further, traditional gender
roles are upheld and reinforced since the price for transgressing is all too
often too painful (Clarke 2001).

Osterman's model (Figure 6.1) provides a useful framework for making
sense of these (in)actions and the failure in the main to challenge homophobia and heterosexism in Physical Education. Osterman uses this model
to explain how people justify their rationale for oppressing others. Looking
at each aspect in term we can see first how 'limited knowledge and/or
isolated experience' in the case of schools in general and PE departments
specifically would apply. Many teachers may have limited knowledge about
lesbian and gay issues and how these pertain to the curriculum and effective
teaching and learning. In relating this directly to PE, teachers may have
limited knowledge about 'out' lesbian and gay athletes, thereby denying
all pupils the knowledge of positive role models. Given the conservative
traditions of PE and sport, it is difficult to name many athletes who are
open about their lesbian or gay identity. Moreover, Section 28 has been
used by some teachers as a way of legitimising their not talking about
homosexuality, yet this is precisely what the PE (and teaching) profession
needs to do. Teachers need to increase (and disrupt) pupils' knowledge
(and perhaps their own) about the diverse sexualities of sports participants. Disrupting knowledge is no easy task when conceptions of
masculinity, femininity and heterosexuality become so 'naturalised' and
'normalised' that they are unquestioned and taken for granted as *the* way
to be. Further, given that schools and PE departments do not exist in a
social vacuum and are part of a broader set of social relations, change

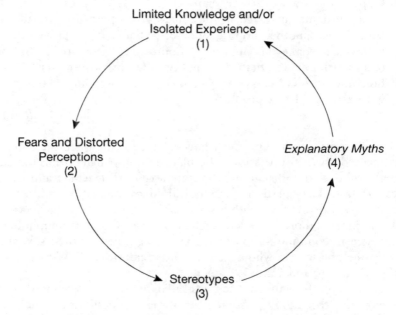

Figure 6.1 Elements of Developing Rationale for Oppression
Source: Osterman 1987: 20.

in schools without wider societal change is inevitably problematic. So
what can PE teachers (and pupils) do?

In terms of the curriculum it is crucial to include specific reference to
the Other. This might occur in examination Physical Education courses
(but *not* exclusively) through for instance discussing the Gay Games
(Hargreaves 2000) and by drawing attention to successful lesbian and gay
athletes like Amelie Mauresmo in tennis or Ian Roberts in rugby (Freeman
1997; Woog 1998). The fact that neither are British says much about the
failure of British sport to be truly equitable and inclusive. Further, teachers
and pupils must cease assuming that heterosexuality is the 'norm' and
engage in a more critical pedagogy (Macdonald 2002).

Turning to the issue of 'fears and distorted perceptions', these perceptions can be seen to be embedded within the discourse of Section 28 and
specifically in point (2), its association of disease, i.e. Aids with homosexuality (Clarke 1966). The Trades Union Congress recently commented
that Section 28 says much about how a society treats its own citizens. It
contends that there would rightly be outrage if the law were to define
any other section of the community in this way. Scotland has repealed
this law, and as Stonewall (2001: 4) pithily comments, 'England and Wales
don't need it.' In connection with this law it is worth considering the

impact that the new Disability Discrimination Act will have on participation in Physical Education. The editorial in the *Observer* (2002: 24),
commenting on the Act's recent implementation, said, 'Laws alone
don't change attitudes. But they transform the landscapes of expectations.'
Much needs to be done if attitudes towards lesbians and gay men are
to change.

The issue of stereotypes forms the third part of the model for the rationale
for oppression in Figure 6.1. Osterman points out how stereotypes feed
myths. The most common and pernicious of these, as we have seen, pertain
to gender roles and appropriate gender behaviour and the participation
of girls and women in PE and sport. The damaging nature of these was
recognised in the Interim Report of the NCPE (National Curriculum for
Physical Education) Working Group (1991). In the section on Equal
Opportunities in Physical Education the Working Group drew attention to:

> the physical nature of physical education, and the emergence of sexu-
> ality during key stages 2, 3 and 4, providing both problems and
> opportunities for physical education in challenging body images, sex
> stereotypes and other limited perspectives which constrain the choices
> and achievements of disabled children, and of both girls and boys
> (NCPE Working Group 1991: 17)

Over a decade later, it is difficult to see substantial evidence of these
'sex stereotypes and limited perspectives' having been transformed.

The transmission of stereotypes is, however, by no means simplistic or
uncontested. It is important to recognise like Woods (1992: 92) that 'In
a society where homosexuals are stereotyped as child molesters who recruit
young children to their so-called deviant lifestyles, female physical educators and coaches are prime targets for homophobic suspicions and
accusations.' These stereotypes of female PE teachers being lesbian have
been well documented (see for instance Squires and Sparkes 1996).
Moreover, Harris and Griffin's research in the United States suggests these
perceptions are widespread. They state that:

> Calling women physical educators lesbians may be used to devalue
> their accomplishments in the eyes of prejudiced people . . . because
> they can then be dismissed as not 'real women' . . . and relegated to
> marginal status . . . Such behaviour serves to protect physical education
> and sport as heterosexual male domains
> (Harris and Griffin 1997: 74)

Harris and Griffin (1997:78) conclude, 'Labeling (or rather mis-labeling)
the majority of women physical educators as lesbian is inaccurate. Such
a term can be used to intimidate, discourage, devalue, and control women'.

Stereotypes also influence the ways teachers treat their male and female pupils, the expectations they have of them and the amount of attention they give them. As Drinkwater (2001: vi) found, 'stereotypical attitudes displayed by some staff encouraged conformity to the female role, thereby denying the girls the support necessary to challenge stereotypical notions of female behaviour.'

Finally, turning to 'explanatory myths', these are used to explain our (in this case oppressive) actions. Osterman (1987: 21) contends that they are 'usually held over long periods of time . . . [and] only when additional information or experience "proves" to us that our myth is distorted or limited will we replace it'. In applying this to PE we can see that one of the most persistent and damaging myths is that of female frailty and the belief that 'sport masculinizes girls and women. Athletic behavior and interest contrast sharply with feminine behavioral standards' (Veri 1999: 357). Other harmful myths are those that see homosexuality as a sickness/mental illness and a deviation from the (heterosexual) norm. If all are to be valued and receive equal treatment in PE then information must be provided to counter these myths, thereby enabling difference and diversity to be respected.

Having sought to explain the cycle of homophobic and heterosexist oppression it is now pertinent to see in more detail how these oppressive practices operate in schools in general and PE departments in particular.

Manifestations of heterosexism and homophobia

Blumenfeld (1992) makes a strong case for recognising that homophobia operates on four distinct but interrelated levels, namely the: personal; interpersonal; institutional; and the cultural or societal. Personal homophobia refers to a personal belief system based on prejudice, stereotyping, misinformation, which 'to put it quite simply . . . [sees homosexuals as] generally inferior to heterosexuals' (Blumenfeld 1992: 4).

Interpersonal homophobia 'is manifest when a personal bias or prejudice affects relations among individuals, transforming prejudice into its active component-discrimination' (Blumenfeld 1992: 4). This includes name-calling which is insulting and often disparaging of girls/women. Duncan's research into bullying in schools reveals that it centres on sexuality and:

> the most prevalent and hurtful accusation levelled at boys by both sexes was to be called 'gay'. Like its counterpart 'slag', the accusation was virtually impossible to refute without a dramatic change in social behaviour and it could be deployed on a continuum of severity or seriousness, from throwaway jocularity to ultimate degradation of the victim, whether true or not.
>
> (Duncan 1999: 106)

Kehily (2002: 145) found 'homophobias to be a routine part of school life, particularly among male peer groups'. One of the manifestations of homophobic bullying within PE lessons is through name-calling. This is frequently levelled at boys whose sporting prowess is deemed inadequate. These unsporty boys or 'wimps' must therefore be 'gay' and not real men, i.e. they become feminised by heterosexual others (Parker 1996). For sporty girls, that is those who perform well and are not stereotypically passive, they must be a lesbian or a 'lezzie', that is, they are exhibiting stereotypical masculine-type behaviours which are viewed as being outside the bounds of the cult of femininity and its association with heterosexual romance. Hence, as Drinkwater (2001: 44) illustrates, 'most girls feel obligated [*sic*] to prove their heterosexuality at every opportunity', and as one of her respondents explained they may be reluctant to engage in any activity which may lead others to question their sexuality.

Related to this discussion about name-calling Wallace (2001: 9) has pointed out that: 'The word "gay" has suddenly become the ultimate put down in schools ... And teachers mindful of Section 28 ... are unsure how to tackle the language of homophobia.' This language is powerful and controlling and leaves little room for resistance. For girls other derogatory and damaging labels seem to be entering the playing field, indeed both Aldridge (1998) and Drinkwater (2001) have detailed the use of the word 'mushbird' to describe girls who have more muscular bodies and a less than stereotypical feminine appearance.

Returning to Blumenfeld's conception of the third level of operationalisation of homophobia, which he sees as institutional homophobia, this refers to the ways educational organisations discriminate on the basis of sexual orientation or identity. In applying this to PE we can see how the National Curriculum (NC) (DfEE/QCA 1999: 3), despite including for the first time 'a detailed, overarching statement on inclusion', fails specifically to address issues that pertain to sexuality and, moreover, it continues to privilege certain activities whilst marginalising others. The section in the NC document entitled 'Inclusion: providing effective learning opportunities for all pupils' describes how effective learning environments can be created by teachers in which 'stereotypical views are challenged and pupils learn to appreciate and view positively differences in others, whether arising from race, gender, ability or disability' (DfEE/QCA 1999: 29). This politics of absence and the issue of silence about sexual identity is complex. Nevertheless, in seeking to understand the concept of silence and its impact on knowledge as it pertains to the official and legitimate discourse of the NCPE we need to ask (see Orner 1992):

- What does silence mean?
- What are the reasons for it?
- What does silence(s) perpetuate?

- What is legitimated?
- What remains unchallenged?
- What relations of power/lessness are implicated?

In essence, silence means that heterosexuality and homophobia remain unchallenged and legitimated, and (hetero)sexual relations retain their power and normalcy. Further, in focusing on silence it is also relevant to note the legal silences around homosexuality.

Cultural or societal homophobia is Blumenfeld's (1992: 6) fourth and final level of homophobia. This he claims takes the form of 'social norms or codes of behavior that, although not expressively written into law or policy, nonetheless work within a society to legitimize oppression.' The so-called hidden curriculum of PE seems a useful way of both unpacking and illustrating this form of homophobia: insofar as the hidden curriculum refers to the ways in which the school, classrooms and playgrounds operate, the underlying rules and rituals, the ways teachers and pupils behave and interact, and the beliefs and values that are transmitted within such practices. The power of the peer group to influence and reinforce hegemonic ways of being male or female is especially significant here. Indeed, we have already seen how name-calling acts as a way of controlling behaviour that falls outside of hegemonic heterosexual norms. Further, Drinkwater's (2001: 39) research reveals how 'Boys were identified by some girls as reinforcing such stereotypical notions [of ways of being] by their perceived attitudes to girls playing sport. As Buffy explained "Boys think we should be in the changing room applying our make-up rather than being out on the rugby pitch." ' The fear of not being seen to be heterosexually desirable/attractive to their male peers leaves many girls regulating their behaviour and policing their appearance so as to appear 'normal'. Thus, these interactions within the peer group involve the communication both implicitly and explicitly of a particular set of values about 'normality' (Nutt and Clarke 2002).

Concluding remarks

This chapter has shown that PE is no neutral, inclusive arena, rather it is an arena that continues to marginalise and exclude those who do not match stereotypical expectations of what it is to be female or male. This situation holds for pupils and teachers alike. Physical Education continues to remain a largely male preserve where status and privilege is ascribed to hegemonic forms of masculinity and others are subordinated. To transgress, at any level of participation, is to risk at best censure and at worst harassment (Clarke 2002).

For PE to be truly inclusive requires an acceptance of the existence of multiple and contested femininities and masculinities, a rejection of a hierarchy of identities and the destabilisation of the heterosexual status quo. Coupled with this is the need to recognise that 'there are other equally damaging oppressions, such as sexism, racism, classism, anti-Semitism, ageism and ableism. These oppressions share common elements that are interconnected through privilege, power, fear and ignorance' (Clarke 1998b: 145–6).

Physical educationalists need to use their privilege and power to ensure that the sporting turf is a safe place, free from discrimination, prejudice and harassment, where all are valued and respected. As such heterosexist and homophobic language and jokes should be challenged and clear policies established for dealing with such incidents. Moreover, such polices need to be enacted at a whole-school level. Teachers need to acknowledge their role in the construction of masculinities and femininities and monitor their own actions and attitudes, and establish within lessons and the co-curriculum opportunities for all pupils to participate in ways (and in activities) that are free from verbal abuse and intimidation to conform to traditional and restrictive notions of what it is to be stereotypically female or male. Further, teachers need to seek out and provide role models and positive, diverse images of masculinity and femininity. Adopting such an approach will likely require training for teachers and trainees to raise awareness about possibilities for change and a shift in ideological and pedagogical approaches so as to emphasise co-operation, self-expression and social responsibility rather than competition. For as Connell (1996: 209) points out, research has shown that the structure of sport (and I would add PE) creates an aggressive masculinity through its structure, 'its pattern of competition, its system of training, and its steep hierarchy of levels and rewards'.

Finally, if we are to have lasting forms of change in PE departments and schools, the dismantling of heterosexism and homophobia must be seen as an integral part of working for equity and social inclusion (Townley cited in Skelton 1998: 103).

Reflective questions

1   Why do teachers, governors and teacher trainers need to address homophobia and heterosexism in Physical Education – what would be gained?
2   If we are to have Physical Education lessons that are devoid of any form of oppression how can we overcome pupils', teachers' and teacher trainers' resistance to change their knowledge base and practices?

Notes

1   I have written elsewhere about the difficulty of identifying gay men in the macho masculine world of Physical Education (Clarke 1998b, 2002). For an account of one male teacher's experiences see the ethnographic fiction written by Sparkes in 1997. Sparkes (2002: 166) explains, 'I produced it for pedagogical reasons, and I had critical intentions, in an attempt like that of Duncan

(1998), to speak for the absent other – in this case, gay, male Physical Education teachers.'

References

Aldridge, M. (1998) ' "On Display and Vulnerable": An Investigation of the Importance and Significance of Body Image and Self Image for Girls in Physical Education', unpublished MA(Ed) thesis, University of Southampton.

Blumenfeld, W. J. (1992) *Homophobia: How We All Pay the Price*, Boston: Beacon Press.

Butler, J. (1990) *Gender Trouble: Feminism and the Subversion of Identity*, London, Routledge.

Clarke, G. (1996) 'Conforming and Contesting with (a) Difference: How Lesbian Students and Teachers Manage their Identities', *International Studies in Sociology of Education* 6, 2: 191–209.

Clarke, G. (1998a) 'Voices From the Margins: Lesbian Teachers in Physical Education', unpublished Ph.D. thesis, Leeds Metropolitan University.

Clarke, G. (1998b) 'Queering the Pitch and Coming out to Play: Lesbians in Physical Education and Sport', *Sport, Education and Society* 3, 2: 145–60.

Clarke, G. (2001) 'Outlaws in Sport and Education? Exploring the Sporting and Education Experiences of Lesbian Physical Education Teachers', in S. Scraton and A. Flintoff (eds), *Gender and Sport: A Reader*, London: Routledge.

Clarke, G. (2002) 'Difference Matters: Sexuality and Physical Education', in D. Penney (ed.), *Gender and Physical Education: Contemporary Issues and Future Directions*, London: Routledge.

Cockburn, C. and Clarke, G. (2002) ' "Everybody's Looking at You!" Girls Negotiating the "Femininity Deficit" they in Incur in Physical Education', *Women's Studies International Forum* 25, 6: 651–65.

Connell, R. W. (1995) *Masculinities*, Cambridge: Polity Press.

Connell, R. W. (1996) 'Teaching the Boys: New Research on Masculinity, and Gender Strategies for schools', *Teachers College Record* 98, 2: 206–35.

DfEE/QCA (Department for Education and Employment/Qualifications and Curriculum Authority) (1999) *Physical Education: The National Curriculum for England*, London: HMSO.

Drinkwater, A. (2001) ' "A Boy Wouldn't Want to Go Out With a Girl Who Had Bigger Muscles Than Him!" Playing the "Femininity Game": The Impact of Stereotypical Images of Femininity on the Physical Education Experiences of Adolescent Girls', unpublished MA(Ed) thesis, University of Southampton.

Duncan, N. (1999) *Sexual Bullying: Gender Conflict and Pupil Culture in Secondary Schools*, London: Routledge.

Fletcher, S. (1984) *Women First: The Female Tradition in English Physical Education, 1880–1980*, London: Athlone Press.

Freeman, P. (1997) *Ian Roberts: Finding Out*, Sydney: Random House.

Gilroy, S. (1997) 'Working on the Body: Links Between Physical Activity and Social Power', in G. Clarke and B. Humberstone (eds), *Researching Women and Sport*, London: Macmillan.

Griffin, P. (1991) 'Identity Management Strategies Among Lesbian and Gay Educators', *Qualitative Studies in Education* 4, 3: 189–202.

Griffin, P. and Harro, B. (1997) 'Heterosexism Curriculum Design', in M. Adams, L. A. Bell and P. Griffin (eds), *Teaching for Diversity and Social Justice: A Sourcebook*, London: Routledge.

Hargreaves, J. (2000) *Heroines of Sport: The Politics of Difference and Identity*, London: Routledge.

Harris, M. B. and Griffin, J. (1997) 'Stereotypes and Personal Beliefs about Women Physical Education Teachers', *WSPAJ* 6, 1: 49–83.

Jeffreys, S. (1990) *Anticlimax: A Feminist Perspective on the Sexual Revolution*, London: The Women's Press.

Johnson, R. and Epstein, D. (2000) 'Sectional Interests: Sexuality, Social Justice and Moral Traditionalism', *Education and Social Justice* 2, 2: 27–37.

Kehily, M. (2002) *Sexuality, Gender and Schooling: Shifting Agendas in Social Learning*, London: Routledge Falmer.

Keyworth, S. A. (2001) 'Critical Autobiography: "Straightening" Out Dance Education', *Research in Dance Education* 2, 2: 117–37.

Kumashiro, K. (2000) 'Towards a Theory of Anti-oppressive Education', *Review of Educational Research* 70, 1: 25–53.

Macdonald, D. (2002) 'Critical Pedagogy: What Might it Look Like and Why Does it Matter?' in A. Laker (ed.), *The Sociology of Sport and Physical Education: An Introductory Reader*, London: Routledge Falmer.

Messner, M. and Sabo, D. (1994) *Sex, Violence and Power in Sports: Rethinking Masculinity*, Freedom: The Crossing Press.

NCPE (National Curriculum for Physical Education) Working Group (1991) *Interim Report*, London: The Department of Education and Science: 8.

Nutt, G. and Clarke, G. (2002) 'The Hidden Curriculum and the Changing Nature of Teachers' Work', in A. Laker (ed.), *The Sociology of Sport and Physical Education: An Introductory Reader*, London: Routledge Falmer.

Observer (2002) 'Lesson in Respect: Disabled Children Get Their Due', 1 September: 24, editorial.

Orner, M. (1992) 'Interpreting the Calls for Student Voice in 'Liberatory' Education: A Feminist Perspective', in C. Luke and J. Gore (eds), *Feminisms and Critical Pedagogy*, London: Routledge.

Osterman, M. J. (1987) *Homophobia is a Social Disease*, Evanston, Ill.: Kinehart Program on Sexuality and Homophobia.

Parker, A. (1996) 'The Construction of Masculinity Within Boys' Physical Education', *Gender and Education* 8, 2: 141–57.

Phelan, S. (1989) *Identity Politics: Lesbian Feminism and the Limits of Community*, Philadelphia: Temple University Press.

Ramazanoglu, C. (1989) *Feminism and the Contradictions of Oppression*, London: Routledge.

Rich, A. (1981) *Compulsory Heterosexuality and Lesbian Existence*, London: Onlywomen Press.

Sears, J.T. (1997) 'Thinking Critically/Intervening Effectively about Heterosexism and Homophobia: A Twenty-Five-Year Research Retrospective', in J. T. Sears and W. L. Williams (eds), *Overcoming Heterosexism and Homophobia: Strategies that Work*, New York: Columbia University Press.

Skelton, A. (1998) 'Eclipsed by Eton Fields: Physical Education and Equal Opportunities', in A. Clark and E. Millard (eds), *Gender in the Secondary Curriculum: Balancing the Books*, London: Routledge.

Smith, A. M. (1994) *New Right Discourse on Race and Sexuality: Britain, 1968–1990*, Cambridge: Cambridge University Press.

Sparkes, A. (1994) 'Self, Silence and Invisibility as a Beginning Teacher: A History of Lesbian Experience', *British Journal of Sociology of Education* 15, 1: 93–118.

Sparkes, A. (1997) 'Ethnographic Fiction and Representing the Absent Other', *Sport, Education and Society* 2, 1: 25–40.

Sparkes, A. (2002) *Telling Tales in Sport and Physical Activity: A Qualitative Journey*, Leeds: Human Kinetics.

Squires, S. and Sparkes, A. (1996) 'Circles of Silence: Sexual Identity in Physical Education and Sport', *Sport, Education and Society* 1, 1: 77–101.

Stonewall (2001) *Equal as Citizens: Action for a New Century*, London: Stonewall.

Swain, J. (2000) ' "The Money's Good, the Fame's Good, the Girls are Good": The Role of Playground Football in the Construction of Young Boys' Masculinity in a Junior School', *British Journal of the Sociology of Education* 21, 1: 95–109.

Sykes, H. (1998) 'Turning the Closets Inside/Out: Towards a Queer-Feminist Theory in Women's Physical Education', *Sociology of Sport Journal* 15, 2: 154–73.

Veri, M. J. (1999) 'Homophobic Discourse Surrounding the Female Athlete', *Quest* 51, 4: 355–68.

Wallace, W. (2001) 'Is This Table Gay? Anatomy of a Classroom Insult', *Times Educational Supplement*, 19 January: 9–10.

Wilkinson, S. and Kitzinger, C. (eds) (1993) *Heterosexuality. A Feminism and Psychology Reader*, London: Sage.

Woods, S. (1992) 'Describing the Experiences of Lesbian Physical Educators: A Phenomenological Study', in A. C. Sparkes (ed.), *Research in Physical Education and Sport: Exploring Alternative Visions*, London: Falmer Press.

Woog, D. (1998) *Jocks: True Stories of America's Gay Male Athletes*, Los Angeles: Alyson Publications.

She seemed to have a sixth-sense about what we would all hate. She kindly introduced us to the medicine ball: A huge brown leather ball that had been gathering dust in the PE cupboard for nigh on a century. We spent the rest of the day dragging our hands along the floor. I suppose it could have been worse. I could have been do-si-do-ing with a boy I didn't like but been paired with. Country dancing. Now what was that all about?

B. Mistry (2002) 'Why I Hated School PE',
PE and Sport Today 9: 56.

7 C'mon PE(TE) it's time to get changed for dance

Saul Keyworth and Fiona Smith

Warm up

As in the Physical Education (PE) lesson, begin with a short warm-up. We want you, the gendered reader, to run your thoughts 'over', 'inside' and 'around' the two job advertisements in Figure 7.1 with a view to answering the following questions – which advert best describes the department(s) where you received your Physical Education, and in which department do you feel pupils are more likely to receive a well-rounded 'broad and balanced' Physical Education?

The learning outcome of this task, and more broadly this chapter, is to engage you in the reflexive process of thinking critically about your PE practice (Tsangaridou and Siedentop 1995). As dance educators, we particularly want you to (re)consider the desirability of delivering dance as part of a broad and balanced PE curriculum to all (male and female) pupils. Are 'breadth and balance' and 'dance' synonymous with your vision of what constitutes PE? If not, what justification do you have for overlooking such an important concept and activity area? Have you ever taken the time to consider why you think and act the way that you do? For example, what influence has your own PE and the teachers who taught you had on your philosophy of what constitutes PE? Was your PE experience largely unproblematic in providing you with a vision/curriculum blueprint that you wish to replicate? Alternatively, if negative, what steps will or are you taking to ensure your practice is different? In terms of gender, how do your gendered beliefs govern your own physical choices, not to mention those you are likely to include/exclude for your pupils? What factors have been central in the formation of these particular gendered beliefs? With specific regard to dance, do you accept its teaching as part of your job specification? If you do/intend to teach dance, how do you/will you go about encouraging boys to participate? If you are not directly involved in teaching dance, will you become a dance advocate by supporting the efforts of teachers/pupils who are? This list of questions is by no means exhaustive; these are just some of the important questions

Teacher PE
For September

We are seeking to appoint a creative and enthusiastic teacher to join this forward-thinking department. The school recently received Sports College Status and Artsmark Silver recognition. GCSE PE and Dance are popular options at KS 4. The successful applicant will be someone who can meet the needs of a broad and balanced curriculum and who values, and can inspire, students of all abilities and interests.

The school boasts excellent facilities including:

- Sports hall
- Playing fields on site
- Dance studio
- State of the art fitness suite
- Dedicated classroom/resource room

The department is committed to achieving the best for each individual student. As part of this commitment the curricular and extensive extra curricular programme is rich and diverse.

The school is a non-selective 11-16 co-educational school that occupies an attractive semi rural site.

Application forms and further details are available from the headteacher
Closing date: 15th April 2002

Teacher of Boys' PE
For September

We are seeking to appoint an enthusiastic teacher to work in this highly successful department. Applicants will be required to teach across the age range, including GCSE PE. The ability to offer expertise in Football, Cricket, Rugby, Athletics and Basketball would be an advantage.

The department enjoys superb facilities including:

- Extensive playing fields
- Floodlit all-weather pitch
- Sports hall

The department supports a wide range of extra-curricular activities and is held in high esteem for its achievements in competitive sport. The school runs a number of successful teams and has an extensive fixture list. A commitment to extra-curricular activities is therefore essential.

The School is an oversubscribed mixed 11-16 school, situated in an attractive site on the edge of the town.

Application forms and further details are available from the headteacher
Closing date: 15th April 2002

Figure 7.1 Mock job advertisements

we feel intending and current PE teachers need to constantly address. As dance educators working primarily within Physical Education (teacher education) PE(TE) we feel it is high time questions like those aforementioned are aired, shared and discussed. Although we recognise PE is one of several homes for dance, we do not wish to rehearse or support the argument for its re-location to departments of the performing/expressive arts (see Sanderson 2001). Much like Flintoff (1990) we do not see location as being of central importance. Our experience has shown us that as long as dance is taught well and treated as an art form (Smith-Autard 1994) it can flourish wherever it may be placed. To suggest this cannot happen within PE is to denigrate a lot of outstanding and committed teaching that has been tuning students into dance for years.

A note towards our technique

Following recent trends in PE research, we encourage male (and female) physical educators to grapple with such questions by engaging in critical autobiographical work (Sparkes 1999a) through which they can begin to publicise and interrogate stories of their teacher socialisation (Dowling Naess 2001).[1] Through engaging in a supportive dialogue with other males (and/or females) a transformative and emancipatory process can begin, enabling marginal male dancers within PE(TE) to 'be heard and understood' (Etherington 2000: 304). In this chapter we endeavour to begin this 'emancipatory storysharing' (Barone 1995) by telling and re-telling stories of several males who have struggled to overcome prejudice to dance. Collating these masculine 'altern(arr)atives' (see Grace and Benson 2000) together, our intent is to form what Richardson calls a 'collective story' which ultimately could serve as a guide to legitimate dance to other males. Upon this issue Richardson argues:

> Collective stories that deviate from standard cultural plots provide new narratives; hearing them legitimates replotting one's own life. New narratives offer the patterns for new lives. The story of the transformed life, then, becomes a part of the cultural heritage affecting future stories, future lives.
>
> (Richardson 1990: 26)

Drawing upon the insights of Polkinghorne (1988), Denison (1996: 359) like Richardson believes that 'narratives are the primary way through which we organise our experiences and come to understand who we are'. Agreeing with this sentiment, we feel hearing the voices of male dancers will provide male physical educators with the narrative resources (Brown 1999; Wright 1999) to step outside of their usual movement range to re-story dance into their lives.

Tension and control

Many male PE teachers see dance as an activity to be avoided as it creates a sense of 'gender trouble' (Butler 1990) that could ultimately shroud their sexual orientation with suspicion. Here Clarke testifies:

> Boys and men who wish to participate in dance or other related activities where they are required to display grace and exhibit emotional characteristics that are not regarded as being traditionally and stereotypically masculine also run the risk of their sexual identity being called into question and the pejorative label gay applied.
>
> (Clarke 2002: 45)

This being the case, males who wish to start and maintain their participation in dance need to be brave. Regrettably, many males find the insidious pressure to 'police' their gendered behaviour too much to bear and this results in so-called 'feminine' activities like dance (see Keyworth 2001) being dropped from their physical repertoires (see Waddell and Schapp 1996). This has the potential to re-affirm a self-perpetuating gender cycle amongst male PE trainees as many gain limited experience of teaching dance whilst on school based placements (Stidder and Hayes 2002). To curb this continued male exodus from dance (in order to fit the traditional and stereotypical hegemonic masculine ideal) we feel male PE teachers and trainees can and should play a central role. This is because their main concerns, experiences of embodiment are central to gender formation (see Connell 1995, Kirk 2002a). As such, male physical educators have the potential to challenge and subvert their own as well as their pupils' understanding of masculinity by 'potentially' doing it differently (Lucal 1999) – for our particular purpose here, 'daring' to become a male role model in dance (see Gough 1999). Unfortunately, challenging traditional gendered pathways through dance remains an opportunity that most male PE teachers miss (Keyworth 2001, Penney 2002). By neglecting to embrace the teaching of dance, many male pupils, therefore, continue to receive a narrow and gendered vision of what it means to be physically educated. More often than not male PE programmes continue to be hijacked by competitive sport, which for many pupils is both alienating (Carlson 1995) and not the precursor to lifetime physical activity (Fairclough *et al.* 2002). In light of this, we are inclined to agree with Murdoch (1997) who called for the PE profession to re-evaluate its conception of what it means to be 'physically educated'. In particular we sympathise with her belief that the physically educated person is more than just 'a good games player, an effective tennis player or an inventive gymnast' (Murdoch 1997: 268). Rather we contend the physically educated person is someone possessing the flexibility to participate with confidence, success and control in a range of activities.

One such individual is the famed American athlete Herschel Walker. Whether on the running track (collegiate record holder), football field (Hall of Fame), ballet stage (regional company) or at the rear of a bob sled (Olympian), Walker always managed to adapt and excel. What is useful for us here is the credibility respected sporting figures like Walker (1991) and English footballer Dion Dublin (Boyden 2002) bring to male dance by demonstrating the desire to share their time between two contrasting physical arenas. 'Performing' on these different stages allows each athlete to experience using their bodies in both an instrumental and expressive fashion. For male pupils who enjoy and want to dance, the availability of such narratives/role models will be much appreciated as they provide an initial foundation upon which their future dancing persona, careers or audience participation can grow. These positive benefits, however, can only come to fruition when male PE teachers start 'daring to be different' (Young 1997) by taking risks with their gender identities and reputations. For some (see Brown and Rich 2002) such 'risk taking' within the profession marks a time that is long overdue and we are inclined to agree. To continue to play it safe in terms of gender displays will not only limit the physical potential and choices for countless numbers of pupils, it will also fuel the continued reinforcement within PE(TE) of recycling and perpetuating narrow minds and gendered visions on broad shoulders.

Dance altern(arr)atives

To encourage more male PE teachers to risk daring to be different, we each tell the stories of male teachers who have embraced teaching dance as part of a broad and balanced PE curriculum. We hope hearing these altern(arr)atives will encourage more male PE teachers to teach dance and in so doing help 'short circuit' (Hickey and Fitzclarence 1999) the gendered legacy of sex differentiated PE teaching (see Kirk 2002b). Regrettably, this still seems a far cry from reality as many PE teachers/trainees continue to view PE as being synonymous with competitive sport. Here I have to confess that upon entering PE(TE) this was the outlook I had. Back then I labelled myself (and was labelled) a footballer and in terms of physical pursuits I did little else. Well, that was until dance came onto the scene during PE(TE). For most of my male peers, dance was a new experience, yet I soon found myself 'capturing a dancing spirit' (Bain 1984: 10). So much so, I quickly replaced football as my activity of choice and I was eager to see/experience as much dance as I could. My relocation from football to dance blew the whistle on my until-then performance of what Keen (1992) calls the 'Gender Game'. As I will indicate, this has and continues to provide the foundation upon which much PE practice and masculine/feminine identity work (see Flintoff 1991) is based.

Fiona's 'fictional' story (see Sparkes 2002) outlines her role in eradicating 'crimes against gender' as an inspector within the Physical Education Gender Police (PEGP). In particular, Fiona shares her report of a recent visit to a school in an area where there had been a worrying outbreak of gender crimes in dance. Fiona gladly reports that on this particular occasion she was pleasantly surprised. The favourable picture of dance that Fiona's final report paints is a composite of her real-life experiences of teaching and observing dance in numerous schools over the years. Indeed, some schools/teachers will be able to identify fragments of themselves within Fiona's narrative. In time we hope this identification will become the rule rather than the exception and that there will no longer be a need for government bodies like the PEGP.

A note on appreciation

Other contributors to this book have highlighted their own personal stories based on biographical accounts of their PE experiences. Likewise the editors have included the testimonials of these individuals, which have preceded each piece. The measure we want you to use in judging our stories is whether they provoke your own storytelling. Are you able to make the stories that we share more personal by relating them to your own experience(s) (see Coakley and Donnelly 1999)? Like John Burt (1987: 168) hoped of his readers, we want you 'to turn the stories we share inside out, to support them, to utilise them to guide your future work – anything but ignore them'. When a story is embraced rather than ignored it will be picked up by others and undergo a gradual process of passing and receipt. We hope this is the plight for the stories we share with you. Following Atkinson (1998: 76) we believe that 'the more we share our stories the closer we will all become'. The potential outcome of this sharing is that the male dancer/curriculum within PE(TE) will become gradually less marginal and a more accepted face of what the male PE teacher/ curriculum can act/look like.

Dancing in time (the time is right)

According to Plummer (1995: 121) stories become tellable when 'a community has been fattened up, rendered ripe and willing to hear such stories'. With particular reference to stories of male dance we would appear to be inhabiting such a time now. Numerous advertisers have utilised dance to promote their wares on television (for example Gap and Nike clothing) while at the cinema the movie *Billy Elliot* became a global box-office hit. Further to this, choreographers are being increasingly employed by pop stars to create dance routines to supplement their music. Many of these routines are easily accessible through satellite TV channels like MTV. It should be pointed out, however, that replicating these routines is not what we would consider a worthwhile dance education, even though this may be what some pupils desire. Rather, we feel dance taught in school should hold the 'art of dance' (Smith-Autard 1994) as its central focus. Here students should have the opportunity to perform, compose and appreciate a variety of dances that pay homage to differing stylistic and cultural conventions. We feel it is important that pupils are encouraged to reflect critically upon the 'challenges' and 'lessons' numerous dance works can provide. For instance the respective works of DV8, Jonzi D and Doug Elkins have challenged my pre-conceived notions of masculinity, race and ethnicity and what can constitute theatrical dance. As I will discuss further below, Lloyd Newson and his company DV8 have challenged dance audiences around the world to heighten their sensitivity towards derogatory sexual politics. For numerous males, including myself, their overt physical style has provided an initial catalyst into further dance exploration. Other dance companies helping me in this regard have been Jonzi D's Lyrikal Fearta and Doug Elkin's own company which is based in New York. Both of these choreographers, like me, have a b-boying (break dancing) background.

PE(TE) should 'observe' Billy Elliot's dance lessons

To return to *Billy Elliot*, Billy's struggle to dance raises many key themes that we feel are pertinent to PE(TE). As Bramley (2001: 47) points out, 'the placing of men as the focus for popular discussion of dance can only be welcomed'. Additionally Quirke (2000: 3) argues that the film's narrative 'resurrects a universal story, be yourself'. Being oneself, however, is not always an achievable goal in a society that places a great deal of pressure on males and females to conform blindly to the traditional and idealised view of masculinity and femininity. The thoughts of two of my favourite choreographers, Doug Elkins and Lloyd Newson, can be drawn upon here. For Elkins, 'one of the hardest things to learn to ignore is other people's explanation of who you are' (cited in Mason and Daniels 1994: 57). This is because, as social beings, we for the most part see and understand ourselves through the reflections of others. This is particularly true when it comes to masculinity and its policing. Here Newson (1996a: 3) outlines, 'The straightjacket of masculinity defines itself in don'ts: don't walk like that, don't talk like that, don't wear particular clothes or colours and don't show certain feelings.'

Newson's 1996 production *Enter Achilles* (Newson 1996b) was largely devised as an attempt to overcome the blind allegiance among men towards their gendered conditioning. In particular it hoped to challenge male viewers to question why the wearing of their 'straight jackets', despite being so restrictive, was considered so comfortable. Despite receiving a fair amount of privilege in the sporting domain, frequenting the dance studio began to show me how I had also been oppressed (see Dewar 1990) by my gendered conditioning. I no longer wanted to be policed to perform the socially sanctioned and approved masculine ideal. Much like Sluder (1998: 117), 'through dance, my story emerged and I found my true self'. Dance enabled me to move with greater flexibility and I 'no longer looked for myself outside of myself' (ibid.: 118).

For Higgins (2000: 17) the plight of Billy Elliot 'could be seen as reflective of the need for communities to break out of old moulds and adapt to new times'. Such a transition, a breaking with tradition, is being called for at present in PE(TE) (Armour 1999; Penney and Chandler 2000). What concerns us most specifically here is the development of a new de-gendered 'vision and voice' (Bain 1990, 1997) for PE(TE). We want to see PE broaden its outlook to welcome and incorporate more readily the teaching of dance and expressive practices. By doing so, more trainee PE teachers are likely to enter PE(TE) seeing dance as centrally their business.[2]

Establishing the 'motif': Boys' limited access to dance education

Fourteen years have passed since Lloyd and West (1988) asked 'where are the boys in dance?' Much of the research has since suggested that in PE(TE) we are still hearing their echoes. As we have argued, countless numbers of boys (not to mention girls)[3] continue to be denied access to dance as part of a 'broad and balanced' PE curriculum (see Sanderson 2001). Numerous attempts have been made to challenge this paucity of male dance provision and we shall pick up and build on these as this chapter proceeds.[4] Before we do this, however, it is first apt to introduce ourselves. Fiona and I first met in 1992 when I turned up to PE(TE) with little to no prior dance experience. Limited exposure to dance is a situation that for many male (and female) trainee PE teachers still rings true (Keyworth 2001). Regrettably, despite the NCPE entering its tenth year, the majority of male PE departments are still failing to embrace the 'challenge' (Penney and Chandler 2000) of teaching dance to their male students (see Waddington *et al.* 1998). More often than not dance teaching becomes the preserve of female PE departments/staff members who on occasion may also teach the boys.

The school I attended did not, however, see the educational benefit of dance for girls. Much like the boys, the girls suffered the similar fate of missing out on the unique contribution that dance can offer: the opportunity to develop knowledge, skill and understanding in the use of their body as a medium for artistic expression and communication. The result of this omission and blatant exclusionary practice was that both sexes were denied the opportunity to appreciate the value of dance within their lives, not to mention how it can contribute to the rich tapestry of social life by bringing them into contact with various issues and cultures to which they would normally not be exposed (see Rorty 1989, Thomas 1993).[5] Furthermore, to not experience dance is to potentially close the door upon an increasingly viable future profession, especially now that dance can be studied at all levels of education.

Contrasting accounts in this regard can be highlighted through the respective stories of Mark Murphy and Ramsay Burt. For Mark Murphy the benefit of having a thriving performing arts department at school, through which he was able to experience a multitude of dance forms, is clearly evident. By his own admission (see Sacks 1995) if he had attended a different school he may never have gone on to dance professionally and set up his own company *Vertical Take-Off and Landing* (V-Tol). Like Murphy, Ramsay Burt would have loved to ply his trade as a dancer. Like many males, however, he was less fortunate and his rather late introduction to the world of dance at the age of 26 put paid to any serious 'performing' plans he may have held. Staying in the dance world, Burt has concentrated his efforts on teaching and writing about dance instead. Emanating from his Ph.D. work, Burt (1995) wrote *The Male Dancer* to begin, amongst other things, dispelling some of the disparaging myths that surround males who want to participate in and/or be seen in dance.

Retracing footsteps and pathways

It is with much sadness that I report following a similar pathway to that of Burt. Like him I, too, have had a noticeable gap in my dance education, and it was only upon meeting my dance 'mentors' that my philosophy towards PE, not to mention my gendered outlook, began to take on a different, 'less blinding' (see Kimmel and Messner 1995) shade. In a similar vein to Murphy, I feel that if I had received my teacher training at a different university my passion for dance may not have been kindled. My reasoning for this assumption is that I had elected (although I didn't realise this at the time) to go to a college with a strong female legacy and foundation. Here, the female tradition (ethos) of championing gymnastics and dance alongside the teaching of games was upheld (Kirk 2002b). I slowly began to see the value of the 'aesthetic' and 'artistic' pursuits of gymnastics and dance and they became central constituents of my philosophy of PE. This philosophy was not always easy to practice in schools, however. Similar to Wright (1995) I soon found that my more central positioning towards dance did not meet much favour in the male departments in which I was located. As Wright (1995: 5) herself found, dance was 'an experience of movement rarely foregrounded in the instrumental and masculinist pursuit of activity in schools'. Due to this climate, upon leaving university I found it extremely difficult to find a department that catered for my vision of PE. It was very seldom that I located a PE job advertisement asking for a male that could, would and wished to teach dance. As Stidder (2002) confirms, secondary schools are restricting employment opportunities for male and female teachers through the vocabulary used in national advertisements, thus perpetuating gender divisions within PE. Needless to say it became quite clear that if I was going to teach PE in school I would have to make some major compromises. I wasn't prepared to do that! So like Ramsay Burt before me, I turned my attention towards research, teaching and writing with the utopian hope that my little pocket of resistance towards the instrumental and masculinist practice of PE in schools could make some positive, even though probably minor, change.

Dancing with PE(TE)

Our intention here as well as in our day-to-day teaching is to encourage more male (and female) PE teachers/trainees to embrace the teaching of dance. We feel it is only through offering dance at school that the majority of pupils will be able to 'capture a dancing spirit' (Bain 1984). Although we realise many current and intending PE teachers have a limited dance knowledge and experience, we feel that this is not an excuse to avoid its teaching and/or to rehearse the argument that dance is better placed elsewhere.

As dance educators within PE(TE) will testify, this initial scepticism should and can be overcome. Our relationship testifies that 'a good dance experience in the teacher preparation programme may be the most critical factor in the process of learning to teach dance' (Downey 1996: 100). Recalling her time as a Physical Education trainee Bain fondly remembers:

> Physical education majors in leotards giggling nervously and averting their eyes from the mirrors – the memory of that first day in my required undergraduate modern dance class remains sharp in my mind. Like most of my classmates, I was drawn to PE because of my love of sports. Teaching dance was not part of my career plans. Four years and several dance classes later I had acquired a dancing spirit if not a dancing body. As a new elementary teacher and later secondary teacher, I taught dance – creative, folk and modern. Although still not a confident mover, I experienced unexpected success and satisfaction. Dance was not just another sport! It was an important and different way of moving, one that provided my students a gateway to the world of creativity and aesthetics.
>
> (Bain 1984: 10)

Capturing a dancing spirit during PE(TE) remains the exception rather than the rule. As Bain alludes to above, the majority of PE teachers are sport lovers first and foremost and this is why they have chosen to teach (see Green 2002). As we shall now argue, much still needs to be done before a significant number of male trainees add dance to their list of passions. It is not a matter of replacing their existing interests but more of adding dance to their repertoire.

Motif development: Using flexibility to remain inflexible

Entering the dance studio during PE(TE) for the first time I felt extremely conscious of my sense of masculinity and heterosexuality. This is how I should have felt, isn't it? Years of playing the 'Gender Game' (Keen 1992) have taught me that my appropriate 'masculine and heterosexual' theatre is the football field. I couldn't help but feel that here in the dance studio all those years of gender and sexual identity work were going to be undone. I quickly scurried to the back so as to blend insignificantly into the distance. Gosh, I'm embarrassed to report that's how I felt just a few short years ago. Should I, however, feel embarrassed? According to Sparkes:

> How I make sense of myself is shaped by the kinds of story that have been made available to me in the various sub-cultures and cultures that I inhabit. That is, I cannot transcend my narrative resources in telling a story about my self or in restorying my self if I desired to do so.
>
> (Sparkes 1999b: 20)

Hetero-normative bodily/identity 'performances' (Butler 1990) held in check by homophobic prejudice pretty much characterised my world. My own Physical Education experiences and immersion into semi-professional football culture had taught me little else. Much like the other males that surrounded me here, I was little more than a narrow mind on broad shoulders. Despite my footballer status bringing me a considerable amount of male status, deep down I felt a burgeoning sense of oppression (see Dewar 1990). As I have written elsewhere

> I felt marginal in the heterosexist environments of semi-professional football and PE in which I was located. I wore the baggage that came with these identifications like an 'ill-fitting coat'
>
> (Keyworth 2001: 118):

Time and time again I felt like the 'odd man out' and I knew I didn't belong. During my remaining years at PE(TE) I knew only a handful of males who were willing to take a more central location in the dance studio. My sense of estrangement from 'normal' male PE culture grew when I came to look for a suitable teaching post.

Be a good sport and play the game

To return to the job advertisements we outlined at the beginning of this chapter (page 108), it was 'The Teacher of Boys' PE' that reared its gender-biased head on more than one occasion. It is with much regret that I found my newly acquired dancing persona being considered an unwelcome intrusion in many of the 'heterosexist' departments I saw advertised. Elsewhere Stidder (2002) has argued that such advertising is highly questionable professional practice within the framework of employment rights. Time after time it was clear that I was not going to be able to retrace the footsteps of the choreographers who so fuelled my love for dance. Mirroring their movements, I wanted to question why I had been conditioned to perform in such a restricted masculine fashion, especially as I was beginning to feel and experience how damaging they could be. For example, as someone who was supposedly 'physically educated' I couldn't touch my toes, not even close. I was the very living embodiment of masculinity – 'inflexible'. Accordingly, given half a chance, I wanted to challenge and subvert the pervasive myths surrounding masculinity and heterosexuality that so impeded my (and other males') sense of embodiment (identity) and experiences of 'expressive' activities like dance. I particularly sympathised with Keen (cited in Hamilton) who feels it's high time the 'Gender Game' was abandoned:

> This question of gender is something, by and large, to be gotten over, to get on the other side of. I don't ask myself the question: Am I a man? Am I manly enough? I ask myself the question what am I about? In other words, I think we need to stop making gender a primary way of asking the question: Who am I?
>
> (Hamilton 2001: 5)

Similarly I feel PE(TE) needs to replace the 'Gender Game' with 'social justice' as the primary way it sees itself. In my teaching I have no intention of reciprocating to pupils the rules of the 'Gender Game'. To do so would be tantamount to closing off their minds and bodies to a world of de-gendered opportunity. I have been there before and I do not wish to return. In describing his notion of the 'Gender Game' Keen has found it useful to draw upon the analogy of setting up and servicing a computer. Sex, gender and sexuality can be thought of in terms of a computer programmer (compulsory heterosexuality), loading software (gendered myths) onto/into the computer's hard drive (sex) and then periodically casting a male gaze over the computer (homophobia) to ensure that no viruses (non-gendered behaviour) had corrupted its smooth operation. As Keen (cited in Hamilton) explains:

> I've got to start with the idea of myth, that a myth is like the software that is inserted into us by society, by our family. Nature gives

us certain hardware. There's male hardware and there's female hardware. But the moment we're born, people start shoving these software disks in, saying, 'Here's what a real man is. Here's what it means to be a man. Here's what it means to be an American man', and things like that. That's what gender is.

(Hamilton 2001: 1)

On recently becoming a father for the first time, I find that Keen's comment that the 'Gender Game' kicks off from birth resonates still more strongly. For the past six months my world has been lit as either pink or blue with a little dash of lemon. Indeed, upon leaving the hospital we were given a personal child health record book in which our son's height and weight would be periodically checked. Even here the respective pages for boys and girls are colour coded blue or pink. Furthermore, when I state that Archie will be going to ballet, I am met with horrified stares and then ... 'Oh, the poor little boy'. To be masculine is, in short, to be not feminine. To recall Newson (1996a), 'doing' masculinity defines itself in various dos (football) and don'ts (dance). On transgressing normal male play through dance I have been labelled gay, queer, a fag, and this has been levelled so as to stop my breaking the rules and to re-align my trajectory along the path that is straight and narrow. Heck, no, I no longer will be policed to perform a role that isn't me. Especially as I'm beginning to see that it is solely to maintain the comfort levels and positioning of those not daring enough to be different. Two wonderfully provocative accounts which demonstrate the pervasiveness of the gendering process can be seen through Gould's (1978) fictitious account *X: A Fabulous Child's Story* and Bem's (1998) *An Unconventional Family*, which more or less brings Gould's fictional account to real life. Through reading deconstructive works such as these and participating in dance, I have been provided with the narrative resources to begin dismantling the masculine ways I have been taught to be and think (see Waddell and Schapp 1996). Regrettably with dance and sociological accounts of the body (for example Kirk 2002a) being marginalised within PE(TE), finding a PE post where I could continue re-writing this new identity/body project as well as those of my pupils has proved to be difficult.

Limited support and resources for dance education

To understand why male PE teachers seldom teach dance, the political, economic and institutional contexts in which they work need to be considered (Penney 2002). For example during key stages 3 and 4 teaching dance remains optional. Upon devising the respective programmes here, teachers have the flexibility to teach gymnastics, dance, or shorter units of both. For male teachers with a limited background and comfort level in dance, this degree of choice (read 'get-out clause') has been nothing short of a godsend. The fears of 'troubling' their gender and/or sexual identity through dance simply no longer have to be confronted. Along with Penney (2002) I feel this becomes a missed opportunity in terms of gender equity, as by and large teachers' and students' traditional and conservative readings of gender remain unchallenged.

OFSTED (1998) reported that a significant number of male PE teachers willingly undertook in-service training in dance. The reality, however, was that many schools omitted dance from boys' PE programmes in favour of gymnastics. A further barrier to dance's inclusion within PE programmes is the perceived responses of both students and parents. Here we can consider the less than positive initial response of Billy Elliot's father to his son's dancing. This strikes a personal chord, as when I first broke the news of my dancing to my father he, too, was less than happy. I wonder what their initial responses would have been if both Billy and I had been taught dance as part of our PE programme? The point I'm making here is that in today's economic climate, whereby schools compete with each other to attract future parents/pupils, being seen to be delivering programmes that are congruent to their needs and desires becomes important. In relation to PE, many parents still appear to see PE as being synonymous with competitive sport and this is what they come to expect for their children. The media has fuelled this relationship as PE in schools on more than one occasion has been vilified as 'responsible for' the decline of our nation's sporting teams. I wonder why the same media panic isn't concocted around the dearth of professional male dancers? Within the internal market of schooling (see Evans *et al.* 1996, Penney and Evans 1997) many PE departments see little option but to play the government's/parents' game of devoting most of their energy/resources towards nurturing a range of successful sports teams. To do so provides the school with an attractive public face that will serve the school well financially by attracting more custom. Returning to the 'Teacher of Boys' PE' advert once more, having an expertise in football, cricket, rugby, athletics and basketball was the 'Gender Game' as usual. Through my participation in dance I was slowly beginning to break these rules and I had every intention for this to continue.

Abandoning the 'Gender Game'

Following Gard (2001) and McFee and Smith (1994) I feel the best long-term solution for promoting male participation in dance is to change boys and men to meet dance rather than changing dance to meet them. In a similar vein Gough (1999) suggests we need to afflict the comfortable not comfort the afflicted. As I write, this is still very much a process I am working through as I have not been wholly successful in breaking free from the shackles of my gendered past. To some degree I have supported the very masculine structure I wish to break down. Although I have dared to be different I still have a long way to go as my movements have pretty much stayed in my comfort zone that advocates the traditional masculine traits of physical robustness and strength. Despite this being an initially attractive position through which to induct males into dance, I have harboured here for too long and stand accused of doing little more than promoting what Willis describes as a 'situated rebirth of ideology' (Willis 1982 cited in McFee and Smith 1994: 69). Even though I very much wish to step outside of my usual masculine movement range, this has been easier to achieve in a theoretical rather than a practical sense. The reason for this is that my usually 'cock sure' (Jackson 1999) male performances experienced through sport have evaded me and I feel vulnerable. I have seldom had a troubled relationship with my body's performance capabilities but in certain dance styles this is very much the case. This experience, however, has been anything but negative; through participating in dance I have developed a heightened sensitivity towards those who have a troubled relationship/experience of sport (see Miller 2002).

Alongside my exposure to dance, I have found the story of Tom Waddell, a gay athlete, dancer and campaigner for social justice invaluable in my ongoing attempts to abandon the 'Gender Game'. Juxtaposing my life with his has taught me that sexuality has very little to do with the actual act of having sex (see Messner 1996, 1999). As a straight male my relocation from sport to dance was met with homophobic prejudice; I was seen to be 'doing' homosexuality. By way of contrast, Waddell's movement from dance to sport was a conscious attempt to closet his homosexuality. Through sport he knew that publicly he would be seen to be 'doing' heterosexuality. This blurring of sexual preference and categorisation indicates to me that sexuality is a form of social control that polices the boundaries of acceptable performance within the 'Gender Game'. As the story of Waddell indicates, much of this behaviour management can be self-policed.

We will now turn to Fiona's fictional account of her role as an Inspector with the Physical Education Gender Police. Through dance's traditional association with feminine identity, many males have been seen to be forsaking this valuable area of the National Curriculum to maintain their heterosexual status. We meet up with Fiona as she embarks on yet another school visit in this most worrying outbreak of gender crimes being committed in dance.

Policing gender crimes in dance

I have now been an Inspector with the Physical Education Gender Police (PEGP) for three years. Following a series of expensive and well-publicised trials, in which a number of former pupils successfully sued their schools for damages resulting from insensitive gender-biased teaching whilst at school, the government set up the PEGP. The Force is based within the newly established Department of Inclusive Policies and Practices (affectionately known as DIPPY). The Force's remit is quite simple; it is to investigate allegations of gender-based malpractice, carry out periodic inspections of PE departments and report back to schools with the findings. Following a period of intensive training in which I was required to familiarise myself with the statutory statement of inclusion within the NCPE I have learnt to detect even the subtlest and most well-disguised signs of gender-biased practice and destructive heterosexist tendencies. I now regularly visit different schools for a period of one week at a time.

I am currently investigating a worrying outbreak of gender crimes in dance and have been sent to school X, as part of the investigation. I am told, by a reliable source, that here I will meet a man who by his own admission was once guilty of crimes against gender. Apparently he has now seen the error of his ways and works to promote equality of opportunity through a fully inclusive, de-gendered PE and dance programme. As a 'born again' PE teacher and disciple of equal opportunity, I am keen to meet him. Mind you, I've become a little cynical of such radical changes over the years. You see, many criminals cleverly disguise themselves as liberal thinkers by 'talking a good gender talk' when the inspector calls. The harsh realty is that once we've gone they revert to their usual practice, which unfortunately sees their actions speaking louder than words.

I arrive at the school on a wet and dreary Monday morning not really expecting this visit to be any different from the majority I undertake. I smile to myself as I weigh up the odds of seeing yet another dance lesson based on a sporting theme and another timetable saturated with traditional competitive games. As I approach the door a rather damp looking young boy, who doesn't seem to possess a raincoat, steps aside to let me pass as his friend holds the door open for me. I make a mental note of the respectful gesture and ask to be directed to the reception desk. The sign says not open until 8.30 a.m., so I sit in the reception and wait. As I sit I am struck by how pleasant the area is and my attention is drawn to a colourful and well-displayed 'Wall of Achievement'. The wall is full of photos of smiling faces with children playing violins, holding various sporting trophies and looking proud as they display bizarre gadgets invented in Design and Technology lessons. Amongst them I notice a slot dedicated to Benjamin James and Sue Thomas, both pupils who went on to perform with Rambert Dance Company. Also, there is a certificate of participation for a year 7 class who performed at a regional dance festival. On the adjacent wall there are photos of a production of Macbeth. It seems that the PE, Art, English and Music department combined forces to present a contemporary version of Macbeth. From the photos it looks like a lavish production with a huge cast of boys and girls of all ages. I am called over by a friendly looking receptionist who guesses who I am and makes every effort to welcome me. She is bursting to tell me that she has had three sons at the school, the youngest of which is presently in year 9, and that all of her sons have enjoyed their PE lessons. She wants to impress on me that she feels the PE department is excellent and I have to agree with her that as a mother of three boys she is probably well qualified to judge. She goes on to explain that her middle son was never home before 6 o'clock in the evening as he was always still at school involved in something. On Mondays and Thursdays it was rugby, dance rehearsals took place on Tuesday while on Wednesdays and Fridays it was either cross-country or athletics, depending on the time of year.

As we pass the photos on the wall again she stops to point out her youngest son who was in Macbeth and tells me with pride that the teacher suggested he join a local youth dance group as he showed a lot of potential. I make another mental note about the number of performances that seem to take place, the links with the local youth group and how her son was able to do such a range of activities. By this time I have reached the PE department and am greeted by Matthew Montgomery (M&M as the children call him, in a clever play on the name of the American white rapper). For some reason I had conjured up a very different picture of the man I was to meet. I imagined he would look different to all the male PE teachers I had seen over the years. But here standing before me was yet another man in a tracksuit with mud on his boots and a whistle around his neck, though, as I was to find out as the week progressed, neither he nor the members of his department could ever be described as average. I was reminded of a foolish comment that I had once made to a female colleague of mine when I commented that she didn't look like a feminist. It was at this point that I realised, even with all my training, that deep down I was quite expecting to be greeted by a man who appeared overtly gay. I checked my thoughts in an attempt to de-programme myself of such prejudicial ideas and hoped that he had not noticed my sense of surprise.

He showed me to a room where all the departmental policies and schemes were laid out ready for my arrival and explained that four year 8 classes were due to burst along the corridor at any moment. We agreed that the best introduction to the school would be for me to spend the day watching some teaching, to give me a feel for the school, and that I could bury my head in the paper work later. That day I watched two mixed-sex year 8 dance classes, a year 9 boys' dance class, and an A level group made up of fifteen candidates, five whom which were boys. It is my custom to jot down notes as I watch. I have developed my own simple system of putting a plus or minus sign by my comments to identify the quality of what I have seen, or a question mark to denote that I need to find out more information. As I look back on my day's notes a rare sight meets me: nothing but plus signs and question marks. The first lesson I observed was a mixed-sex year 8 class that got off to an unusual but interesting start. Written on the board was the name Rio Ferdinand (the Manchester United and England footballer) and a comment, 'it could have all been so different'. I was already intrigued, and so were the pupils who had already started to guess why it could have all been so different.

Following a series of wrong guesses M&M explained that he had read an article in a Sunday magazine explaining that the now-most expensive defender in the world of football could have been a dancer. According to his uncle, Rio was 'more into dancing than football' when he was younger. But because he grew so fast he was forced to give up dancing because of potential ligament damage. One bright spark in the class says 'he wouldn't be half as rich' and another under his breath makes a rather rude comment about his ball handling skills. I was impressed with the way M&M dealt with this. He simply said that this was an inappropriate comment and asked the pupil if he could think of any benefits that dancing might have for footballers. A brief conversation followed in which various pupils offered ideas such as flexibility, fast, fancy footwork and jumping high. M&M then publicly congratulated the children from the class who were involved in the recent production of Macbeth. He told them how much he enjoyed the performance, and it was obvious to see that they were delighted by his recognition of their efforts. The lesson then continued and the pupils remained attentive and active throughout. I was impressed by M&M's willingness to demonstrate and by how hard the pupils worked. The pace of the lesson was demanding yet there was a calmness and sensitivity in his delivery that was refreshing to see.

Towards the end of the lesson I noticed that the young boy on crutches, who had admirably been doing his best to offer directions and suggestions to his friends whilst hobbling about or resting precariously on one crutch, had sat down for a well-deserved rest. Wherever possible I like to take account of pupils' views when I write my report. In light of this I asked him to tell me about the dance, and what had happened in the lessons running up to this. He enquired if I meant this particular dance or the dance they had done before half term. Surprised by how articulate the pupil was, and pleased that there had actually been a before, meaning that this was not a school where six weeks of dance was the total sum of the pupils' experience, I said I would be interested to know both. He proceeded to tell me that the first dance they did was about traffic. That they had had to show lots of different speeds within their dance, depicting fast motorway driving, the slow stopping and starting of a traffic jam and the idea of moving up through the gears. He went on to say that he really liked the music, it was 'wicked, as it came from *The Matrix*. He also said that his favourite part was the crash scene where they had to show the idea of a pile up.

Having visions of a class full of excited 12-year-olds, all colliding into one another, leaving a scene of devastation requiring a fleet of ambulances, I asked how they did this without getting hurt. At this point he looked at me, hesitated, then explained as politely as he could, obviously assuming that I did not understand the way dance works, that when you dance you do not have to copy the idea exactly. He explained that person one made contact with person two, who made contact with person three which showed the type of crash where a series of cars go into the back of one another. Also, that for a really big crash the group would all contact one another then spin off in different directions, or even end up upside down or on top of one another. I remember thinking to myself how exciting it all sounded, and a far cry from my own PE lessons at 12 years of age. I asked him about the dance that they were currently working on and he explained that it was very different because it was based on a dance called *Covering Ground* that was performed by Phoenix Dance Company. He said that it had lots of different pieces of music, some very slow and some fast, and that it was more difficult because the mood kept changing and the steps were more complicated and you had to learn to learn to lift your partner safely.

The four lessons I watched that day, along with all the lessons that I observed that week, were a pleasure to watch. Throughout the week the pupils had, for the vast majority of the time, worked with great integrity, commitment and enthusiasm. Clearly being male in this school was not accepted as an excuse when it came to teaching or participating in dance. I was amused to see a note pinned to the wall of the PE office, which simply read 'Dance – being male is an explanation not an excuse. Football – being female is an explanation not an excuse!' I clearly saw evidence of this philosophy in practice throughout the week in a number of different ways. Most importantly, the unique contributions that dance makes to a pupil's Physical Education was recognised. Dance was considered of equal value to both boys and girls and of equal value to other activity areas. This went beyond lip service, as the per centage of time allocated to dance on the timetable was the same for boys and girls and the same as other activity areas. The department did not appear to make assumptions about what boys or girls will or will not like. As M&M said, for boys dancing is a bit like trying foreign food. They are a little suspicious of it to start with, but once they try it they are often pleasantly surprised by how much they like it. They then get braver and more adventurous about what they are prepared to try and then actually go out searching for it in preference to their normal diet.

Whilst acknowledging that the developing male ego of teenage boys is a fragile and easily bruised thing, and that many boys come to dance with a certain amount of 'baggage' gained through years of socialisation, this school demonstrated that it was possible to 'offload' this baggage quite quickly. Part of the offloading process in this school seemed to be a very accessible introduction to dance which built on boys' interests and cultural experiences, without alienating the girls. But, most importantly, they moved beyond this stereotypical physical challenge introduction quite quickly, recognising that one six-week block is not enough time to facilitate this shift.

Another factor in the 'offloading' process in this school seemed to be the abundance of positive role models. Four out of the six members of the department taught dance, two males and two females. Negative stereo-types were challenged by a barrage of positive images that it would be hard for even the most stubborn of boys to deny. Every available inch of wall space was covered with photos of male and female pupils and professionals in the full spectrum of activities. Visiting guest artists and video extracts within classes were carefully selected to reinforce positive images of male dancers. Older pupils were used to motivate younger pupils and parents. I attended a year 9 options evening during which both male and female candidates demonstrated their work and spoke to year 9 pupils about what they would be expected to do if they opted for GCSE Dance.

There was also an absence of those throwaway comments that seem so light-hearted, yet eat away at all the good work being done. I think back to some of the comments I have heard – 'If you lot don't shut up I'll make you go and dance with the girls', or 'Well, lads, it's not really my cup of tea, I like getting muddy . . . but if you like dancing it's fine with me as long as you don't expect me to do it with you'.

It is now the end of the week and for once I feel energised and cannot wait to tell my colleagues back at DIPPY what an inspirational week I've had. I stop at the garage on the way back and as I stand in the queue to pay I find myself reading the covers of various glossy magazines. Three headings in particular catch my attention, the first promising me 'a six-pack in six weeks'. This reminds me of the constant pressure we face to conform to an ideal 'pre-ordained goal'. The second says 'Beckham wears pink nail varnish'. This headline I find fascinating as I stop and wonder whether if David Beckham were not such a good footballer would he get away with wearing pink nail varnish. I wonder about how many other men would also like to wear nail varnish but do not dare to. I think back to my week in school and I now realise one of the great strengths of the department I had visited. So often boys that are exceptional get away with dancing without ridicule as their skill provides them with a shield to defend them against prejudice. Yet within the school I visited they had succeeded in creating a culture in which it was as acceptable to dance as it was to kick a football, regardless of your ability to do it well. The final headline reads 'swimming against the tide'. It is a provocative heading as it leaves you guessing who is swimming against what tide and in what context. I read it as being my story and M&M's story. We swim against the tide, working in little pockets of resistance, struggling against outdated practices. We dream of a time when we can just swim (dance) without all the extra effort, when we can work in a way that gender is not an issue, it is just simply about dancing.

Cool down – A work in progress

Following Rorty (1989) and Plummer (2001) we believe that the telling and re-telling of stories can perform important moral work. The moral of the stories we've shared here is that gender crimes, much like appropriate gender displays, need to be self-policed. Each and every time you teach your students you should be reflecting upon what the Inspector from the PEGP would say. Surely if any profession knows the benefit of 'perfect' practice it should be us. To put it another way, we should stop impressing our visitors with our best crockery or untypical lessons. In practice we need to break free from our gendered pasts to begin 'daring to be different'. The de-gendered vision we are proposing, although feeling strange at first, will become habitual with practice. As a result, with the passage of time, it will be viewed as being the rule rather than the exception. So with this in mind, let's stop seeing/teaching the curriculum and our pupils through gendered lenses. We realise we've probably asked more questions than provided answers about how to proceed and we are not apologetic for this. The de-gendered future we see for PE needs to be made, it won't just happen. Let's get to work. Come on PE(TE) we shouldn't have to tell you again – Get Changed for Dance!

Reflective questions

1   Has your own PE experience influenced your vision of what it means to be physically educated?
2   Are you able to identify the unique contribution that dance makes to the curriculum?
3   Do you consider dance to be an integral part of the PE curriculum and accept that it is part of the contemporary PE teacher's repertoire of skills?
4   Do male trainee PE teachers require a greater awareness of gender issues in PE/Dance in order to challenge their own attitudes and beliefs regarding dance education?

Notes

1   The socialisation of PE teachers begins long before the PE(TE) programme commences. By the time each new recruit arrives at university s/he has already experienced ten years of formal PE, what Lortie (1975) calls the 'apprenticeship of observation'. During this time a philosophy of what constitutes PE will be formed. Lawson (1983) calls this the 'subjective warrant' which according to Schempp and Graber (1992) will not be easily overturned during the training process.
2   Feel free to argue here if you have had a positive experience of dance at school; in fact shout it from the rooftops!
3   Although this chapter is concentrating on the lack of male exposure to dance, we fully recognise that this too is a pertinent issue for a number of females. In fact in our role as dance educators working primarily within PE(TE) we are often surprised by how many of our possible recruits, whether male or female, have not had the opportunity to experience dance at school.
4   At the 1999 annual conference of the National Dance Teachers' Association (NDTA) *'Access and Entitlement: The Dance Curriculum and Beyond'*, Bruce

Gill (2000: 17) asked the cogent question during his keynote address, 'how can we begin to create the future we want if all pupils do not have the chance to dance, the chance to consider careers in dance, the chance to reflect on the place of dance in their lives?'

5   Dance offers a rich potential resource for the new curriculum area 'citizenship' (QCA 2000). For example, 'dancing bodies and the stories they tell' (Albright 1997) have the ability to 'mirror our deepest concerns, our fondest hopes, our crassest dreams, our most starry-eyed idealism and ultimately our truest selves' (Carbonneau 1998: 5). Drawing upon Rorty's (1989) idea of the narrative turn, dance has the ability to sensitise its audience towards the pain felt by the marginalised other. We're sure you can add your own examples here.

References

Albright, A. (ed.) (1997) *Choreographing Difference: The Body and Identity in Contemporary Dance*, London: Wesleyan University Press.

Armour, K. M. (1999) 'The Case for a Body-Focus in Education and Physical Education', *Sport, Education and Society* 4,1: 5–15.

Atkinson, R. (1998) *The Life Story Interview*, London: Sage.

Bain, L. (1984) 'In My View: A Dancing Spirit', *Journal of Physical Education Recreation and Dance* September: 10.

Bain, L. (1990) 'Visions and Voices', *Quest* 42,1: 2–12.

Bain, L. (1997) 'Transformation in the Postmodern Era: A New Game Plan', in J. Fernandez-Balboa (ed.), *Critical Postmodernism in Human Movement, Physical Education and Sport*, Albany, NY: State University of NY Press.

Barone, T. (1995) 'Persuasive Writings, Vigilant Readings, and Reconstructed Characters: The Paradox of Trust in Educational Storysharing', in J. Amos Hatch and R. Wisniewski (eds), *Life History and Narrative*, London: Falmer Press.

Bem, S. L. (1998) *An Unconventional Family*, New Haven, CT: Yale University Press.

Boyden, M. (2002) 'New Theatre of Dreams for Dion', *The Times (The Games Section)* 21 October: 2–3.

Bramley, I. (2001) 'High Art? No Thank You', *Dance Theatre Journal* 16, 4: 44–7.

Brown, D. (1999) 'Complicity and Reproduction in Teaching Physical Education', *Sport, Education and Society* 4, 2: 143–59.

Brown, D. and Rich, E. (2002) 'Gender Positioning as Pedagogical Practice in Teaching Physical Education', in D. Penney (ed.), *Gender and Physical Education: Contemporary Issues and Future Directions*, London: Routledge.

Burt, J. (1987) 'Three Dreams: The Future of HPERD at the Cutting Edge', in J. Massengale (ed.), *Trends Toward the Future in Physical Education*, Champaign, Ill.: Human Kinetics.

Burt, R. (1995) *The Male Dancer: Bodies, Spectacle, Sexualities*, London: Routledge.

Butler, J. (1990) *Gender Trouble: Feminism and the Subversion of Identity*, New York: Routledge.

Carbonneau, S. (1998) 'Dance at the Close of the Century', *U.S. Society and Values USIA Electronic Journal* 3, 1 (5 pages).

Carlson, T. B. (1995) 'We Hate Gym: Student Alienation from Physical Education', *Journal of Teaching in Physical Education* 14, 4: 464–77.

Clarke, G. (2002) 'Difference Matters: Sexuality and Physical Education', in D. Penney (ed.), *Gender and Physical Education: Contemporary Issues and Future Directions*, London: Routledge.

Coakley, J. and Donnelley, P. (1999) *Inside Sports*, London: Routledge.

Connell, R. W. (1995) *Masculinities*, Cambridge, MA: Polity Press.

Denison, J. (1996) 'Sport Narratives', *Qualitative Inquiry* 2, 3: 351–62.

Dewar, A. (1990) 'Oppression and Privileges in Physical Education: Struggles in the Negotiation of Gender in a University Programme', in D. Kirk and R. Tinning (eds), *Physical Education, Curriculum and Culture: Critical Issues in the Contemporary Crisis*, Lewes: Falmer Press.

Dowling Naess, F. (2001) 'Sharing Stories about the Dialectics of Self and Structure in Teacher Socialisation: Revisiting a Norwegian Physical Educator's Life History', *European Physical Education Review*, 7, 1: 44–60.

Downey, P. (1996) 'Preparing Physical Education Majors to Teach Dance', *Impulse* 4: 90–101.

Etherington, K. (2000) *Narrative Approaches to Working with Adult male Survivors of Child Sexual Abuse: The Clients', the Counsellors' and the Researchers' Story*, London: Jessica Kingsley Publishers.

Evans, J., Penney, D. and Davies, B. (1996) 'Back to the Future: Education Policy and Physical Education', in N. Armstrong (ed.), *New Directions in Physical Education: Change and Innovation*, London: Cassell.

Fairclough, S., Stratton, G. and Baldwin, G. (2002) 'The Contribution of Secondary School Physical Education to Lifetime Physical Activity', *European Physical Education Review* 8, 1: 69–84.

Flintoff, A. (1990) 'Physical Education, Equal Opportunities and the National Curriculum: Crisis or Challenge?' *Physical Education Review* 13, 2: 85–100.

Flintoff, A. (1991) 'Dance, Masculinity and Teacher Education', *British Journal of Physical Education* 22, 4: 31–5.

Gard, M. (2001) 'Dancing Around the Problem of Boys and Dance', *Discourse Studies in the Cultural Politics of Education* 22, 2: 213–25.

Gill, B. A. G. (2000) 'Special Measures', *Dance Matter* 27: 15–17.

Gough, M. (1999) *Knowing Dance: A Guide for Creative Teaching*, London: Dance Books.

Gould, L. (1978) *X: A Fabulous Child's Story*, New York: Daughters Publishing Company.

Grace, A. P. and Benson, F. J. (2000) 'Using Autobiographical Queer Life Narratives of Teachers to Connect Personal, Political and Pedagogical Spaces', *International Journal of Inclusive Studies* 4, 2: 89–109.

Green, K. (2002) 'Physical Education Teachers in their Figurations: A Sociological Analysis of Everyday Philosophies', *Sport, Education and Society* 7, 1: 65–83.

Hamilton, C. (2001) 'A Men's Movement Pioneer Calls for the End to the Gender Game: An Interview with Sam Keen', *What is Enlightenment?* issue 16, online, available HTTP: <http://www.wie.org/j16/keen1.asp> accessed 3 July 2002.

Hickey, C. and Fitzclarence, L. (1999) 'Educating Boys in Sport and Physical Education: Using Narrative Methods to Develop Pedagogies of Responsibility', *Sport, Education and Society* 4, 1: 51–62.

Higgins, C. (2000) 'What to Say About ... Billy Elliot', *Guardian (Editor Supplement)* 13 October: 17.
Jackson, D. (1999) 'A Cock Sure Body', in A. C. Sparkes and M. Silvennoinen (eds), *Talking Bodies: Men's Narratives of the Body and Sport*, Jyvaskyla: SoPhi.
Keen, S. (1992) *Fire in the Belly: On Being a Man*, London: Piatkus.
Keyworth, S (2001) 'Critical Autobiography: Straightening out Dance Education', *Research in Dance Education* 2, 2: 117–37.
Kimmel, M. S. and Messner, M. A. (eds) (1995) *Men's Lives*, London: Routledge.
Kirk, D. (2002a) 'The Social Construction of the Body in Physical Education and Sport', in A. Laker (ed.), *The Sociology of Sport and Physical Education: An Introductory Reader*, London: Routledge.
Kirk, D. (2002b) 'Physical Education: A Gendered History', in D. Penney (ed.), *Gender and Physical Education: Contemporary Issues and Future Directions*, London: Routledge.
Lawson, H. A. (1983) 'Toward a Model of Teacher Socialisation in Physical Education: The Subjective Warrant, Recruitment and Teacher Education', *Journal of Teaching in Physical Education* 2, 3: 3–16.
Lloyd, M. L and West, B. H. (1988) 'Where are the Boys in Dance?' *Journal of Physical Education Recreation and Dance* 59, 5: 47–51.
Lortie, D. C. (1975) *Schoolteacher: A Sociological Study*, Chicago: University of Chicago Press.
Lucal, B. (1999) 'What it Means to be Gendered Me: Life on the Boundaries of a Dichotomous Gender System', *Gender and Society* 13, 6: 781–97.
McFee, G. and Smith, F. (1994) 'Let's Hear it for the Boys: Dance, Gender and Education', in A. Tomlinson (ed.), *Gender, Sport and Leisure: Continuities and Challenges* Volume 3, University of Brighton: Meyer and Meyer.
Mason, F. and Daniels, D. (1994) 'A Conversation with Doug Elkins', *Ballet Review* 22, 3: 50–63.
Messner, M. A. (1996) 'Studying up on Sex', *Sociology of Sport Journal* 13: 221–37.
Messner, M. A. (1999) 'Becoming 100 Percent Straight', in J. Coakley and P. Donnelley (eds), *Inside Sports*, London: Routledge.
Miller, A. (2002) *Tilting at Windmills: How I Tried to Stop Worrying and Love Sport*, London: Viking.
Murdoch, E. (1997) 'The Background to, and Developments From, the National Curriculum for PE', in S. Capel (ed.), *Learning to Teach Physical Education in the Secondary School: A Companion to School Experience*, London: Routledge.
Newson, L. (1996a) 'Talkback', *Dance Europe* February/March.
Newson, L. (1996b) 'Enter Achilles', text from original handbill, online, available HTTP: <http://www.dv8.co.uk/ENT_ACH/p.release.html> accessed 11 March 2002.
OFSTED (Office for Standards in Education) (1998) *Secondary Education 1993–1997: A Review of Secondary Schools in England*, London: HMSO.
Penney, D. (2002) 'Gendered Policies', in D. Penney (ed.), *Gender and Physical Education: Contemporary Issues and Future Directions*, London: Routledge.
Penney, D and Chandler, T. (2000) 'Physical Education: What Future(s)?' *Sport, Education and Society* 5, 1: 71–87.
Penney, D and Evans, J. (1997) 'Naming the Game: Discourse and Domination in Physical Education and Sport in England and Wales', *European Physical Education Review* 3, 1: 21–32.

Plummer, K. (1995) *Telling Sexual Stories: Power, Change and Social Worlds*, London: Routledge.

Plummer, K. (2001) *Documents of Life 2: An Invitation to a Critical Humanism*, London: Sage.

Polkinghorne, D. E. (1988) *Narrative Knowing and the Human Sciences*, Albany: State University of New York Press.

QCA (Qualifications and Curriculum Authority) (2000) *Citizenship at Key Stages 3 and 4: Initial Guidance for Schools*, London: QCA.

Quirke, A. (2000) 'Get your Heart Punched by a boy called Billy', *Independent on Sunday (Culture Supplement)* 1 October: 3.

Richardson, L. (1990) *Writing Strategies: Reaching Diverse Audiences*, London: Sage.

Rorty, R. (1989) *Contingency, Irony and Solidarity*, Cambridge: Cambridge University Press.

Sacks, A. (1995) 'Driving Himself up the Wall', *The Sunday Review*.

Sanderson, P. (1996) 'Dance within the National Curriculum for Physical Education of England and Wales', *European Physical Education Review* 2, 1: 54–63.

Sanderson, P. (2001) 'Age and Gender Issues in Adolescent Attitudes to Dance', *European Physical Education Review* 7, 2: 117–30.

Schempp, P. G. and Graber, K. C. (1992) 'Teacher Socialisation from a Dialectical Perspective: Pre-training Through Induction', *Journal of Teaching in Physical Education* 11: 329–48.

Sluder, S. S. (1998) 'Her Story', in S. Shapiro (ed.), *Dance, Power and Difference: Critical and Feminist Perspectives in Dance Education*, Champaign, Ill.: Human Kinetics.

Smith-Autard, J. M. (1994) *The Art of Dance in Education*, London: A & C Black.

Sparkes, A. C. (1999a) 'Beyond Romantic Views of the Self: Critical Autobiography as a Challenge to Teacher Development', Paper presented at the Physical Education Association (UK) Centenary Conference, University of Bath 8–11 April.

Sparkes, A. C. (1999b) 'Exploring Body Narratives', *Sport, Education and Society* 4, 1: 17–30.

Sparkes, A. C. (2002) 'Fictional Representations: On Difference, Choice, and Risk', *Sociology of Sport Journal* 19, 1: 1–24.

Stidder, G. (2002) 'The Recruitment of Secondary School Physical Education Teachers in England: A Gendered Perspective?' *European Physical Education Review* 8, 3: 253–73.

Stidder, G. and Hayes, S. (2002) 'A Survey of Physical Education Trainees' Experiences on School Placements in the South-East of England (1997–2001)', *The British Journal of Teaching Physical Education* 33, 2: 43–8.

Theroux, P. (1986) *Being a Man: In Sunshine with Seamonsters: Travels and Discoveries*, Boston: Houghton Mifflin.

Thomas, H. (ed.) (1993) *Dance, Gender and Culture*, London: Macmillan.

Tsangaridou, N. and Siedentop, D. (1995) 'Reflective Teaching: A Literature Review', *Quest* 47: 212–37.

Waddell, T. and Schapp, D. (1996) *The Life and Death of Dr Tom Waddell*, New York: Alfred A. Knopf.

Waddington, I., Malcolm, D. and Cobb, J. (1998) 'Gender Stereotyping and Physical Education', *European Physical Education Review* 4, 1: 34–46.

Walker, H. (1991) 'Herschel Walker: All-American Football Player' (interview 28 June, New York) The Hall of Sports, online, available HTTP: <http://www. achievement.org/autodoc/page/wa10int-1> accessed 19 July 2002.

Wright, J. (1995) 'A Feminist-Post-Structuralist Methodology for the Study of Gender Construction in Physical Education: Description of a Case Study', *Journal of Teaching in Physical Education* 15, 1: 1–24.

Wright, J. (1999) 'Changing Gendered Practices in Physical Education: Working with Teachers', *European Physical Education Review* 5, 3: 181–97.

Young, J. (1997) 'DV8 Dares to Challenge the Instinct to Conform', *Bucks Free Press* 4 April.

Sport does have a meaningful and powerful role to play in the social transformation of (South African) society if care is taken to provide the necessary conditions for success.

Archbishop Desmond M Tutu in Keim, M. (2003)
'Nation Building at Play: Sport as a Tool for Social Integration in Post-Apartheid South Africa', Aachen, Meyer and Meyer: 10

8 Sport and social inclusion across religious and ethnic divisions

A case of football in Israel

Gary Stidder and John Sugden

Introduction

In this chapter we examine the value of using sport as a vehicle through which to promote community relations and social inclusion in politically and socially fractured societies. We begin with a general discussion about the pacifist potential of sport, followed by a brief consideration of the context of sport and community relations in Northern Ireland. The main body of the chapter concerns an in-depth look at one particular sport-based community relations project run by the World Sport Peace Project (WSPP) in Israel's historic Galilee region. This is a three-year programme that, at the time of writing, is entering its third and final phase. Particular attention is paid to the experiences and reflections of trainee Physical Education teachers who worked on the project during 2002 and the implications this had for their teaching of children with distinct cultural differences.

Sport – peacemaker or war monger?

What then, if anything, is the value of sport to processes of peace and reconciliation? Throughout the world, in places like Northern Ireland, South Africa, the Balkans and in the Middle East there are one-off initiatives and more lengthy programmes that aim to use sport as a tool for engineering peaceful co-existence in otherwise deeply divided societies. More often than not, however, ideology, sentiment, and hope rather than hard, empirical evidence drive the rationale that lies behind such interventions (Sugden and Bairner 2000).

The mythology of the social and political healing powers of sport can be traced back to the fabled ancient Olympic truce, when the warring city states of ancient Greece laid down their weapons for the duration of the Olympic festival, as an exemplar of the contribution that sport can make to peace (McIntosh 1993). Likewise, the reputed soccer match played between British and German soldiers in no man's land on Christmas Day 1914 during an impromptu truce in World War I, is used to exemplify the capacity of sport to divert potentially hostile communities. In this scenario sport is viewed as a temporary escape from war.

Others, mainly sports administrators and allied politicians – those who have career-vested interests in sport development – are even more optimistic about sport's ongoing and incremental capacity to promote peace and understanding. Such sports evangelists preach that sport offers more than a temporary haven for the suspension of conflict. For this group sport, locally and globally, can solve those problems that politicians and militarists palpably cannot. Most of these people will have been long-time sports participants and enthusiasts. If sport was good for them, their thinking goes, then it must be good for others and the intrinsic value of sport as a social good is rarely questioned. They believe in the fraternal and character-building qualities of sports and in its capacity to bring diverse people and peoples together in global festivals, such as the modern Olympics or the football World Cup Finals. The literature of the International Olympic Committee and other national and world sports governing bodies reflects this and is littered with the rhetoric of sports evangelism (Hill 1992). In their hands sport is offered as a vehicle through which to resolve community conflict and to end war permanently.

There is some support in the academic community for an amalgamation of these positions. According to Elias and Dunning (1986) and their followers, the experience of sport has a progressively moderating effect on social behaviour beyond the playing field itself and as such makes a positive contribution to peace and harmony. It is a long game. Nevertheless, sport, by offering opportunities for the socially approved arousal of moderate excitement, leads people to exercise stricter control over their public behaviour in society in general. In short, sport is a civilising influence, both within and between nations.

George Orwell's statement that sport is 'war minus the shooting' (Orwell 1970: 63) is often quoted by those who would use sport as a servant of peace. They invoke Orwell to help demonstrate that sport can serve as a cathartic alternative to war. In this vision, the playing of competitive sports provides distinctive communities (nations, regions, towns and so forth) with opportunities to express distinctiveness and rivalry without threatening the wider social order. In other words, sport instead of war (Goodhart and Chataway 1986).

It is this optimistic reading of sport that dominates the thinking of sports administrators and politicians. In an interview in 1998, Joao Havelange, then the outgoing President of FIFA, the governing body of international football, spoke eloquently of his last great ambition:

One day during the World Cup (USA '94) I had a telephone call from Al Gore (vice president of the United States). At that time Gore was involved in negotiating for a peaceful settlement in the Middle East. Mr Gore said he really had no experience of football before, but he was amazed that the World Cup could be so perfectly organised and that so many people could become so passionately involved. He was greatly inspired by this and asked would it not be possible to have a match between Palestine and Israel, organised by FIFA? The project is now indeed to have such a match, Palestine versus Israel, ideally in New York – New York being the seat of the United Nations – just to show the politicians football can do things that they cannot!

(Sugden and Tomlinson 1998: 240)

This vision would not have been shared by Orwell himself, who harboured bitter memories of his experiences of sports at public school. He observed that sport was a training ground for elitist bullies who would go on to use their experiences within sport to promote violence and conflict in later life. He coined the phrase 'war minus the shooting' in an essay about the Moscow Dynamo soccer team's post-war tour of Britain in 1945. In this essay Orwell argued that far from helping to improve international relations between the West and the Soviet Union, by providing opportunities for public and collective displays of aggressive nationalism, tours such as this made the Cold War even icier and the threat of global nuclear war greater.

Few sports optimists/evangelists quote the first half of Orwell's statement when he states, '[sport] is bound up with hatred, jealousy, boastfulness, disregard of all rules and sadistic pleasure' (Orwell 1970: 63). Orwell continues:

If you wanted to add to the vast fund of ill-will existing in the world at this moment, you could hardly do it better than by a series of football matches between Jews and Arabs, Germans and Czechs, Indians and British, Russians and Poles and Italians and Jugoslavs, each match to be watched by a mixed audience of 100,000 spectators.

(Orwell 1970: 64)

Who is right, Orwell or Havelange? Can sport make a significantly positive contribution to peace processes in deeply politically divided regions like the Middle East or does it make matters worse? And how do such interpretations of the core value of sport drive or inhibit the potential of school-based sport in Physical Education?

The Northern Ireland experience

There is evidence that under clearly thought-out and well-managed circumstances sport can help to improve cross-community relations. From 1982 until 1996, when he moved to the University of Brighton, one of the authors of this chapter lived and worked in Northern Ireland. He was involved in a range of sport-based activities, the broad intentions of which were to make a contribution to conflict resolution and peacemaking in what was then an undeclared war-torn Province. Much of these efforts were devoted towards helping to change policy in the overlapping areas of sport development and community relations. The main tools for this were systematic research and sustained critical argument.

At another level there was engagement with a variety of grass-roots and hands-on sport and community relations projects. Chief among these was Belfast United, a programme that provided opportunities for young Protestants and Catholics to play and learn together in a politically neutral environment. The peak experience of Belfast United came when integrated football and basketball teams spent time in the United States, coaching and being coached and playing in competitions with and against the American hosts. While this was going on pairs of Protestant and Catholic youngsters lived together with US families. At the end of these projects (Sugden 1991, McLaughlan 1995) it was clear that under such carefully managed conditions the participants did in fact experience positively changed perceptions about the nature of 'the other' and equally positively altered views about the potential for mutual co-existence. At the same time, follow-up research revealed that, because of the institutionalised depth of sectarianism and its geographical consequences, it was virtually impossible for those youngsters who went through the Belfast United experience to build on cross-community friendships once they returned home from the US. On balance, however, it is believed that, albeit in a small way, projects such as this could make a direct contribution to improving community relations.

Indirectly the impact of such initiatives is much more difficult to gauge. However, because they did not occur in isolation from policy debates – some of the same people lobbying for political change and policy development in terms of sport and community relations were the same ones engaged in this grass-roots work – they can be viewed as part of a wide-ranging series of interventions that have led to significant changes in the way sport is considered and provided for in Northern Ireland (Bairner 2002). Today Northern Ireland is grappling with a political peace process and sport is viewed there as one of a number of accompanying and important social and cultural support mechanisms. For instance, since 1998 the Sports Council for Northern Ireland has had a declared policy for sport and community relations, many of the region's sport governing bodies have community relations specialists working for them and almost all of the Province's twenty-six district councils have sport and community relations workers. Although the context is vastly different, a similar story could be told with regard to how, in South Africa, sport, which was once used as a blunt instrument to help dismantle the apartheid regime, is now likewise being used as a vehicle to foster peace and reconciliation (Keim 2003). Based on the experiences of Northern Ireland and South Africa, is it possible that similar roads can be travelled in the Middle East and what, if any, is Physical Education's template for fostering comparable initiatives?

The World Sport Peace Project in Israel

It was with this question in mind that the authors, as representatives of the University of Brighton, agreed to take part in a three-year pilot scheme that set out to use football as a means of promoting improved community relations in the Galilee region of Northern Israel. It is naive to think that, like flat-pack furniture, projects designed to achieve reconciliation in one country can simply be transported and reassembled to work in regions with vastly different social and political histories. Before embarking on such endeavours it is essential to learn as much as possible about the nature of the political terrain into which you are entering and adapt your ideas accordingly. Because we came to this particular project when much of the logistical development work had been done we had to work hard to develop a level of understanding of the detailed contours of social and political division that feed into the Middle East crisis. There have been volumes written about this subject (Elon 2000, Said 2000) and while there is no room here to provide a critical summary, in the context of project design and process it is nevertheless worth noting some key observations that can be drawn from such a review.

1   The Middle East conflict is thousands of years old. Its current manifestation has certain unique features, but it can only be fully comprehended with an appreciation of its history ancient and modern.
2   Given the scale and depth of the conflict it is unrealistic to claim that sport alone can achieve what politicians have spectacularly failed to do. But it can have a small and nonetheless important part to play.
3   Israel is an intensely politically sensitive place and everything is subject to political interpretation. It is wrong to assume that sport and sports people are automatically neutral in this regard.
4   Sport has its own political history and political legacy in Israel and, like all other economic, social and cultural resources, it, too, is contested terrain.
5   The participants in such a contest are not simply monolithic blocks of Arabs and Jews. Each category has multiple sub-groups that are often antagonistic within a supposed shared religious and/or ethnic identity. Understanding the subtleties of this and how it feeds into the political process is vital to the success of any peace work.

With this contextual information in hand, the primary task of WSPP in the region was to provide an opportunity, through football and social education, for children from Arab and Jewish communities to meet and participate together in teams and groups. Football was the obvious choice as the medium through which to pursue a community relations agenda because it is a popular team game with young people throughout the country, irrespective of ethnicity, national identity or religious affiliation (Johnson 2001). It was hoped that by setting up coaching and playing camps and having children from different communities playing on the same teams, trust and support, personal development, friendship and an appreciation of the perspective of 'the other' could be facilitated in order begin to establish communities that are more inclusive.

There was an element of serendipity in how this project evolved and our involvement in it. It was the idea of a small group of like-minded individuals based in Sussex in the south of England who, like many others, had become sick and tired of the images of violence and death in Israel and Palestine broadcast into their living rooms on a daily basis. Unlike most others they decided to try and do something about it and set up WSPP. The broad aims of this small organisation were dedicated to finding ways of using sport to help bring peace to troubled societies, with a specific remit to develop projects in the Middle East. It was to be financed through sponsorship raised by generous people running the London Marathon.

Initially there was nobody on WSPP's co-ordinating committee who had undertaken this kind of work before in a sporting setting. We (the authors) were brought on board in late 2000 when one of WSPP's founder members learned of the Northern Ireland connection. This was timely as, for personal reasons, another founder member withdrew from the project. Amongst other things he had responsibility for recruiting volunteer soccer coaches. The University of Brighton has dedicated undergraduate programmes in Physical Education, Sport Science, and Sport Studies and because of this we were able to fill the coaching void by recruiting some of our own students who were also well qualified soccer coaches.

Ibillin 2001

The project was scheduled to run over three years. One member of the project development team had been working in the region for many years and had particularly strong links with the town of Ibillin which was in the centre of the province of Galilee and about forty miles from Israel's northern frontier with Lebanon. It was agreed that, because of existing connections, the first phase of the project should be based in this town. Like the rest of Israel, Galilee's social geography is sectarian. The bigger cities and towns have clearly and sharply delineated Jewish and Arab quarters while smaller towns, villages and settlements tend to be almost exclusively either Arab or Jewish. Ibillin is essentially an Arab town and, in order for the basic aims of the project to be met, it was necessary to establish relations with a nearby Jewish community. This proved to be extremely difficult as, at the time, the country was enduring one of its more destructive periods of cross-community hostility. At a political level peace negotiations had broken down completely. The then Israeli Prime Minister, Ariel Sharon, was on the war path; Yasser Arafat, the veteran leader of the Palestine Liberation Organization (PLO), was sounding equally uncompromising from his bunkered headquarters in Ramala. The Palestinian intifada, or uprising, was intensifying, and was to resort to suicide bombings of Jewish civilian targets and Israeli Defence Forces (IDF). The re-occupation of large tracts of the Palestinian Authority by the IDF with ensuing violence and death was a regular occurrence and the construction of Jewish settlements on Arab land in the West Bank and Gaza continued apace. The worst, or perhaps best, of times to launch yet another peace initiative.

It was, therefore, no small achievement that in the nearby town of Misgav we managed to secure a partner Jewish community that agreed pro-rata to provide children to participate in the Ibillin-based initiative. The project development team was under no illusion, however, that this was a very tenuous partnership that could be caused to collapse by events beyond our control in the broader political landscape. With this in mind, back in the UK the authors set about selecting student coaches and providing them with a crash-course in the politics of the Middle East, while, at the same time, preparing them to do both the coaching and the team-building exercises that were to be the practical centre pieces of the first project in Galilee.

At one level the first project in the summer of 2001 was a spectacular failure; at another, in terms of learning, it was a huge success. It was a failure because, at the eleventh hour, the Jewish partners pulled out, citing fears about the security of their children. A car bomb had exploded in the region, killing passengers on a bus, and the parents of the children from Misgav, not unreasonably, had decided that it was too risky to transport their loved ones into the heart of an Arab community. Even at the earliest stages of our planning we had realised that, given the volatile nature of the region and the contingent nature of the security situation there, the project may have to be cancelled at the last minute. Thus, even before we got going, our primary aim of bringing young Jewish and Arab children together was defeated. Nevertheless, it was too late to cancel flights and other logistical deployments so we decided to go anyway.

It was successful to the extent that, from a practical point of view, we proved to ourselves that we could mount a project such as this: raise the money; recruit the coaches; transport them and their equipment to the site of the project; and coach children. It was also successful in an unforeseen way in that hitherto we had not realised the extent of the divisions within the Arab town between Muslim Arabs and Christian Arabs. Approximately 20 per cent of Israeli citizens are Arabs and of them less than 10 per cent are Christians, most of whom live in the north of the country close to the Lebanese boarder. Ibillin, the site of the 2002 project, is roughly fifty-fifty Muslim Arab and Christian Arab and the town betrays the same sectarian geography that can be found in parts of Belfast. Most of Ibillin's children live in neighbourhoods differentiated by religion and attend separate schools. There is little or no opportunity for the kind of fun-filled socially inclusive activity provided by our 2001 project. In this regard we believe our decision to carry on regardless of the Jewish withdrawal was a good one. Learning about the depth of division and potential antagonism between the Arabs of Ibillin would also serve us well for future project development. We also learned that we would have to do a lot more work with local partners if a further project in 2002 was not to suffer the same fate. In particular, helped by our own evaluations and the observations of an official from Olympic Aid (a branch of the International Olympic Committee), who accompanied the 2001 project team, we realised we needed more Jewish involvement in the planning stages and a wider range of feeder communities involved.

Galilee 2002

For the 2001 project the vast majority of the planning and co-ordination had taken place from London. Our evaluations showed that the length of lines of communication had been one factor that contributed to the loss of the Jewish partners. For the 2002 project development we decided that we needed a neutral broker to work on the ground on our behalf in Israel to help us identify partner communities and work with them with regard to local planning. To this end, three of the WSPP's coordinating committee visited Israel in early spring 2002 and met with a variety of agencies that were involved in peace-related work and had bases in the Galilee region. Our most productive contacts were with representatives of the British Council, who supported our objectives and proved eager to help. Working with them we managed to persuade two Jewish communities to join with Ibillin and provide children for the 2002 event. The identification of a second Jewish partner was important: should one pull out there would still be a chance that we could work with Jewish children from the remaining town. In the event, all three communities stayed on board, which was extremely reassuring since the political situation had dramatically deteriorated from that which was considered to be dire a year earlier.

The local co-ordinating work of the British Council worked on several levels. It helped to arrange a series of regular planning meetings so that the representatives of the three partner communities were much more likely to fulfil their commitment to seeing the project through. It also operated as a vital medium through which the planning decisions of the WSPP coordinating committee could be disseminated, considered and adapted to local conditions. Finally, and most importantly, it facilitated the establishment of a network of Arab and Jewish sport and community development workers who otherwise would never have worked together. This is of vital significance for the long-term aims of the WSSP initiative.

After months of exhaustive planning and preparation, eight trainee PE teachers from the University of Brighton embarked on the peace mission in August 2002. The students were escorted by their university lecturers/coaches and a former university chaplain. In 2001 all of the coaching and competitions had taken place in Ibillin. For 2002, after consulting our local partners, it was decided to rotate the football/peace camp around the three participating communities of Ibillin, Misgav and Tivon. First the children were to be split into two age categories so that the numbers for the coaching sessions would be manageable within the facilities available. The children were then to be organised in groups mixed according to religious/ethnic affiliation. Each group would be assigned two English coaches and two coaches (one Arab and one Jewish) drawn from the participating communities. This helped to overcome the language difficulties associated with English coaches instructing children whom, for the most part, knew little English and only spoke either Hebrew or Arabic. More importantly, by allowing these local coaches to get to know each other and work co-operatively, it provided another layer of cross-community contact.

On the first morning of the first day of the project, the teams of English and local coaches were introduced to one another and spent some time discussing the day-by-day project plans. The first three days were to be spent taking the children through a basic soccer skills coaching programme. On the fourth day the children would be re-mixed into teams according to ability as well as religious affiliation/ethnicity. This was to ensure that teams would be evenly matched on the day of the tournament. The rest of the fourth day was spent engaging the groups with a series of team-building games and activities. We believed that the community relations dimension of the programme would be best served by emphasising the sport team-building process. This was to be supplemented by a series of recreational activities organised by local volunteers that would take place alongside the football programme as the different age groups were rotated. The final day consisted of a six-a-side tournament.

What follows is an account of the project as it unfolded. It is based upon the reflections of one of the leaders, supported by extracts taken from both a video diary kept throughout the time in Israel by the student coaches, as well as informal interviews and discussions that took place during debriefing sessions at the end of each day.

Leader and trainee teacher perspectives on Galilee 2002

The UK team personnel arrived in the capital city of Tel Aviv late in the afternoon and were taken to a guesthouse in Ibillin in the northern part of Israel about two hours away. Later that day we met with all the partners from the Jewish and Arabic communities with whom we would be working over the next week and spent the evening, over tables groaning with local food, talking about politics, sport, peace and conflict resolution. The project proved to be a very sharp learning curve for the trainee teachers, all of whom had a pre-trip briefing but little appreciation of politics in general, let alone the complexities underlying the conflict in the Middle East. The preparation and training of the UK team prior to the project had helped in their understanding of the political and cultural divisions and the importance of their contribution to the overall aims.

The coaching began that weekend and the trainee teachers worked with children from the two Jewish communities of Misgav and Tivon and the Palestinian community of Moslems and Christians from Ibillin. All the children were put into mixed groups of Jewish children, Arab-Muslim and Arab-Christians. Several of the trainees reflected on their initial observations as the children first arrived:

> At the start of the week the kids were really apprehensive, you could see the division. You had Muslim and Jewish kids at separate ends of the training grounds. But as time went on they would go straight into their teams with no hassle.
>
> (Male soccer coach)

> You could feel the tension between the different communities. Once we got into the football that disappeared.
>
> (Male soccer coach)

> It was obvious that they were sitting together in their villages at the start and were very quiet. It was hard for us in terms of coaching but must have been just as hard for them but once we got over the first hurdle things really worked out well – soon as you got a football out and got them working in pairs they were fine.
>
> (Male soccer coach)

The second day was spent in one of the Jewish communities and the coaches worked with the children in the afternoon. This involved them participating in many individual, co-operative and competitive tasks through the use of modified and adapted small-sided conditioned games.

The third day was spent working with the youngsters in the other Jewish town. By now the children had got to know each other and had become accustomed to playing in their respective groups. Much of this could be attributed to the coaching strategies used during the project. An example of this was highlighted by one of the trainees:

> It was important for them to share their ideas amongst each other and to focus a lot on their input as well. We made sure that they worked as a team and gave them some responsibility like 'You're going to teach the group your free kick'.
>
> (Male soccer coach)

Whilst they learnt new skills and developed competencies through progressively more difficult tasks they had also begun to respect the abilities of each other and the co-operative nature in which they worked became more and more visible. We recognised that such evidence of co-operation may be temporary but, given the surrounding socio-political climate, it was nonetheless significant.

The fourth day was spent in the Arab community that had hosted us during our stay. The trainees organised a number of trust games, problem-solving and team-building activities for the children in preparation for the final tournament the next day. Children engaged in pair and group work that aimed to develop positive personal and social skills.

The tournament itself, on the final day, was a huge success, with children mixed in teams and competing for trophies and prizes. A Jewish child passes the ball to an Arab team-mate to score a goal before sharing happy high-fives in celebration. It was an unlikely image in a country devastated by religious conflicts, political turmoil and suicide bombings but it happened and it happened many times. Throughout the day the children competed against each other for a place in a play-off game which culminated in a dramatic penalty shoot-out in the final game. As each child received commemorative awards, T-shirts and other gifts from the British Deputy Ambassador in front of a large crowd of parents and community representatives, there were handshakes, hugs and embraces between team members and opposition. One of the coaching team observed:

> They were just like children anywhere – they just wanted to play and didn't care who with. By the end of the week during the tournament they were happily chatting and playing together.
>
> (Male soccer coach)

In many ways the Galilee project encompassed many of the UK government's aims for citizenship and social inclusion in PE and sport through which children develop mutual respect and understanding for each other and learn to become informed and responsible citizens (DfEE/QCA 1999a). As one member of the coaching team remarked:

> Physical education and sport have a major part to play in developing citizenship amongst young people and the challenges we were presented

with in Israel made us all think carefully about our teaching strategies in this respect.

(Male soccer coach)

In addition, the pedagogical skills employed in such situations enabled
the trainees to reflect upon their coaching and on the importance of careful
planning and organisation. For example, some of the trainees remarked:

You're thinking all the time – I must make sure he demonstrates, I ask
a question to one kid and must try to get an answer from another. We
also had to make sure that they really did mix in their teams so you were
always thinking about pair work and competitive games so that you
had a roughly even mix of Jewish and Arabic kids working together.

(Male soccer coach)

You were always conscious of selecting an even split so that they'd
have some idea of the qualities of the Jews and Arabs and felt equally
respected. After every demo we'd get the rest of group to clap or
sometimes used group demos to the rest of the group. It's about taking
the initiative and making things happen.

(Male soccer coach)

For some of the trainees, working with these children, across three
different languages of instruction, presented a number of challenges to
their teaching and highlighted a number of issues that they had neither
experienced during their teacher training nor were likely to experience
during their teaching careers:

They were all so keen to learn and really receptive to advice, although
at times this was a bit frustrating as everything I said had to be trans-
lated from English into Hebrew and Arabic.

(Male soccer coach)

Because of the language difficulties I had to use many more demon-
strations in my teaching and economise with instructions. It made me
more aware of different teaching styles and approaches to learning.
This is something that everyone should do if they are lucky enough
to get the opportunity.

(Female soccer coach)

For others, the experience of working with Jewish and Arabic children
had certain similarities to teaching pupils in schools in the UK and had
particular relevance to PE. As one trainee pointed out:

I think it's very similar, in theory, to classroom management. I go on
a [teaching] placement where there may be a disruptive influence or
maybe girls and boys don't mix together. So it's basically getting

people from different social groups and thinking about putting them elsewhere whilst ensuring that they enjoy themselves.

(Male soccer coach)

In this context, the unique contribution of PE through sport enabled the coaching team to provide opportunities and experiences for young Israeli children to become sensitive to their different cultural beliefs and the historical and political context in which it had evolved. Whilst we are yet to accumulate sufficient empirical evidence to support such a claim, our own observational evidence showed that many of the young people gained both personally and educationally from such experiences.

Whilst the project was successful in enabling children from different religious and cultural backgrounds to participate together through physical activity, mixed-sex groups were not an option. In this context, boys and girls worked separately, not because of significant differences in technique or skill, but because of strong cultural beliefs. It has been argued that girls might not respond to competitive sport in the same way as their male counterparts, or in the presence of them (Clarke and Nutt 1999), but our experience suggested that the boys and girls with whom we worked were equally attuned to competitive situations.

Despite the gender divisions that continued throughout the week both the boys' and girls' groups worked, played and celebrated together through fun, friendship and football, a game that has traditionally been associated with the male gender. If anything, the girls' participation in football-related activities and the way in which the project was staffed by both male and female coaches had the potential to challenge any stereotypical assumptions about the girls' ability to perform. Indeed, as the week progressed it soon became evident that the girls wished to compete against rather than with the boys during the final tournament. As one of the female trainees observed, this was the choice of the girls themselves:

> The girls I worked with were brilliant and kept going throughout the session even though it was scorching hot for some of the time. On the final day the girls wanted to play against the boys so we let them and they really did well. I've definitely got a different attitude about girls now when it comes to football.
>
> (Female soccer coach)

Similarly, one of the trainees remarked on the attitudes of many of the girls during the week:

> From what I saw I was very impressed with the girls' abilities and commitment. They seemed to be more mature and aware of the reasons for why they were there. With the girls they were more supportive of each other, particularly during the tournament.
>
> (Male soccer coach)

The Israel experience enabled the UK team to assess the impact of sport: how it can make a small difference in transcending, however temporarily, conflict and addressing peace and coexistence within a divided society. It also highlighted the relationship between sport and PE and the implications for practice within schools. The lessons learnt have been a valuable learning curve for trainee teachers and qualified practitioners alike. Many of the issues that confronted the coaching team in Israel are issues that have arisen and will continue to arise in the context of teaching and learning within UK schools. One of the trainees was able to reflect on the experience, stating:

> It's definitely important not to have any preconceived ideas, other-wise the kids will pick up on that straight away. You've got to be objective and treat the kids with equal respect. To me they were just children, not Jewish or Arab.
>
> (Male soccer coach)

Conclusion

There are several indicators that have led us to believe that our work had a positive impact even though, at the time of writing, the project still has one more year to run. Whilst we acknowledge that it may not be possible to reflect fully on how successful it has been, the 2002 event brought together more than 100 Jewish, Muslim Arab and Christian Arab children who mixed together and shared a very harmonious inclusive experience. As with the situation in Northern Ireland two decades earlier, given Israel's sectarian geography and high levels of community polarisation, it is too much to hope that friendships formed across religious/ethnic boundaries would last long after we left. It was, however, a potentially significant and formative experience for many of these youngsters and the memory of it may linger much longer. This may, in the long run, make a small contribution to community reconciliation.

At another level, the planning for and practice of the project necessitated the establishment of cross-community networks of local administrators, coaches and related facilitators. Indeed, one of the most poignant moments of the 2002 trip was the sight of a Jewish groundsman and his Arab counterpart sitting in the shade of an olive grove eating ice cream together and sharing stories and ideas about the upkeep of their respective playing fields: grass-roots diplomacy at its best. Even as we prepared to leave we were privy to animated discussions between Jewish and Arab coaches about things such as more cross-community sports camps and the setting up of a regional cross-community soccer league. The fact that these networks will be built upon in the planning and development of the 2003 expedition leads us to hope that more lasting cross-community links are being forged.

One thing of which we are certain is that the trainee teachers in their capacity as coaches reaped huge benefits from their participation in the Galilee project. As the commentaries cited above clearly demonstrate, it was a significant horizon-expanding experience for them. They had to learn about one of the world's most intractable political problems and experience the social and cultural consequences of it first hand. Despite being made aware of such problems, they were privileged to be the beneficiaries of exceptional hospitality and friendship from both Arab and Jewish hosts. Of most significance was the fact that they came to realise that, even in the most fractured of societies, if such a project is approached in a professional manner and handled with skill and sensitivity, through the co-operative teaching of sports and games, children (and pupils in schools) can learn and experience fun in each others' company, regardless of perceived difference.

At the micro-level, teachers are faced with similar issues with their pupils and are constantly challenged in resolving disputes and differences that children often have, whether or not such circumstances are culturally or religiously motivated. Many of the comments from the trainees who took part in the project have highlighted the need to plan for inclusive pedagogy and practice and have important implications for teaching and learning in the context of social inclusion and PE.

Finally, even as we began our planning for what is to be the third and final phase in the summer of 2003, there were strong indications that the project would be extended and expanded. Impressed by the success of the 2002 event, the British Council approached WSPP and asked if they could have more involvement and eventually adopt the project's aims, objectives and practices within their own cultural programme for the region and, eventually, throughout Israel. This would mean the involvement of more Jewish and Arab villages and towns and an expansion in the numbers of children, coaches and leaders. It was proposed that the latter be facilitated by inviting other UK universities to join WSPP, thus allowing more British trainee teaches and coaches to share in some of the positive experiences outlined herein. Thus, what started as a noble idea of a few well-minded individuals, funded by personal donations and voluntarist money-raising, looks set to become a significant and established feature of the cultural dimension that must necessarily accompany any movement toward any political peace in Israel. If such expansion does take place, however, it will be essential that it features more systematic research, the findings of which will help us to understand, rather than merely hope for, the precise impact of such interventions and its potential benefits for pupils, teachers and trainees.

Having reviewed the evidence surrounding the 2002 Galilee project, can we now answer the question posed earlier in this chapter: 'Can sport make a significantly positive contribution to peace processes in deeply politically divided regions like the Middle East or does it make matters worse'? The answer, we believe, is neither. Grand gestures out of context, such as that suggested by Al Gore to Havelange, may have a cosmetic political value, but have little potential to have a long-term impact on the prospects for peace. Orwell's view with regard to the augmentation of conflict through sport, on the other hand, is too sweepingly pessimistic. If the dynamics of the social intervention featured in sport are handled correctly, the Galilee project has convinced us that, little by little, sport can make a positive and progressive contribution to peace processes. And, concomitantly, such interventions can illustrate the potential of sport to contribute to inclusive models of socio-cultural participation and citizenship.

Reflective questions

1   How can PE and sport address cultural and religious differences between pupils in schools?
2   What teaching and learning strategies can be employed in order to ensure an inclusive experience of PE and sport for pupils from different cultural and religious backgrounds?
3   How can the teacher training process contribute to the development of pedagogical skills when teaching pupils from different social and cultural backgrounds?

References

Bairner, A. (2002) 'Sport, Sectarianism and Society in Ireland Revisited', in J. Sugden and A. Tomlinson (eds) *Power Games: A Critical Sociology of Sport*, London: Routledge: 181–95.

Clarke, G. and Nutt, G. (1999) 'Physical Education', in D. Hill and M. Cole (eds), *Promoting Equality in Secondary Schools*, London: Cassell: 211–37

DfEE/QCA (Department for Education and Employment/Qualifications and Curriculum Authority) (1999a) *Citizenship: The National Curriculum for England*, London: HMSO.

DfEE/QCA (Department for Education and Employment/Qualifications and Curriculum Authority) (1999b) *Physical Education: The National Curriculum for England*, London: HMSO.

Elias, N. and Dunning, E. (1986) *Quest for Excitement: Sport and Leisure in the Civilizing Process*, Oxford: Blackwell.

Elon, A. (2000) *A Blood Dimmed Tide: Dispatches from the Middle East*, London: Penguin.

Goodhart, P. and Chataway, C. (1968) *War Without Weapons*, London: W. H. Allen.

Hill, C. (1992) *Olympic Politics*, Manchester: Manchester University Press.

Johnson, P. (2001) *Sport and the Reconciliation Process in Israel: A Case Study of Ibillin 2001*, unpublished Masters dissertation, University of Brighton.

Keim, M. (2003) *Nation Building at Play: Sport as a Tool for Social Integration in Post-apartheid South Africa*, Aachen: Meyer and Meyer.

McIntosh, P. (1993) 'The Sociology of Sport in the Ancient World', in E. Dunning (1993), *The Sports Process: A Comparative and Developmental Approach*, Leeds: Human Kinetics.

McLaughlan, J. (1995) *Sport and Community Relations in Northern Ireland*, unpublished Ph.D. thesis, University of Ulster.

Orwell, G. (1970) *In Front of Your Nose: The Collected Essays, Journalism and Letters of George Orwell*, Volume 4, Harmondsworth: Penguin.

Said, E. (2000) *The End of the Peace Process*, London: Granta.

Sugden, J. (1991) 'Belfast United: Encouraging Cross-community Relations Through Sport in Northern Ireland', *The Journal of Sport and Social Issues* 15, 1: 59–80.

Sugden, J. and Bairner, A. (1999) 'Sport in Divided Societies', in J. Sugden and A. Bairner (eds) *Sport in Divided Societies*, Aachen: Meyer and Meyer: 1–11.

Sugden, J. and Tomlinson, A. (1998), *FIFA and the Contest for World Football: Who Rules the Peoples' Game?* Cambridge: Polity Press.

Their opportunities in sport are therefore restricted to Physical Education lessons; but for the victims, Physical Education is no different from any other aspect of their daily existence. Personal racist abuse – both verbal and physical – is as prevalent there as elsewhere.

> I was tackling Mark and he didn't want me to take the ball off him, and by mistake I just pushed him, so he started swearing at me, very rude – 'You "Paki" bastard, idiot, get back to your own country' (Aslam)

The harsh reality is that for the victims, sport through Physical Education is not the 'great equalizer' that it is often claimed to be.

S. Fleming (1991) 'Sport, Schooling and the Asian
Male Youth Culture', in G. Jarvie (ed.),
Sport, Racism and Ethnicity, London: Falmer Press: 35.

9 'Race', racism and education

Racial stereotypes in Physical Education and school sport

Ian McDonald and Sid Hayes

Introduction

Physical Education (PE) teachers are generally committed to delivering high quality Physical Education and sport programmes to all of their pupils. There will not be many in the profession, if any, who would take issue with the legal requirement on them and their schools 'to provide all pupils with an education free from racial discrimination' (Teacher Training Agency, cited in Waller *et al.* 2001: 166). Indeed, many PE teachers suggest that PE and school sport is one area least affected by racial discrimination, as it is not unusual to see African Caribbean pupils doing well in PE and shining in school sport.

But is this view a form of racial stereotyping? Can success in PE and sport by, for example, African Caribbean pupils be the result of racial ideologies? If this is the case, is *dis*-couragement of African Caribbeans in PE and sport a necessary corollary? Yet, discouragement of any pupil of whatever ethnicity *would* clearly be discriminatory. Racial stereotypes also relate to the diversity of pupils from South Asian descent, who are framed by the opposite stereotype of being non-physical, and, therefore, not inclined to take PE and sport too seriously (Fleming 1995). The fact that racial stereotyping tends to incorporate physical attributes, such as South Asian bodily frailty or African Caribbean athleticism, means that school PE and sport are logical and even likely places where such ideologies are perpetuated.

These questions raise some contentious issues that the PE profession has to navigate in its attempt to deliver 'race' equality, and which we will address in this chapter. In order effectively to engage with 'race', racism and school PE and sport we need to clarify some conceptual frameworks and provide a social and historical context. We therefore begin the chapter with a discussion of the ways in which key concepts such as 'race' and racism have been understood. Then we give a brief overview of the debates and nature of contemporary racism in the UK. This is followed by a discussion of the relationship between 'race' and racism in education, before we examine how it affects school sport and PE. We conclude this chapter by looking at the importance and potential of Initial Teacher Training in contributing to a genuinely socially inclusive PE and sport curricula.

Personal reflections: Sid Hayes

Interest in this area of study arrived part way through my career. As a pupil I was relatively unaware of the phenomenon associated with stereotypes and ethnicity. It was not until I embarked on my teacher training course that 'race' issues in relation to sporting performance were addressed, albeit at a somewhat superficial level. I was schooled into the genetic explanation of sporting performance by selected 'racial groups' in certain sports and it seemed very plausible at the time. With the simplicity of the argument and the media evidence in the form of national television coverage of football and athletics, etc. there seemed little reason to question its logic. It was not until I embarked on further study programmes that I was exposed to alternative viewpoints and began to question the folklore explanation of sporting performance by certain ethnic groups. I was also fortunate to work in an inner city environment as a teacher of Physical Education where I could be reflective with regards to my perceptions and expectations of pupils from minority ethnic backgrounds in PE and sport. It was whilst at this secondary school that I came across viewpoints of colleagues who were also seeking explanations for sporting performance in the field of genetics associated with 'race'. Whilst I had and still have the utmost respect for the work of all my colleagues during my teaching days in schools, I did sense that there were some mixed views surrounding expectations, in the sporting arena, of pupils from different ethnic backgrounds. It was such perceptions that have motivated me to research into this area further. My present position as a teacher trainer allows me some reflective time relating to this issue, and it still appears that the question of ethnicity in relation to education, and specifically in the area of PE and sport, is under-represented as a discussion point.

Understanding 'race' and racism

A common distinction made by many writers is to distinguish chronologically and conceptually between biological and cultural racism. Where racial characteristics such as skin colour, temperament and physicality are invoked to justify discrimination, it is said to be biological racism. Where cultural characteristics are foregrounded in the process of excluding social groups, such as religion and language, it is said to be cultural racism. Biological racism, it is argued, evolved in the seventeenth and eighteenth century in an attempt to rationalise the practice of slavery. It then developed to justify the expanding British Empire in the nineteenth century (Fryer 1984).

The experience of the Nazi-inflicted holocaust during World War II, however, made biological racism politically unacceptable. Advances in genetics rendered the idea of biological 'races' scientifically invalid. Rather than resorting to a biological rationale, writers such as Barker (1981) asserted that racism now operates predominantly through the medium of culture, whereby culture is mapped onto nations to constitute national cultures (Barker 1981, Short and Carrington 1998). So cultural racism manifests itself in the declaration that different ethnic groups, however they are defined, are culturally distinct, each group having their own incompatible lifestyles, customs and ways of seeing the world, and that attempts to mix the cultures will lead to social breakdown. In stark political terms it is often employed to defend the notion of a white and Christian British identity with the aim of excluding those who are deemed to be different or 'alien'. It can also be seen, for example, in the increase in anti-Muslim sentiments in the UK recently, which has been termed 'Islamophobia' (Runnymede Trust, 2000).

It is important not to overstate the difference between the two forms of racism, nor to overstate the shift from a crude biological racism to cultural racism. For example, anti-Jewish sentiment at the turn of the twentieth century was often cloaked in cultural terms (Holmes, 1988), while British-born blacks and Asians continue to live under the threat of racist violence, as the murder of Stephen Lawrence highlighted. Though conceptually distinct, in reality biological and cultural racism tend to interface, to produce 'a matrix of biological and cultural racism' (Cole 1998: 39).

As Britain emerged as an increasingly multicultural society in the post-war period, the concept of ethnicity emerged to replace 'race' as a means of identification and categorisation. Whereas 'race' categorised people according to assumed fixed biological make-up, ethnicity emphasised the fluidity of identities based on culture (Hesse 2000). In the context of cultural racism, however, the dynamic and processual meaning of ethnicity has undergone a process of racialisation, leading to the development of what Paul Gilroy (1987) has called 'ethnic absolutism' – the process of fixing cultural identities so as to be seen as innate rather than socially constructed. As Malik argues (1996: 104), 'though the political use of racist science was discredited, its conceptual framework was never destroyed. The discourse of race was reformulated, but the concept never disappeared'. The fixing of cultures, so that they effectively come to represent 'races', reflects a stubborn persistence in the belief of 'race', even if it is articulated through the language of ethnicity, nation and culture. This problematic status of 'race' as 'biologically meaningless, although still socially explosive'

(Rose 1998: 37), explains the placing of the word in inverted commas, a common convention amongst researchers in this area.

An initial definition of racism, then, is that it exists where a group of people is *discriminated against* on the basis of *racial* and/or *cultural* characteristics that are held to be *inherent* within them as a group. Such a definition focuses on:

- fixed racial/cultural differences
  and
- discriminatory action.

The focus on the former identifies the process of stereotyping of social groups on the basis of 'race' and/or culture. Such stereotypical thinking becomes racist where it leads to, or feeds into, or sustains discriminatory practices against the targeted social group. Crucially, it highlights that racism is an expression of a power whereby the disadvantaged position of subordinate social groups is reproduced (Bhattacharyya *et al.* 2002).

'Race', racism and society

In the period following the publication of the Macpherson report in 1999, after the racist murder of the black teenager Stephen Lawrence, there was a widespread sense of optimism that, at last, a political resolve existed to combat racism wherever it surfaced, be it on the streets, in the police force, or in any public body or organisation. In fact, such expectations have on the whole not been met. Issues of 'race', racism, and national identity remain one of the most contentious areas of politics in Britain. The riots in the northern towns of Oldham, Burnley and Bradford in the summer of 2001, and the subsequent election of three British National Party members to Parliament, is evidence of the central place occupied by 'race' in contemporary British politics and society. The Labour Government's position in this is interesting. The establishment of the cross-departmental Social Exclusion Unit in 1998, and the amendment to the Race Relations Act in 2000, so that public authorities now have a statutory duty to promote race equality, suggests a belief in the benefits of inclusivity and justice. In contrast to the previous Conservative administrations, it would be fair to say that anti-racism is now part of official discourse in the UK. And yet numerous commentators, campaigning groups, activists and scholars have argued that, in practice, the Labour Government has done little to alleviate racial injustice and inequalities faced by Britain's ethnic minority communities. What is clear is that much of the discourse of racism is focused on immigrants, asylum seekers and Muslims (Kundnani 2002). One writer suggested that Labour's strategy is based on:

[a] double game of rhetoric about 'toleration' and 'inclusion' while en-
acting the harshest barrage of racist anti-asylum and anti-immigration
measures seen for a generation

(Mahamdallie 2002: 3)

Indeed, the new Nationality, Immigration and Asylum Bill introduced
in the wake of the 2001 riots has been widely condemned as racist, as it
combines an exclusive notion of British citizenship, targeted at South
Asians, with a battery of controls to stop non-whites and the poor from
entering the UK. The thinking underpinning this controversial piece of
legislation was made explicit by David Blunkett's statement, 'We have
norms of acceptability, and those who come into our home – for that is
what it is – should accept those norms' (Mahamdallie 2002: 4). In targeting
migrants seeking a better life in Britain, Blunkett simultaneously recast
many Asians who were either born in Britain or who have lived in the
country for decades as foreigners and, therefore, to be tolerated only if
they become 'more English'.

'Race' and racism in education

Current discriminatory ideologies and practices are rooted in history.
For example, a legacy of British colonialist ideologies of race and empire,
which posited non-white people variously as the inferior, threatening,
and exotic 'Other', was influential in framing young black people in the
1950s and 1960s as 'a problem'. Anxiety amongst many white parents
led to a policy of dispersion in the 1960s to ensure that ethnic minority
children did not constitute more than 30 per cent of the school population (Blair and Cole 2000). This 'monoculturalist' approach to education
sought to make all newcomers socially and culturally British; 'The idea
was both to prevent "a lowering of standards in schools" and to ensure
rapid assimilation of the children into the "British Culture"' (Blair and
Cole 2002: 63).

It was during the 1970s that 'the imagery of violence and decay became
synonymous with those inner-city localities in which black migrants had
settled and established themselves' (Solomos 1993: 135). An important
factor in this was the 'moral panic' about mugging in the early 1970s,
which was constructed as a new 'black juvenile' crime, and perceived
by the public as constituting a major social problem (Hall et al. 1978).
In response, there was a growing sense of frustration within the black
communities and an increasingly antagonistic relationship between black
youths and the police, reflecting 'a deep crisis in the relationship between
these communities and the state, especially the police' (Witte 1996: 59).

Racial stereotypes of black youngsters not only as 'disruptive' but as
physically threatening abounded in the media and official reportage of the

riots that erupted across Britain in the early 1980s. Instead of understanding the riots as an expression of extreme frustration and anger caused
by lack of decent employment opportunities, police harassment and
poverty, the perception emerged that black youths were 'trouble'. As Blair
and Cole (2002: 64) comment, 'The view which carried into the classroom was that black children were not only disruptive, but violent'. The
notion of the physically able but educationally inferior black child was
established. And with it emerged an educational discourse of 'under-
achievement', which placed the 'failing' black pupils with low 'self-esteem'
under the spotlight in the search for explanations and solutions.

Ironically, the first official recognition that racism was adversely affecting
the education of black children came with the Rampton Report in 1981
– the year of the riots. This report, however, was not received well by
the right-wing Thatcher government, especially in the wake of the riots,
and so the Prime Minister commissioned another study with a brief to
cover all pupils from minority ethnic backgrounds. The Swann Report,
Education for All (Swann Report 1985), while confirming the findings of
the Rampton Report, made its mark more for its recommendation that
children in all schools should be educated for life in an ethnically diverse
society. The belief that underpinned the Swann Report was that if all children, but especially white children, were taught about different cultures,
then prejudice and racism would be undermined. This represented a real
shift from a 'monocultural' approach to education, based on the concept
of assimilation, to multicultural education. Though multiculturalism is a
complex and multi-layered term (Hesse, 2000), we concur with Waller *et
al.* (2001) in defining multicultural education as the acceptance of cultural
difference and the attempt to forge a greater understanding of diverse
cultures.

The principles underpinning multicultural education and the practicalities of its effective implementation in the school setting have stimulated
extensive debate with educational research over the past few years. With
developments in multicultural education, it was necessary to develop further the understanding of racism to account for the continuing inequalities
in experiences and attainment. Gillborn (1998) argued that a definition of
racism based on a degree of intentionality – that is, where racially discriminatory action is conscious and deliberate – is a necessary component
but not by itself sufficient. It does not account for the 'possibility of "unin-
tentional" or institutional racism, where individuals and organisations
act in ways that are discriminatory in their *effects*, though not in intention' (Gillborn 1998: 43). The salience and credibility of this observation
was confirmed with the publication of the Macpherson Report in 1999,
which identified institutionalised racism as a key issue in combating racial
inequalities. The report defined institutional racism as:

The collective failure of an organisation to provide an appropriate and professional service to people because of their colour, culture, or ethnic origin. It can be seen or detected in processes, attitudes and behaviour which amounts to discrimination through unwitting prejudice, ignorance, thoughtlessness and racial stereotyping which disadvantage ethnic people.

(Macpherson 1999: 321)

Following the publication of the Macpherson Report, a range of British institutions have been subject to accusations of institutional racism, including the police force, the army, the legal profession, the National Health Service, and of course the educational system. Indeed, long before Macpherson, many writers had identified institutional racism within the educational system (Gillborn and Gipps 1996).

A key report by Gillborn and Mirza (2000), however, gives an insight into where progress has and has not been made. Before we look at the report, an important caveat to consider is that the 'progress' is narrowly interpreted here as attainment in GCSEs. It does not consider a number of other important factors relevant in understanding racial equality in schools, such as the qualitative experiences of pupils from minority ethnic backgrounds and the type and structure of subject provision. We will return to these other factors when reviewing the impact of 'race' on school PE and sport. Gillborn and Mirza (2000) confirm that the 1990s saw a dramatic improvement in the proportion of pupils completing their compulsory schooling with five or more GCSE higher grade passes (A–C) or their equivalent. Of the principal ethnic groups looked at – white, Indian, Pakistani, Bangladeshi, African Caribbean – all are now more likely to attain five higher grades than ever before. This rising overall profile notwithstanding, there are less encouraging trends.

Considerable differences in attainments exist between ethnic groups, suggesting that pupils of different ethnic origin do not experience equal educational opportunities. African Caribbean, Pakistani and Bangladeshi pupils are less likely to attain five higher grade GCSEs than their white and Indian peers. Indian pupils achieved the largest improvement in performance. Indeed, during the period from 1997 to 1998, the gap between Indian pupils and white pupils was erased. Bangladeshi pupils had also improved at the same rate as white pupils, thus leaving the pattern of inequality intact. While Black and Pakistani pupils have improved, however, it is not enough to close the gap with their white peers, in fact the gap has widened. Gillborn and Mirza conclude that 'African Caribbean and Pakistani pupils have drawn least benefit from the rising levels of attainment: the gap between them and their white peers is bigger now than a decade ago' (Gillborn and Mirza 2000: 14).

Disturbingly, in one large urban local education authority cited in the report, the experience of schooling proved detrimental to black pupils:

> At the start of their compulsory schooling black pupils are the highest attaining of the main ethnic groups in the LEA; recording a level of success 20 percentage points above the average for the authority. At Key Stage 2 pupils in the same group are attaining below the LEA average and in their GCSE examinations they attain 21 points below the average.
>
> (Gillborn and Mirza 2000: 16)

Encouragingly, one of the most important findings to emerge from the report is that for each of the main ethnic groups there is at least one LEA where that group is the highest attaining. Gillborn and Mirza conclude that:

> It suggests that even for the groups with the most serious inequalities of attainment nationally, there are places where that trend is being bucked. The significance of this finding should not be overlooked and is a reminder of the variability of attainment and the lack of any necessary or pre-determined ethnic ordering.
>
> (Gillborn and Mirza 2000: 9)

The report, in common with most other studies on educational achievement (Abbas 2002, Haque and Bell 2001), does not give any clues as to levels of attainment by ethnicity in PE. It would be interesting to see if the under-attainment of black pupils is replicated or contradicted in PE. It would also be useful to know how pupils of Indian and Pakistani origin fare in PE given their contrasting experiences of attainment more generally. A further issue that requires examination is the relationship between ethnicity, gender and social class. Most studies of school PE and sport focus on the impact of racial ideologies on the experience and delivery of school PE and sport, and, given the differential experiences of Britain's ethnic minorities, we would expect to see that ideologies of experiences of racism are expressed in a diversity of ways.

'Race' and racism in school sport and Physical Education

It is clearly the case that pupils of African Caribbean origin are not performing as well in schools as their white and Indian counterparts. Indeed, young people of African Caribbean origin are over-represented in suspensions and expulsions from school and in units for pupils with emotional and behavioural difficulties (Gillborn and Gipps 1996). Assumptions about the supposed disruptive, aggressive and violent natures of youths from African Caribbean backgrounds have informed a number of strategies intended to contain such behaviour. For example, many of the testimonies of successful black sportsmen of the 1970s and early 1980s recalled how they were encouraged by their teachers to concentrate on sport at the expense of their academic studies (Cashmore 1982). Such personal accounts were further exemplified by a study conducted by Carrington and Wood (1983) that illustrated how school teachers used school sport as a tool of social control over black pupils. By encouraging them to do well in PE and play school sport, physical activities in which black pupils were seen as most likely to excel, it was felt that their self-esteem would improve. Furthermore, the teachers would be better able to secure their peaceful compliance in the classroom by threatening to prevent black pupils from having access to sport.

What these studies show is the need to situate the experience of PE and sport in its context, because they clearly illustrate how success in sport can be the consequence of racial ideologies. As Back and Solomos point out:

> Racist discourses need to be rigorously contextualised. This means that racism needs to be situated within specific moments. The effect of a particular racist discourse needs to be placed in the conditions surrounding the moment of its enunciation.
>
> (Back and Solomos 2000: 230)

Hoberman's *Darwins Athletes* (1997) has reminded us of the importance of this approach with his devastating, though ultimately flawed, analysis (see Carrington and McDonald 2001: 10–12 for a critique) of the deleterious impact of black athletic success in the USA. The subtitle of his book neatly encapsulates his argument: 'How sport has damaged black America and preserved the myth of race'. For Hoberman, the over-emphasis on achievement in sport may be reflected in success at school level but, for the vast majority of young blacks, it will not lead to success in professional sports. Furthermore, such a 'sports-fixation' directly contributes to an anti-intellectualism in the black community and black underachievement in schools.

The theoretical significance of this observation is that it is naive to correlate racism simply to levels of exclusion from sport and low attainment in PE. It may well be those high levels of attainments in PE and success in school sport are related to processes of racial stereotyping. An adequate understanding of racism, then, should not only refer to negative impacts and characterisations, but should also include 'seemingly positive characteristics':

> Negatively evaluated characteristics include such instances of biological and intentional racist discourse as 'black children are not as clever

as white children', but excludes such seemingly positive though biological statements as 'black children are good at sports'. While this latter
assertion can lead to individual and/or group short-term enhancement
(an unmerited place in the school football team for the individual or
enhanced status for the group as a whole in an environment where
prowess at sport is highly regarded), it is potentially racist and likely
to have racist consequences. This is because, like most stereotypes, it
is distorted and misleading and typically appears as part of a discourse
which works to justify the channelling of black children into sport,
rather than academic activities.

(Cole 1998: 41)

Hayes and Sugden (1999) showed how the PE profession still considers
some aspects of performance in PE and sport by ethnic groups to be
founded in racial biology. They challenged this notion and identified the
racial stereotypes this may reinforce, and which may be implicated in
the under-achievement of black pupils:

The physiological mythology surrounding blacks in sport seems deeply
entrenched within the physical education profession. This evokes
a set of beliefs on behalf of teachers and pupils which maintains a
mutually reinforcing and vicious circle.

(Hayes and Sugden 1999: 105)

While racial ideologies help to explain the over-representation and
narrow focus on sport amongst youngsters of African Caribbean background, a different set of racial ideologies frames the discussion of the
lack of participation of South Asians in sport generally and school sport
specifically. For example, Fleming's research (1991, 1995) on South Asian
male youth and sport has highlighted how the existence of stereotypes
about Asian physical frailty and cultural priorities have adversely impacted
upon the school-based experiences of Asian male youths. His research
showed that rather than sport and PE bringing different communities
together, it instead provided an opportunity for the dominant ethnic group,
the white pupils, to bully racially and abuse South Asian pupils. The South
Asian pupils in turn adopted various coping strategies, such as avoiding
school sport and internalising the stereotypes. Fleming outlines the different
ways that racism is experienced and responded to according to the religious, class, and linguistic backgrounds of the pupils. Such differences in
cultural responses, however, should not lead to a preoccupation with the
differences in cultural backgrounds, as 'the preoccupation with cultural
difference is a diversion and a distraction from the most fundamental issue
– the pervasive impact of racism in all its guises' (Fleming 1994: 172).

Without a critical understanding of the nature and development of
stereotypes, PE teachers are more vulnerable to such myths, especially

when they seem to be confirmed by the limited number of role models from the Asian community in high profile sports such as football (Bains and Patel 1995, Johal 2001). As with pupils of African Caribbean origin, success in some sports can actually serve to perpetuate racial ideologies. So, the successes of some South Asians in activities like cricket and badminton serve to bolster ideas that they are good only at sports that require limited or no contact. Pedagogically, the concern is that as Fleming suggests:

> Perceived aptitude for a particular sport became the basis on which many schools focused their PE curricula to accommodate a large south Asian population in the school. That is to say, emphasis was placed on those activities that were considered popular with south Asian and other ethno-cultural groups, invariably cricket and hockey. Indeed, assertions based upon 'natural ability' which have been overwhelmingly rejected elsewhere have become prominent as an expedient rationalisation of the situation. Some south Asians have internalised the self-image and even 'swallowed the myth' themselves.
>
> (Fleming 1995: 40)

The gender aspects of ethnicity were focused on by Benn (2000) in her research on Asian females. Benn notes the difficulties that occur when cultural norms conflict with traditional practices in a PE department. For example, dress codes are often considered to be indicators of standards within departments, which can be problematic. The adherence to a specific form of dress attire in PE and sport in schools is felt to be appropriate by professionals in terms of its health and safety in practical activities. This conflicts, however, with a cultural norm shared by many Asian girls that requires them to cover most parts of the body and to avoid public nudity, even amongst members of the same sex. This clearly poses challenges during practical mixed-sex classes as well as in the pre- and post-lesson environment in the changing rooms, and points to the importance of Initial Teacher Training in preparing PE teachers for the challenges of delivering an equitable and just educational experience for all pupils.

Conclusion: The importance of Initial Teacher Training

Gainge (2001) correctly argues in our opinion that 'schools that recognise "race" and ethnicity as issues are more likely to be successful in serving minority pupils' needs than a "colourblind" approach' (2001: 119). Although racial equality is accepted as an ideal in education, it is not clear how far it is embedded in the structures of school provision and in professional practices. This makes it even more important that newly qualified teachers are aware of equity issues and inclusive practices. As Tomlinson and Craft acknowledge, 'If such matters are not addressed in initial teacher training they are unlikely in future to be addressed anywhere' (1995: 10). There is evidence, however, that 'Neither initial nor in-service training pays sufficient attention to race and racism issues' (Richardson and Wood, 2000: 35). It is an observation that is confirmed by our investigations into the amount of time spent on multiculturalism and ethnicity on undergraduate courses taken by trainee PE teachers. As expected, all of the institutions we contacted covered issues of multiculturalism and ethnicity, because they are required to do so by the Teacher Training Agency (TTA). Most of the institutes were able to show that they satisfy TTA requirements by showing that these issues were being covered *somewhere*, albeit for just a couple of hours within a full degree programme. Only a small minority went beyond this tokenistic approach, with evidence of a more sustained and developmental engagement with the issues.

Trainee PE teachers need to have a sound sociological understanding of how 'race', ethnicity and racism operate within society, schools and in the curriculum. This is not just a question of technique that can be left to 'professional practice', based on a superficial understanding of different cultures. What we are advocating is the incorporation of anti-racist education that encourages teachers to:

> Engage in 'critical reflection' to question their own practice and that of their schools, with a commitment to working within a morality of social justice and egalitarianism and a concomitant determination to raise issues of racism and anti-racism within the classroom, the school and society.
>
> (Waller *et al.* 2001: 166)

It is a call for teachers to become more self-reflexive so that they understand the complex dynamics of racism and multiculturalism, and can deliver PE and sport that eschews stereotyping and actively combats all forms of racism. To do anything less would mean our newly qualified teachers would continue to be ill-prepared to question established structures of provision, unable to challenge entrenched stereotypical thinking, and, therefore, culpable in perpetuating a culture of racial inequality in school PE and sport.

Reflective questions

1   Are pupils from a variety of minority ethnic backgrounds catered for in the structures and processes adhered to within the PE department?
2   What views are held within the PE department regarding access to and performance within the PE curriculum?
3   Does the school have a policy surrounding issues related to
     (a) ethnicity?
     (b) anti-racism?

4 Are issues relating to ethnicity and anti-racism considered when planning takes place within the PE department?

References

Abbas, T. (2002) 'The Home and the School in the Educational Achievement of South Asians' in *Race, Ethnicity and Education* 5, 3: 291–316.

Back, L. and Solomos, J. (2000) 'Introduction: Theorising Race and Racism', in L. Back and J. Solomos (eds), *Theories of Race and Racism*, London: Routledge.

Bains, J. with Patel, R. (1995) *Asians Can't Play Football*, Midlands Asian Sports Forum.

Barker, M. (1981) *The New Racism*, London: Junction Books.

Benn, T. (2000) 'Towards Inclusion in Education and Physical Education', in A. Williams (ed.), *Primary School Physical Education*, London: Routledge.

Bhattacharyya, G., Gabriel, J. and Small, S. (2002) *Race and Power: Global Racism in the Twenty-First Century*, London: Routledge.

Blair, M. and Cole, M. (2002) 'Racism and Education', in M. Cole (ed.), *Education, Equality and Human Rights*, London: Routledge Falmer.

Carrington, Ben and McDonald, I. (eds) (2001) *'Race', Sport and British Society*, London: Routledge.

Carrington, Bruce and Wood, E. (1983) 'Body Talk: Images of Sport in a Multi-racial School' in *Multiracial Education*, 11, 2: 29–38.

Cashmore, E. (1982) *Black Sportsmen*, London: Routledge and Kegan Paul.

Cole, M. (1998) 'Racism, Reconstructed Multiculturalism and Antiracist Education', *Cambridge Journal of Education*, 28, 1: 37–48.

Fleming, S. (1991) 'Sport, Schooling and the Asian Male Youth Culture', in G. Jarvie (ed.), *Sport, Racism and Ethnicity*, London: Falmer Press: 30–58.

Fleming, S. (1994) 'Sport and South Asian Youth: The Perils of False Universalism and Stereotyping', *Leisure Studies* 13: 159–77.

Fleming, S. (1995) *'Home and Away': Sport and South Asian Male Youth*, Aldershot: Avebury.

Fryer, P. (1984) *Staying Power: The History of Black People in Britain*, London: Pluto Press.

Gainge, C. (2001) 'Promoting Equality and Equal Opportunities: School Policies', in D. Hill and M. Cole (eds), *Schooling and Equality*, London: Kogan Page.

Gillborn, D. (1998) 'Racism and the Politics of Qualitative Research: Learning from Controversy and Critique', in P. Connolly and B. Troynas (eds), *Researching Racism in Education: Politics, Theory and Practice*, Buckingham: Oxford University Press.

Gillborn, D. and Gipps, C. (1996) *Recent Research on the Achievements of Ethnic Minority Pupils*, OFSTED Report, London: HMSO.

Gillborn, D. and Mirza, H. F. (2000) *Educational Inequality Mapping Race, Class and Gender*, OFSTED Report, London: HMSO.

Gilroy, P. (1987) *'There Ain't No Black in the Union Jack': The Cultural Politics of Race and Nation*, London: Routledge.

Hall, S., Critcher, C., Jefferson, T., Clarke, J. and Roberts, B. (1978) *Policing the Crisis: Mugging, the State, and Law and Order*, London: Macmillan.

Haque, Z. and Bell, J. F. (2001) 'Evaluating the Performances of Minority Ethnic Pupils in Secondary Schools', *Oxford Review of Education* 27, 3: 357–68.

Hayes, S. and Sugden, J. (1999) 'Winning Through "Naturally" Still? An Analysis of the Perceptions held by Physical Education Teachers Towards the Performance of Black Pupils in School Sport and in the Classroom', *Race, Ethnicity and Education* 2, 1: 93–107.

Hesse, B. (ed.) (2000) *Un/Settled Multiculturalisms: Diasporas, Entanglement, Transruptions*, London: Zed Press.

Hoberman, J. (1997) *Darwin's Athletes: How Sport has Damaged Black America and Preserved the Myth of Race*, Boston: Mariner Books.

Holmes, C. (1988) *John Bull's Island: Immigration and British Society 1871–1971*, London: Macmillan.

Johal, S. (2001) 'Playing their Own Game: A South Asian Football Experience', in B. Carrington and I. McDonald (eds), *'Race', Sport and British Society*, London: Routledge.

Kundnani, S. (2002) 'The Death of Multiculturalism', online, available HTTP: <http://www.irr.org.uk/cantle/index.htm> accessed 13 March 2003.

Macpherson, Sir W. (1999) *The Stephen Lawrence Inquiry: Report on the Inquiry by Sir William Macpherson of Cluny*, Cm 4262, London: HMSO.

Mahamdallie, H. (2002) 'Racism: Myths and Realities', *International Socialism Journal* 95: 3–39.

Malik, K. (1996) *The Meaning of Race: Race, History and Culture in Western Societies*, London: Macmillan.

Richardson, R. and Wood, A. (2000) *Inclusive Schools, Inclusive Society*, Stoke-on-Trent: Trentham.

Rose, S. (1998) *Lifelines: Biology, Freedom, Determinism*, London: Penguin.

Runnymede Trust (2000) *Commission on the Future of Multi-Ethnic Britain*, online, available HTTP: <http://www.runnymedetrust.org/meb/TheReport.htm> accessed 13 March 2003.

Short, G. and Carrington, Bruce (1998) 'Reconstructing Multicultural Education: A Response to Mike Cole', *Cambridge Journal of Education* 28, 2: 231–4.

Solomos, J. (1993) *Race and Racism in Britain*, 2nd edition, London: Macmillan.

Swann Report (1985) *Education for All: The Report of the Committee of Inquiry into the Education of Children from Ethnic Minority Groups*, Cmnd 9543, London: HMSO.

Tomlinson, S. and Craft, M. (1995) 'Education for All in the 1990s', in S. Tomlinson and M. Craft (eds), *Ethnic Relations and Schooling: Policy and Practice in the 1990s*, London: Athlone: 1–11.

Waller, T., Cole, M. and Hill, D. (2001) 'Race', in D. Hill and M. Cole (eds), *Schooling and Equality*, London: Kogan Page: 161–85.

Witte, R. (1996) *Racist Violence and the State*, London: Longman.

Playing rugby, as I had to, is to look fear in the face every week. When you get hold of the ball, a load of six foot tall fat marauding hooligans, yelling war cries, comes after you intent on diminishing your chances of walking home that night. I remember my PE teacher running up the field with the ball shouting: 'Come on lads, try and tackle me, tackle me'. Given half the chance now, I would try and take him down.

S. Ball (2001) 'Why I Hated School PE', *PE and Sport Today* 5: 52.

10 Class, inequality and the body in Physical Education

Ian McDonald

Introduction

The statement on social inclusion in the National Curriculum for Physical Education (NCPE) document identifies three key principles for the development of a more inclusive curriculum. These are (1) setting suitable learning challenges, (2) responding to pupils' diverse learning needs, and (3) overcoming potential barriers to learning and assessment for individuals and groups of pupils (DfEE/QCA 1999: 28). In serving these principles, issues of 'race', gender, disability, sexuality, religious and cultural differences, special needs, and ethnicity tend to be foregrounded. But what about social class? Often, social class is either forgotten or disregarded in discussions of social exclusion in education and Physical Education. Indeed, social class seems to be marginal to the discourse of social inclusion more generally. In this chapter the marginal status of class in combating social exclusion will be challenged through three distinct but connected arguments.

One argument will be a general critique of the politics of social inclusion. The marginalisation of class from the social inclusion agenda is not an oversight. Rather, it follows from the dominant political interpretation of social inclusion, in which a resolution to the symptoms of social exclusion, such as deprivation and disadvantage, is sought without questioning the key structural relations of power that created such conditions.

A second argument draws attention to a tension in the relationship between social inclusion/exclusion and notions of equality and equity. In terms of public policy, social inclusion is not synonymous with equality. For example, the explicit emphasis in government educational policy on raising standards in achievement can and does sit very comfortably with increasing inequalities, as I outline later. Furthermore, the emphasis on social inclusion downplays the gross inequalities and privileges enjoyed by the elite private schools within a hierarchical educational structure. In other words, the social inclusion/exclusion agenda detaches disadvantage and deprivation from a relational analysis of the social structure of society in general and education in particular. Solutions to social exclusion tend not to be based on principles of redistribution of resources, but on creating the frameworks for people/communities to access opportunities to become socially included. Social equality is at best an incidental policy outcome. It follows then that we should not confuse the achievement of social inclusion with greater equality. Indeed, 'social inclusion/exclusion' and 'inequality/equality' represent alternative policy paradigms. While the former paradigm tends to foreclose questions of social structure, inequality/equality paradigms tend towards a more critical interrogation of structural relations. The battle to alleviate social exclusion does not necessarily create greater equality.

It was within an inequality/equality paradigm that *Equality, Education and Physical Education*, edited by John Evans (1993), examined the impact and significance of a range of issues including sexism, racism, disability, and social class, on the philosophy, culture and practices of Physical Education. In setting out the approach taken in the book, Evans and Davies tied the quest for equality in Physical Education to a more general political project. They declared that 'Our own perspectives and choice of company in this volume are informed by our value commitments to the politics and philosophies of democratic socialism', which they argued placed an emphasis on 'individuality, diversity, plurality both in the curriculum and schooling and in wider society. It is a view which has equity uppermost in its concerns' (Evans and Davies 1993: 12).

As with *Equality, Education and Physical Education,* equity and social inclusion in Physical Education are uppermost in the considerations of contributors to this volume. Unlike the 1993 collection, however, absent from the current text is an explicit linking of the quest for equality to a transformative political project – be it democratic socialism or any other system. The emphasis in this volume is more on practitioner relevance – to assist PE teachers in developing a more socially inclusive, just and fair curriculum. Such a practitioner emphasis, however, does not necessarily mean that broader questions of politics should be avoided. Also, not to declare a political position is not the same as being neutral; rather, it lends de facto support for the government's political project, which, with reference to alleviating social exclusion, is a project that is highly problematic and limiting in fundamental ways. The question that is then raised is the following: to what extent is it viable to create a genuinely socially inclusive, equal and fair PE curriculum within the government's own framework – that is, within a social inclusion/exclusion paradigm? Another way of posing the question is to ask whether the solution to potential equality issues in PE lies simply in amending individual attitudes and practices, while leaving the structure of PE in particular and education in general intact. These questions form the point of departure for the chapter in setting out the case for a class-based analysis of PE. A class-based analysis enables a serious examination of how particular class-based bodies are produced in PE, which enables the subject to connect with wider relations of power that reproduce disadvantage and confirm privilege. My broad aim in this chapter then is to reveal the problematic and limiting nature of the social inclusion/exclusion agenda in realising the goal of a PE curriculum based on the principles of social justice, fairness and equality.

Class, PE and the body

A pivotal concept in understanding the relationship between class, sport and PE is the body. It is the body that is at the centre of Physical Education and sport as an activity. Until recently, the body was studied more as a biological machine that needed to be exercised to increase its performance, rather than as a form of identity, and a site of social difference and division. As sociologists and cultural critics have discussed for some time now, our bodies are not merely natural entities, but are also socially 'produced', or 'constructed' (Shilling 1993). The fact that, for most of the time, we more or less experience our embodied selves as natural and taken for granted (for example, we do not consciously think about everyday uses of our body) should not conceal the fact that attitudes to and uses of bodies are socially learnt. Socially produced bodies carry symbolic values which are indicators of social class position. How we manage our bodies in terms of diet and exercise, how we carry our bodies in terms of posture and deportment, how we present our bodies in terms of clothing, and how we use our bodies in social and physical activities, carry significant social and class meanings. And, in a society in which class is still a significant social category, the body is a marker of class differences. This could also manifest itself in the types of activity that pupils engage in and pursue later in life. Golf, rugby and cricket have traditionally been associated with middle-class English society whilst football has historically been linked with the working classes (Holt 1989).

Pierre Bourdieu (1984) outlined the place of the body in his theory of social reproduction. For Bourdieu, the social location of bodies (the material circumstances of our lives such as where and how we live, our age and geographical location) shapes the formation of our body *habitus*. By habitus, Bourdieu is referring to bodily dispositions that arise out of the social location and shape people's reactions to familiar and novel situations. The habitus then gives rise to the development of *taste,* that is the preference for particular lifestyle choices including diet, fashion, and sports, for example, which marks out a person's social location, such as class identity. For example, historically upper-class people generally prefer going to opera rather than pop concerts. Working-class families tend to favour the sun and sand of Spanish resorts rather than the solitude of walking in scenic surroundings. These distinctive practices are not arbitrary or accidental, but arise out of their class-based body habitus. In Bourdieu's schema, social locations and habitus are relatively durable, but taste is more dynamic, as it develops in relation to the taste of other classes. In other words, the development of particular taste emerges out of a strategic attempt by different classes for distinction. Typically this involves a constant process of emulation by the lower classes of higher class habits, which then causes the higher classes to cultivate more distinctive tastes, so as to distinguish themselves from 'the lower orders'.

In *Distinction* (1984) Bourdieu empirically maps out the distinct body habitus developed by the main classes. The upper classes treat their bodies as a 'project', akin to a form of investment. The elite strata of the upper classes favour a macrobiotic cult of health and distinction, as witnessed in the ways the elite members of the upper classes seek out exclusivity in physical activities in private and expensive clubs. This is also a convenient method to combine social networking and business contacts, thus ensuring the reproduction of their class power and privilege. The non-elite sections of the upper class, the middle classes, also treat the body as a project, but less for intrinsic benefits and more for extrinsic display, in what Bourdieu called a 'body for others'. This leads to an attraction to fitness and health activities, in which a desirable body is produced. For both sections of the dominant classes, sport and physical activities offer a means of socialising with similarly located people, and a way of inculcating a way of carrying the body and instilling a desirable set of characteristics suited to their leadership positions in society. Members of the manual working class meanwhile, as befitting their positions as labourers (whether inside or outside the home), have an instrumental orientation to their bodies, based on the metaphor of the body as a machine. The body is valued for its functional utility, and is expressed in a preference for sporting activities that require stamina, power and strength.

The different body habitus of the respective classes is reflected and reinforced by schools, and especially in PE. In what J. E. Hargreaves (1986) has referred to as 'schooling the body', class divisions were inscribed from the beginning in PE. During the latter part of the nineteenth century, sports and games emerged in the elite public school and university system as a means of creating future leaders of Britain and its Empire (Dixon *et al.* 1973, Mangan 1981). Games such as rugby, cricket and lacrosse, requiring plenty of space and specialised equipment, were favoured not only because they demonstrated distinction from the masses, but also because of their putative character-building qualities. It was a very different rationale, however, that underpinned the military drill exercises that were served up to working-class pupils at the beginning of the twentieth century. Here the concern was with providing an activity that required minimal space and equipment and maintained a rudimentary level of health coupled with establishing a regime of obedience training (Penn 1999). The emerging bourgeoisie, located between the working class and the ruling elite, enthusiastically adopted the public school games ethic. As Kirk notes, 'Part of the success of competitive team games among the bourgeoisie was their symbolic value as a mark of social superiority, through which they could simultaneously emulate their social superiors and distance themselves from their inferiors' (1992: 85).

The inequalities in the quality of sports facilities, and the contrasting pedagogic frameworks, highlight the centrality of the body in establishing a class-based philosophy and politics of PE. Reflecting the class nature of education at the turn of the twentieth century, PE played a critical role in preparing and training the bodies of pupils for their expected designation in society. PE was one site where pupils' bodies were literally worked on as a disciplining mechanism in accordance with their respective position in society.

The post-World War II expansion of secondary schooling resulted concomitantly in an expansion of PE as a subject. Team games, which had occupied a central role in the education of upper-class males from the mid-1880s, and were later adopted by upper-class females (J. A. Hargreaves 1994), soon became the most important part of PE in the state sector. 'Within a decade and a half', writes Kirk (1992: 84), 'a version of Physical Education that had until the 1950s only been "traditional" to the private schools in Britain became "traditional Physical Education" for everyone, for the masses as well as the wealthy'. This was not a simple process of diffusion, however. Whereas the games ethic was intended to inculcate leadership qualities into upper-class pupils in private schools, it was developed as a means of ameliorating social ills amongst the masses, especially working-class and, from the 1970s, black males (J. E. Hargreaves 1986).

To enable PE to play this role, it was necessary first to shift its ideological basis in the public schools as a symbol of class superiority, and to reposition itself as an element of national culture. 'In keeping with [the] spirit of social reconstruction', writes Kirk, 'the elitism and separatism of the public schools' use of team games was turned on its head, so that team games became the natural inheritance of all, and the common denominator that proved British society was "equal"' (1992: 159). Such a view of sport and games as a common denominator and a unifying medium in society developed in order to facilitate the integration of the working-class pupils as part of the social reconstruction of post-war Britain. This was especially important because of the academic differences experienced by pupils allocated into grammar, secondary modern and remedial schools. But with the provision of playing fields and other sports facilities on a mass scale, it was thought possible to consolidate a sense of national identity through the playing of sport and games in PE. As Kirk states, it necessitated 'the eradication of the idea that games playing demonstrated social superiority, in order to accommodate the alternative notion that games were a common denominator that could transcend barriers of class and wealth' (1992: 115). But, of course, as Kirk, following

J. E. Hargreaves, unequivocally states, this idea was a myth that served to incorporate the working class into 'respectable' bourgeois society.

Such a Bourdieuan-inspired analysis throws light on the ways in which dominant power relations are maintained and reproduced in Physical Education. The fact that, since World War II, many working-class pupils were encouraged to participate in sport and do well in PE (not only to integrate them into bourgeois values, but also as a compensation for their academic failure) is not without ideological significance. To what extent PE continues to play such an ideological role is open to question, but it is not one that is contradicted by the commitment to social inclusion by contemporary physical educationalists.

A more immediate aspect of how class is impacting upon PE, however, is the effect of cutbacks in school budgets over the past decade or so. The constraint on resources available to schools has led to the selling off of playing fields in many areas, affecting the opportunities available to pupils from working-class areas to benefit from wide-ranging PE curricula. Though the situation is uneven, it is clear that cutbacks in school budgets, especially in deprived urban and rural areas, have disproportionately affected schools serving predominantly working-class pupils, of whatever ethnic origin they may be. Furthermore, with the introduction of literacy and numeracy hours, the time spent on Physical Education is being increasingly squeezed, as schools are pressured to raise standards and their positions in 'league tables'. Unfortunately, statistics on attainment in GCSE PE are not available in relation to class but it would be interesting to see whether working-class pupils succeed in this particular subject.

The key point is that deep structures of embodied power and the reproduction of class inequalities in Physical Education are left untouched by the focus on combating social exclusion. To substantiate such a claim it is necessary to examine the nature of social inclusion within the Labour Government's agenda for addressing deprivation and disadvantage.

Social inclusion: Concept, politics and policy

Since the early 1990s, it seems that discussions of the relevance of social class have faded into the background in the field of social policy. Instead, as any academic publisher's catalogue will illustrate, social inclusion/exclusion has emerged as a central concept in analyses of social policy. A concern with overcoming social exclusion may appear to be similar to overcoming class disadvantage, but these ideals represent competing ways of analysing social inequalities, suggesting different policy responses. Social inclusion/exclusion has replaced class as an explanatory factor in producing social disadvantage and, while concerned with alleviating forms of poverty, it leaves untouched fundamentally asymmetrical power relations and their associated social inequalities.

In the opinion of Burchardt *et al.*, social exclusion is 'a contested term' (2002: 1). It is perhaps more accurate to say, however, that social exclusion is more of a promiscuous than a contested term, appearing in diverse social and political contexts. Percy-Smith traces its conceptual lineage back to Max Weber's understanding of exclusion as one form of social closure, but stresses that its currency in policy debates first arose in France in the 1980s where it was used to refer to those who had slipped through the social insurance system. It was subsequently taken up and generalised by the European Union to relate to social and economic cohesion (Percy-Smith 2000). It wasn't until the latter part of the 1990s, with the creation of the interdepartmental Social Exclusion Unit (SEU) in 1997 by the Labour Government, that the term became a familiar part of British political discourse. And yet, as Hills *et al.* note (2002: 226), 'the new familiarity still leaves the danger of talking at cross-purposes, with the phrase being used in different ways'. In contrast to academic discussions of social exclusion, however, the SEU has a precise operational definition:

> A shorthand term for what can happen when people or areas suffer from a combination of linked problems such as unemployment, poor skills, low incomes, poor housing, high crime environments, bad health and family breakdown.
>
> (Social Exclusion Unit 1997: 1)

As can be deduced from this definition, social exclusion is often taken to be more or less synonymous with poverty or disadvantage. Whereas in discussions of poverty and disadvantage per se in social policy the focus tends to be on the need to redistribute resources and goods to those deemed to be in need, the current discourse of social inclusion/exclusion tends to eschew such principles (Burden 2000). Thus, the aim of the SEU is to 'empower' individuals and/or communities to lift themselves out of their excluded position, of which poverty and disadvantage are key indicators, to become part of mainstream society. The causes of social exclusion are often rooted in structural problems, such as those caused by shifting forms of economic production from manufacturing to information technology. In government-based discussions of social exclusion, however, its perpetuation lies in the failure or inability of people to access the 'networks of opportunity' (Dean and Woods 1999: 10) that are assumed to exist within society for all its members. Bennington and Donnison (1999: 64) point out that 'the concepts of social inclusion/exclusion are used to signify a shift in focus away from the poor and the state of poverty, towards the processes, policies and institutions which cause or reinforce poverty by excluding people'. It is argued, therefore, that what is required is not a redistribution of income, but a promotion of the means to ensure that individuals are included in the labour market and within the wider community. In short, people who are socially excluded need a 'hand-up' not a 'hand-out'. It follows that if, despite the state's efforts, people remain stubbornly unemployed or uneducated, then this is their own fault and reflects their own personal inadequacies and/or failure to take the 'new opportunities' they have been offered. 'In this', argues one critic, 'they represent a return to Victorian liberalism' (German 1999: 11). Another critic, Chantel Mouffe (2000), comments that the discourse of social exclusion abstracts the analysis of poverty, unemployment, and poor education from the wider structures of power in society, most notably in the economic and political spheres. In short, we should be careful not to conflate the alleviation of social exclusion with the creation of a more equal society.

Social class: Is it still relevant?

The emergence of social inclusion/exclusion as the key concept for discussions of social disadvantage is based on the supposed irrelevance of social class. Class, it is often argued, is an anachronistic concept that carries little value in understanding modern lifestyles and contemporary social structures. Or, if it is accepted that class still exists, then a common argument is that 'we are all middle class now'. In this view, the idea of class struggles is dismissed as outdated, as class barriers are no longer the obstacle they once were in preventing working-class people from moving up the social hierarchy. There are different ways of formulating this idea, such as the 'two-thirds–one-third' society, in which the majority is comfortably off, while a minority (sometimes referred to as the 'underclass') is excluded from the benefits and comforts of mainstream society.

A common concept of class that underpins assertions of its declining significance is based on an association of class with mass industrial economy that sustained and gave meaning to distinct class-based cultures. The fact that, in the UK at least, we live in what some people refer to as a post-industrial, postmodernist consumer society means that the old class-based divisions and cultures have died out. Much sociological commentary has been devoted to confirming this trend, and to the nature of new identities created in the post-industrial/capitalist/modernist society, prompting Bradley and Hebson to lament the 'sequestration of class' from the sociological mainstream. They note how academic fashion has shifted interests 'from structure to culture, from production to consumption, from history to identity' (1999: 178). In other words, relations of power and the social reproduction of privilege have been displaced within the academy, as postmodern preoccupations with identity, style and consumption have emerged.

Yet, despite the attempts of politicians, academics and other privileged people (classes) to promote the 'end of class' thesis, recent surveys show that *increasing* numbers of people believe in the significance of class in shaping life-chances and the nature of society. From 1983 to 1991 the *British Social Attitudes* survey included a self-assignment question on social class. Reid (1998: 32) has summarised the results from these questions and found that around two-thirds of respondents classify themselves as upper working or working class, and about a quarter see themselves as middle class. The 1997/8 *British Social Attitudes* survey revealed that 87 per cent of people believe that the gap between those with high incomes and those with low incomes is too large, and 59 per cent think big business operates for the benefit of its owners at the expense of the workers (Heath and Park 1997: 10–11). Following on from this signficant level of class consciousness, the 2002/3 British Social Attitudes survey asserts that 'Britain remains a heavily unionised society . . . almost one-third of employees are union members: this makes trade unions the largest voluntary organisation in Britain' (Bryson and Gomez 2002: 43). Set against the class-based inequalities in wealth, these subjective perceptions of class identity and unequal class relations offer compelling evidence of the continuation of class divisions and exploitation within the UK. The work of Adonis and Pollard (1997) and Reid (1998) also presents ample evidence of how class differences differentially affect lifestyle and life-chances. Furthermore, beyond the borders of the UK, there is clear evidence that class division, inequality and exploitation is increasing on a global scale (for example, see Klein 2000: 196–257), as is the size of the industrial working class (see Harman 2002).

A key obstacle facing any class-based analysis is that, in the UK at least, social life may no longer be represented so readily in class terms, social relationships may not be articulated in class terms, and social issues may not be popularly understood in class terms. But herein lies the power of class exploitation. Lynch and Lodge's observations about the hidden nature of social class in contemporary Ireland are equally apt for the UK:

> Social class differences in Ireland have been denied, hidden behind the language of nationalism, community and, more recently, social partnership. Although class permeates the micropolitics of our lives, it hides behind the face of 'differentials' in trade union language; it is catalogued in the form of 'careerism' among the middle classes; it is sidelined into debates about work versus welfare in the 'poverty' debates, and it is depoliticised in educational debates as 'disadvantage' . . . The language of social class is not part of the vocabulary of either politics or education.
>
> (Lynch and Lodge 2002: 55)

Clearly, the issue of whether and how class manifests itself hinges on how class itself is defined and theorised. Perhaps the most common way in which class is represented is in terms of occupational categories. The most commonly cited method of social class classification is by the Registrar General, which is used in the census, and is based on the following scale: Social class I, Professional; II, Intermediate occupations; IIIN, Skilled non-manual; IIIM, Skilled manual; IV, Partly skilled occupations; V, Unskilled occupations. But there are many other variations on the same theme, such as the Hope-Goldthorpe Scale, the Hall-Jones Scale and those used for market research purposes (see Reid 1998). Apart from the implicitly ideological suggestion that social mobility and success in life can be measured by one's ability to climb into a higher category, what such scales have in common is that they are descriptive frameworks, and crude ones at that. They exclude large swathes of the population that cannot be categorised by occupation.

Crucially, left out of this framework is the really significant division in society between the relatively small number of massively wealthy members of the upper classes and the vast majority of people in society. The extent of class inequality in the UK is indicated by a governmental *Social Trends* report on the distribution of wealth in the late 1990s. It shows that the poorest 50 per cent of the population owns only 5–6 per cent of the total national wealth, whereas around 25 per cent of all wealth is owned by the richest 1 per cent (cited in Hill and Cole 2001: 138). The distinctions within the vast majority of people in society, be they in social class I or social class III, are likely to be insignificant compared with their differences with a senior manager of a multinational company or a top financial broker in the City, for example. In other words, descriptive sliding scales omit both the relational aspect of class inequality and, therefore, the significance of power, be it economic, political or cultural, to ensure the maintenance of the status quo. Thus, class as a description of differences existing within the majority of people (working or not working) focuses on fine gradations of differences and so empirically misses the significant divisions in society, and analytically ignores class relations as a form of power.

The relationship between social class and education

Extensive and authoritative research has been conducted on the class nature of the educational system in general, and in how it works to reproduce social inequalities (Bowles and Gintis 1976, Bourdieu and Passeron 1977, Willis 1977). More recent research and commentary confirms the significance of class in education, and of education in reproducing class privilege. As Lynch and Lodge observe, in an increasingly globalised geo-political order, credentialised knowledge plays a powerful role in determining the pattern of occupational opportunities, it 'is a key player in legitimating and ordering socio-cultural relations' (2002: 1). And, as Bourdieu's study of education in elite institutions shows, those who are able to benefit from such education are privileged over those who do not (Bourdieu 1996). Recently gathered data continues to highlight the significance of class on the educational experiences and fortunes of pupils. For example, according to the 2001 report on social trends, 'around two-thirds of young people with parents in non-manual occupations attained five or more GCSEs at grades A* to C in year 11 in 2000, compared with a third of those with parents in skilled and semi-skilled manual occupations' (cited in Hill and Cole 2001: 139). This is in tune with the findings of Gillborn and Mirza (2000), whose report for OFSTED showed children from the most advantaged backgrounds were more than three times as likely to attain five or more higher grade GCSEs than their peers at the other end of the class spectrum. More worryingly, they state that 'there is evidence that the inequality of attainment between social classes has grown since the late 1980s' (Gillborn and Mirza 2000: 18). The analysis of research findings provided by Gillborn and Mirza is particularly useful, as it is sensitive to the intersecting nature of class, 'race' and gender. The determining influence of class, however, can be discerned from the fact that pupils from non-manual backgrounds have significantly higher attainments, as a group, than their peers of the same ethnic origin but from manual households. Furthermore, Gillborn and Mirza graphically demonstrate that inequalities in attainment by social class are considerably larger than the disparity by 'race' and gender. As they comment, 'In contrast to the media attention, our data shows gender to be a less problematic issue than the significant disadvantage of 'race' and the even greater inequality of class' (Gillborn and Mirza 2000: 23).

While critics have blamed government policy for increasing the class-based inequalities (see Plewis 2000, Hill 2001), the relationship between class and educational achievement seems to be a problem across several countries in Europe (Ambler and Neathery 1999), prompting Lynch and Lodge to suggest that 'class inequality in education is endemic to the education process' (2002: 37). From their research on twelve single-sex and coeducational schools in Ireland over a two-year period, Lynch and Lodge summarise the complex but systematic ways that class division affects education, in what they refer to as a 'Class Act with four stages'.

The first stage begins with a set of politics and practices institutionalised in law and in economic and social policy which advantage the economically powerful and reinforce their dominance. Public policy places upper- and middle-class families at a considerable advantage in education as they have the economic resources to exercise choice in what is, in many respects, a free market education system.

The second stage is set when the parents 'choose' a school for their children. Low-income working-class households are seriously disadvantaged at this stage as they frequently lack the money, transport, time and, sometimes, even the knowledge, to discriminate between schools. It is middle-class families who exercise the freest choice.

The third stage starts with the grouping of students by so-called 'ability' in schools. It is suggested that social class influences the types and experiences of student groupings. Other research has also shown that white working-class pupils and black pupils from all class backgrounds are likely to be over-represented in lower ranked teaching groups where schools adopt selective grouping according to ability. This disproportionate grouping has been explained by differential teacher expectations, which tend to be lower for working-class and black pupils, thus institutionalising disadvantage. Middle-class students are least likely to be in low streams or bands (Plewis 2000: 87).

The fourth stage moves inside the classroom door, where the learning environment in the higher bands was found to be more conducive than in the lower bands where working-class students were disproportionately situated (Lynch and Lodge 2002: 38–54). Working-class pupils have tended historically to be disadvantaged in many school settings, be it in traditionally academic subjects or in traditionally non-academic subjects such as Physical Education.

Concluding comments

The emphasis on social inclusion as it is presented in government-dominated policy discourse magically conjures away the hierarchical social structure to leave individual schools with their individual challenges to make sure that all of their pupils are included. Gillborn and Mirza (2000) identify a number of common themes in inclusion strategies aimed at the school and LEA level. They include: strong leadership on equal opportunities and social justice; procedures for recording and acting on racist incidents; developing and communicating high expectations accompanied by a clear view that under-performance by any group is unacceptable; curricular and pastoral approaches to ensure their sensitivity and appropriateness. Of course, all these are important points, and it would be a cause for concern if schools weren't implementing these policies. They are, however, all concerned with internal processes of the school, thus ignoring the much more significant barriers to attainment such as class inequalities in society.

Such an approach does not seriously tackle the chronic under-resourcing of education that has disproportionately impacted on schools in deprived areas. Neither does it address the increasing levels of demoralisation among the teaching profession brought about by successive governments' policy. A survey by the *Guardian* published in January 2003 revealed that over a third of teachers plan to quit the profession within five years due to overwork, overcrowded classrooms and increasing bureaucracy (Woodward 2003). As this chapter has outlined, however, there are also deeper structural reasons for the underachievement of pupils from lower-class backgrounds. Hill contends that 'the policy of social inclusion is contradicted, and to an extent, interdicted, by the widening social and educational gaps consequent upon selection and hierarchy in schooling' (2001: 24). It follows then that a meaningful social inclusion strategy should include a considerable investment of resources so that all schools are adequately funded, and raised to the point where the same privileges enjoyed by upper-class pupils in the independent schools and the public schools are available to all. If we are to make sport and PE in schools genuinely inclusive, it is important to develop a critical understanding of the politics and limitations of social inclusion. Indeed, if the arguments set out in this chapter are persuasive, then it calls for a radical overhaul of the concept of social inclusion which itself is found to be exclusionary in fundamental ways.

With thanks to Mike Cole and Alan Tomlinson for their critical comments and suggestions.

Reflective questions

1 What can PE teachers do to reduce class inequality in PE?
2 To what extent is the PE curriculum influenced by traditional class values associated with certain areas of study?
3 Independent schools are able to structure their own PE curricula. To what extent does this autonomy allow for the perpetuation of traditional activities associated with differing socio-economic groupings?

References

Adonis, A. and Pollard, S. (1997) *A Class Act: The Myth of Britain's Classless Society*, London: Hamish Hamilton.

Ambler, J. S. and Neathery, J. (1999) 'Education Policy and Equality: Some Evidence from Europe' *Social Science Quarterly* 80, 3: 437–56.

Bennington, J. and Donnison, D. (1999) 'New Labour and Social Exclusion: The Search for a Third Way – or Just Gilding the Ghetto Again?' in H. Dean and R. Woods (eds), *Social Policy Review II*: 45–70.

Bourdieu, P. (1984) *Distinction: A Social Critique of the Judgement of Taste*, London: Routledge.

Bourdieu, P. (1996) *The State Nobility: Elite Schools in the Field of Power*, Oxford: Polity Press.

Bourdieu, P. and Passeron, J-C. (1977) *Reproduction in Education, Society and Culture*, London: Sage.

Bowles, S. and Gintis, H. (1976) *Schooling in Capitalist America*, New York: Basic Books.

Bradley, H. and Hebson, G. (1999) 'Breaking the Silence: The Need to Re-articulate "class"' *International Journal of Sociology and Social Policy* 19, 9: 178–203.

Bryson, A. and Gomez, R. (2002) 'Marching on Together? Recent Trends in Union Membership', in A. Park, J. Curtice, K. Thomson, L. Jarvis, and C. Bromley (eds), *British Social Attitudes: The 19th Report*, London: Sage.

Burchardt, T., Le Grand, J. and Piachaud, D. (2002) 'Introduction', in Hills, J., Le Grand, J. and Piachaud, D. (eds), *Understanding Social Exclusion*, Oxford: Oxford University Press.

Burden, T. (2000) 'Poverty', in J. Percy-Smith (ed.), *Policy Responses to Social Exclusion: Towards Inclusion?* Buckingham: Open University Press: 43–58.

Byrne, D. (1999) *Social Exclusion*, Buckingham: Open University Press.

Dean, H. and Woods, R. (1999) 'Introduction', in H. Dean and R. Woods (eds), *Social Policy Review II*: 7–27.

DfEE/QCA (Department for Education and Employment/Qualifications and Curriculum Authority) (1999) *Physical Education: The National Curriculum for England*, London: HMSO.

Dixon, J. G., McIntosh, P. C., Munrow, A. D. and Willetts, R. F. (1973) *Landmarks in the History of Physical Education*, London: Routledge and Kegan Paul.

Evans, J. (ed.) (1993) *Equality, Education and Physical Education*, London: Falmer Press.

Evans, J. and Davies, B. (1993) 'Equality, Equity and Physical Education', in J. Evans (ed), *Equality, Education and Physical Education*, London: Falmer Press: 11–27.

German, L. (1999) 'The Blair Project Cracks', *International Socialism: A Quarterly Journal of Socialist Theory* 82: 3–37.

Gillborn, D. and Mirza, H. S. (2000) *Educational Inequality: Mapping Race, Class and Gender: A Synthesis of Research Evidence*, London: OFSTED.

Hargreaves, J. A. (1994) *Sporting Females: Critical Issues in the History and Sociology of Women's Sports*, London: Routledge.

Hargreaves, J. E. (1986) *Sport, Power and Culture: A Social and Historical Analysis of Popular Sports in Britain*, Oxford: Polity Press.

Harman, C. (2002) 'The Workers of the World' *International Socialism Journal* 96: 3–45.

Heath, A. and Park, A. (1997) 'Thatcher's Children?' in R. Jowell, J. Curtice, A. Park, L. Brook, K. Thomson and C. Bryson (eds), *British Social Attitudes: The 14th Report*. Aldershot: Ashgate.

Holt, R. (1989) *Sport and the British: A Modern History*, Oxford: Oxford University Press.

Hill, D. (2001) 'Equality, Ideology and Education Policy', in D. Hill and M. Cole (eds), *Schooling and Equality: Facts, Concept and Policy*, London: Kogan Page: 7–34.

Hill, D. and Cole, M. (2001) 'Social Class', in D. Hill and M. Cole (eds), *Schooling and Equality: Facts, Concept and Policy*, London: Kogan Page: 137–59.

Hills, J., Le Grand, J. and Piachaud, D. (eds) (2002) *Understanding Social Exclusion*, Oxford: Oxford University Press.

Kirk, D. (1992) *Defining Physical Education: The Social Construction of a School Subject in Postwar Britain*, London: Falmer Press.

Klein, N. (2000) *No Logo*, London: Flamingo.

Lynch, K. and Lodge, A. (2002) *Equality and Power in Schools: Redistribution, Recognition and Representation*, London: Routledge Falmer.

Mangan, J. A. (1981) *Athleticism in the Victorian and Edwardian Public School*, Cambridge: Cambridge University Press.

Mouffe, C. (2000) *The Democratic Paradox*, London: Verso.

Penn, A. (1999) *Targeting Schools: Drill, Militarism and Imperialism*, London: Woburn Press.

Percy-Smith, J. (ed.) (2000) *Policy Responses to Social Exclusion: Towards Inclusion?* Buckingham: Open University Press.

Plewis, I. (2000) 'Educational Inequalities and Education Action Zones', in C. Pantazis and D. Gordon (eds), *Tackling Inequalities*, Bristol: Policy Press.

Reid, I. (1998) *Class in Britain*, Cambridge: Polity Press.

Shilling, C. (1993*) The Body and Social Theory*, London: Sage.

Social Exclusion Unit (1997) *Social Exclusion Unit: Purpose, Work Priorities and Working Methods*, London: HMSO.

Willis, P. (1977) *Learning to Labour: How Working Class Kids get Working Class Jobs*, Aldershot: Gower.

Woodward, W. (2003) 'A Third of Teachers Plan to Quit', *Guardian*, 7 January, 1.

In the classroom, those of a lesser ability could hide at the back. Not so in the gym. My inadequacies were on display as a spectator blood sport for all to jeer at. I saw absolutely no sense in somersaulting over a vaulting horse only to be saved from serious injury by an inch of matting made from a camel's pubic hair. The worst ordeal, however, was the cross country run. This particularly sadistic ritual was reserved without fail for days when you could see your own breath inside the classroom, let alone outside. They reasoned that you would perform better if there was a serious chance you could freeze to death if you spent too long on the spot. Appeals to my parents for a day off were usually met by tales of how, in their day, they had walked 40 miles to school every morning in bare feet.

S. Chadbourne (2002) 'Why I Hated School PE',
PE and Sport Today 8: 56.

11 Accreditation in Physical Education

Meeting the needs and interests of pupils in key stage 4

Gary Stidder and James Wallis

Introduction

> We are seeking to underpin the training and support for young people aged 14–19 to develop their leadership skills both in sport and their local communities. They will act as role models for younger children and perhaps prepare themselves for careers in sport.
>
> (Hoey 2001: 22)

These comments by the former UK minister for sport outlined the government challenge for teachers of PE and sport in secondary schools. Many of the initiatives that have been developed at key stage 4 are reflective of the dramatic increase in the number of pupils currently taking examination and leadership qualifications in PE. This chapter discusses the opportunities for teachers in guiding all pupils towards nationally accredited courses in PE and considers the implications of this type of approach to learning and teaching. Moreover, the chapter asks some critical questions concerning the revised National Curriculum for Physical Education (NCPE 2000) in England (DfEE/QCA 1999) and whether accredited courses in PE can encompass a more inclusive approach for pupils in key stage 4 (ages 14–16) compared with more conventional types of provision.

Externally accredited courses in PE such as examinations, national governing body awards and leadership qualifications, have continued to gain support amongst teachers during the past decade, reflecting the evolving nature of the subject and the government's attention to raising academic standards. Current trends in PE curriculum development at key stage 4 has meant that non-examination or 'core' programmes of physical activity are competing for timetable space with other forms of PE in the 14–16 age range, such as examination courses and other related award schemes. To date there has been a paucity of research evidence to suggest that a move towards these alternative programmes of PE would be in the best interests of all pupils and the question of whether they have greater potential in meeting the government's aims for social inclusion remains unanswered. There is, however, recognition that the continued growth of accredited PE courses is an important issue for teachers and in this respect the Qualifications and Curriculum Authority (QCA) have stated:

> Qualifications in PE attract many young people and are growing in popularity. There is a need to ensure that these qualifications continue to meet the needs of young people as the national infrastructure for PE and school sport is put into place.
>
> (QCA 2002: 6)

Personal reflections

During the past thirty years our own experiences of PE as pupils, trainees and teachers have become progressively influenced by the introduction of accredited forms of learning and teaching during key stage 4. As pupils neither of us had the opportunity to engage in any accredited forms of PE, and we tended to participate in optional recreational activities throughout our secondary and post-16 schooling. As trainees our teaching experiences of examination courses and other related awards were limited and only began to develop once we were established in our institutions during the 1990s. In many ways this challenged our professional development and informed our own critical thinking. This has led us to re-examine the ways in which pupils could best develop their cognitive and physical abilities within the context of PE and sport during the latter stages of their compulsory education in the context of accredited programmes. Like other chapters in this book, our own experiences of PE have provided our impetus and are a result of critical self-reflection on contemporary practices in the subject. Consequently, our experiences as teacher educators in higher education have led us to explore possible curriculum developments within key stage 4 and a framework within which all pupils can enhance their learning.

Background

Traditionally, PE departments in British secondary schools offered a range of options to pupils aged 14–16 years that focused upon non-accredited forms of participation. This provided pupils with the opportunity to escape from the confines of the classroom, relax without the academic pressures of other examination courses, participate in different forms of physical activity and socialise with each other in a more informal setting. These types of PE, however, may have done little to increase the status or profile of the subject within secondary schools or enabled pupils to achieve certified evidence for their achievements during their senior years of schooling (Stidder 2001a, 2001b). This has raised the issue as to whether accredited forms of PE should replace traditional non-examination 'core' PE programmes and become an entitlement to all pupils in secondary schools (Dickenson 1989, 1997).

Since the introduction of the General Certificate of Secondary Education (GCSE) in PE in 1986 and the first GCSE PE examination in 1988 the number of entries has expanded rapidly. National UK statistics have shown that an increasing number of pupils are currently following GCSE examination courses in PE and their results are continuing to improve (OFSTED 1999, 2000). Similarly, courses such as National Governing Body Awards (NGBA) and sports leadership qualifications have grown in popularity amongst pupils aged 14–16. For example, the increasing number of schools showing interest in accredited PE courses has resulted in many secondary schools re-designing their PE curricula at key stage 4 (OFSTED 1998) and the number of pupils achieving alternative awards in PE, compared with examination courses, at the end of key stage 4 has increased significantly (OFSTED 2001).

Accreditation in PE

The unprecedented growth of accredited awards in PE and the increasing number of candidates engaged in such courses has partly been a response to professional accountability, which has continued to have an impact on the teaching profession in general. Much of the drive and impetus, however, has come from PE teachers who have expressed dissatisfaction with their marginal status in schools and the lack of promotional opportunities within their subject (Carroll 1998). Furthermore, increased opportunities in vocational courses and sports-related occupations have also contributed to the expansion of accredited PE courses in secondary schools (OFSTED 1995) and provided further justification for their place within the secondary school curriculum.

The number of schools moving away from 'core' programmes of PE can have a very beneficial effect on curriculum design and has the potential to improve pupil achievements in an increasing number of schools. For example, UK inspection evidence (OFSTED 1995, 2000, 2001) suggests that the best work observed in key stage 4 PE is often seen in examination classes, and that the teaching of examination groups tends to be better than in the 'option' classes traditionally offered to pupils. In this respect, non-accredited courses rarely have fully planned outcomes and standards are often poor compared with examination classes. Furthermore, pupils' achievements are highest when they are following an accredited course and the links between informal and formal assessment in examination lessons is stronger than in core PE lessons, where the assessment of non-examination pupils is often neglected (OFSTED 2001).

The shift towards examination courses and alternative PE qualifications has enabled many teachers to address issues related to inclusion and provide a PE curriculum based upon pupils' individual ability and particular needs. These types of arrangements have provided greater motivation for pupils and a potential blueprint for future developments and innovation in PE at key stage 4 (Stidder 2001a, 2001b). As Dickenson (1997: 144) has commented, 'it is becoming increasingly likely that all study [in PE] at key stage 4 will lead to accreditation'.

National accredited courses have been revised to take into account the statutory requirements for PE within the NCPE in England (DfEE/QCA 1999). Teachers have a legal obligation to report on the progress of pupils in key stage 4 but there are no mandatory requirements to assess pupils according to the NCPE (2000) criteria or guidance concerning the expected attainment for the vast majority of pupils at the end of their compulsory schooling. The document states, 'At key stage four, national qualifications are one means of assessing attainment in Physical Education' (DfEE/QCA 1999: 42).

The flexibility within the revised NCPE has, therefore, encouraged teachers to think critically and reflectively about the best forms of provision for their pupils. Findings from previous studies (Stidder 2001a, 2001b) and the professional autonomy within the revised NCPE (2000) suggests that it might be a logical step for PE teachers to adopt 'Assessment strategies used for national qualifications as another means of assessing at this key stage' (PEA UK 2000: 6).

Core PE – the traditional approach

The increasing popularity of accredited courses in PE and subsequent myriad of opportunities afforded to 14–16 year olds may have done little to placate the PE purists. Authors and researchers are consistent in their views on the promotion of the vital humanistic, social, moral and physical values of PE (Van Dalen and Bennett 1971, Almond 1997, Capel 1997, Theodoulides and Armour 2001). A major point of contention when addressing accreditation at key stage 4 may be the extent to which the essential values of PE, that is educating the body and developing one's physicality, are undermined by the requirement of assessing or validating and the need to evidence pupils' knowledge or expertise. Sceptics of further accreditation in the critical 14–16 age group may also point towards the volume of testing that already exists at this pivotal time, not to mention the prospect of recurrent external exams brought about by Curriculum 2000. Far from adding to this burden upon young performers, it can be argued that, in the current examination climate, there is an increased need for the traditional therapeutic value of PE with a strong emphasis on personal and social development. Pro-accreditation voices may direct attention towards the need to raise the profile of PE in certain quarters and to combat its marginal status by following the same direction as other core subjects in providing examination courses for all students.

We recognise that there are some compelling arguments for retaining non-accredited core PE programmes during which pupils receive a worthwhile experience. We also accept that a widespread move towards accredited PE courses at the expense of traditional 'core' programmes could be considered as short-sighted and may be detrimental to the subject, rather than being seen as having its own value in the curriculum. Equally, the 'academicisation' of PE can promote the assumption that physical movement is only worthwhile if it can be understood, analysed and responded to cognitively through a test or exam and, therefore, physical knowledge is not valuable, as it reinforces the notion that factual knowledge is the primary form of knowledge. Hence, other types of knowledge such as physical knowledge become marginalised.

This section will not, therefore, be 'selling' the concept of accredited awards as the solution to raising the marginal status of PE. It is recognised that the distinctive and unique nature of PE should not be jeopardised in favour of further certification. Discussion will, however, direct practitioners towards a range of accredited awards which may uphold the humanistic values of PE whilst also providing opportunities for all pupils to experience the benefits associated with achieving externally accredited awards. Examples of practice within specialist sport colleges are provided which may help others in re-examining current curriculum arrangements within their own institutions. Reference will also be made to the government's vision for a 14–19 curriculum and the need for PE departments to provide a coherent framework through which pupils can progress. Finally, we present our own research associated with partnership training that highlights current practice in schools in the south-east of England.

The growth of examination courses in PE – a rationale

The success of GCSE PE has been acknowledged and recognised as a key innovation in the development of contemporary PE (Carroll 1990) and has made a significant contribution to the learning process and understanding of pupils (Walters 1991). Likewise, the rapid growth of examination courses in PE has reflected the development of 'increasing subject maturity, occupational professionalism and enhanced subject status' (Nutt and Clarke 2002: 156). For example, there has been a significant increase in the number of pupils entered for GCSE PE examination courses in secondary schools, and this now accounts for 17.5 per cent of all pupils taking a GCSE examination (Hodgson 2001).

Provisional data from the Joint Council for General Qualifications (JCGQ) (2000) showed that 117,294 candidates were entered for a GCSE PE course in June 2000, representing a rise of nearly 100,000 candidates compared with 1988, and more pupils are entered for GCSE PE courses in secondary schools than in Business Studies, Drama, Information Technology and Music. Furthermore, OFSTED (2000) reported that 52 per cent of pupils achieved a grade A*–C at the GCSE PE examination, just below the national average for all subjects and higher than Design and Technology, Mathematics and Humanities (JCGQ 2000).

Advocates for examination courses in PE have argued that PE teachers have a professional responsibility to address both the content and form of PE for pupils entering the final two years of compulsory schooling, and that the development of examination courses in PE could have a profound effect on the future of PE in secondary schools (Alderson 1988, Casbon 1988, Aylett 1990). Furthermore, Carroll (1998) observed that specialised courses in games and short courses in PE and games have been particularly suited to schools where time and facilities were restricted and that these types of courses could have the potential to enable other schools to do the same.

New courses such as the GCSE Short Course and Certificate of Achievement (COA) have also become increasingly popular within schools. OFSTED (1998) suggested that these types of arrangements may provide better structure for the large majority of pupils who have a limited amount of timetabled curriculum PE each week and that a qualification which provides a limited range of activities in a shorter period of time could prove to be a highly motivating factor for pupils.

Much of the impetus for these developments has arisen as many pupils find the theoretical aspects of GCSE PE particularly challenging. UK inspection evidence has shown that there was a wide gap between achievements in the theoretical and the practical aspects of GCSE PE, as many pupils had poor literacy skills (OFSTED 2000). Similarly, the standards of attainment and distribution of higher grades in GCSE courses have continued to plateau over the last two years despite the increasing numbers of candidates achieving the award (OFSTED 2002). Consequently, over a third of all maintained secondary schools have introduced a certificate of achievement for low attaining pupils in key stage 4.

The rise of alternative accredited awards

In this respect, some have argued that PE is becoming too academic and that examination courses such as the GCSE are not suitable for every pupil. Fisher (1997), for example, has extolled the virtues of a vocational programme of activities for less able pupils in key stage 4 and has shown how this can be a very positive experience for pupils in one particular school. Others (for example Scott 1997) have proposed a National

Curriculum key stage 4 certificate for those pupils who achieve the required National Curriculum level but who do not take a GCSE examination.

In 1994 the Central Council for Physical Recreation (CCPR) launched the Junior Sports Leader Award (JSLA) in response to teachers who called for a nationally recognised leaders' award for pupils under the age of 16. Following the success of the JSLA older pupils were able to progress to the Community Sports Leader Award (CSLA), the Higher Sports Leader Award (HSLA), and General and National Vocational Qualifications (GNVQ).

One of the significant advantages of the JSLA has been its assistance in delivering aspects of the NCPE (2000). This has enabled teachers to address the knowledge, skills and understanding required in the programmes of study and involve pupils in the processes of 'acquiring and developing skills', 'selecting and applying skills, tactics and compositional ideas', 'evaluating and improving performance' and 'knowledge and understanding of fitness and health' (DfEE/QCA 1999).

This has the potential to be integrated into key stage 4 PE teaching without any added time required and causes minimal disruption to normal PE lessons. It can also be an alternative for, or complementary to, GCSE PE courses and may be more appropriate for pupils who find theoretical aspects of examination PE more difficult. In this respect, OFSTED (2000) has indicated that accredited courses in PE can increase the participation and enthusiasm of pupils aged 14–16.

> The Junior Sports Leadership Award provides the opportunity for pupils to become more responsible for their own learning. National Governing Body Awards are also providing a more clearly structured PE programme in Key Stage 4. The accredited outcomes to such courses are having a positive impact on the motivation and engagement of pupils.
>
> (OFSTED 2000: 2)

In addition, many national governing bodies (NGBs) such as the Amateur Swimming Association (ASA) and the English Table Tennis Association (ETTA) provide a range of young leadership awards developed as 'bolt-on' extras to the CSLA. Pupils are able to apply leadership skills to specific activities that qualify them to assist in the delivery of sports-specific sessions. This has helped to prepare pupils for roles within sports clubs as paid or voluntary leaders, coaches and officials, and has also prepared pupils for further intermediate and advanced awards (*The Leader* 2001: 5).

Tulley (1990) remarked that alternative accredited awards, such as the CSLA, have the capacity to develop not only sporting skills, but also management, leadership, academic and performance skills. In this respect, the introduction of the JSLA into key stage 4 and the CSLA at post-16 has become a real strength within PE departments in England (OFSTED 2001). Moreover, case study research (Reilly 2002) has shown the potential benefits and advantages that the JSLA course can have on disaffected pupils. In this context, this type of course can help schools to retain pupils at risk of exclusion through improving concentration, developing key skills, controlling impulsive behaviour and building trust with peers and teachers, and thus raising self-esteem and confidence (Reilly 2002).

Future directions and implications of PE at key stage 4

If accredited courses in PE are to be further embedded within key stage 4 PE programmes of study for all pupils in secondary schools, it is important to consider the implications for PE teachers. For example, can the PE profession continue to rely upon the goodwill of committed PE departments and realistically expect teachers to provide extension and enrichment to the formal PE curriculum through extra-curricular sports and activities? Carroll has warned that in these circumstances there is a real danger of PE teachers having too much responsibility, which could do more harm than good.

> It remains to be seen whether the PE teachers can retain a footing in the three camps, recreation, academic examinations and vocational, or, whether they will trip up trying to meet too many demands.
> (Carroll 1998: 350)

Likewise, Nutt and Clarke have stressed that the impact of examination courses in PE on teachers' professionalism and quest for subject status could be detrimental in developing an equitable PE experience for all young people.

> (PE) teachers engaged in the development and teaching of examination courses must begin to reconcile the tensions that will inevitably emerge between the multiplicity of role definition and identity they are currently expected to fulfil.
> (Nutt and Clarke 2002: 162)

Nonetheless, there is no doubting that the status of PE needs to be further increased, along with staffing, pay incentives and other benefits that might accrue. We believe that accreditation may help to address some of the status problems that PE endures and that some accreditation is necessary for pupils who exhibit a keen interest in PE and sport and for those who want to follow a career in the sport, leisure or PE industry. The validation of pupils' physical experience through this process is one way of making these experiences worthwhile.

Whilst claims that accreditation has a profound effect on the interest, motivation and value pupils place upon PE may be largely unsubstantiated, the concept does possess a degree of intuitive appeal. Previous research (Scott 1997, Stidder 2001a, 2001b) has shown a number of positive benefits resulting from the introduction of examination courses in PE. These include benefits to the school, community, department and pupils as well as pedagogical practice. For example, the prospect of accredited awards may raise the expectations of pupils in core lessons to be taught rather than merely supervised. Also, a direct influence upon their expectation is that they will receive formal assessment on their progress at the end of a block of work and that their efforts are being monitored. Pupils may yield personal and social esteem from their achievements whilst investigating alternative pathways for progression and developing their Records of Achievements (ROA) and personal resumes.

Examination courses in PE, in particular, often have clearer criteria for assessment (OFSTED 2002). This can also help to provide formal grades that can be cross-referenced with other subjects and, therefore, contribute to the overall academic profile of a pupil. There are systematic assessment procedures that are consistent amongst staff and the reporting of pupil achievement is, therefore, more relevant and informative. Consequently, strategies and target-setting for pupils' learning can be clearly defined based on achievements and used to determine predicted outcomes of achievement. Pupil performances can be quantified and more substantial data can be provided, demarcated and moderated against the actual grades achieved. Moreover, there is potentially greater quality of feedback to parents and an increase in the number of parents seen during formal academic reviews.

Aside from the potential elevation of the status and kudos of the subject in the eyes of significant others, in particular peers in the teaching profession, the likelihood of increasing pupil numbers may become appealing in terms of finance, staffing and time allocation for PE. Retaining PE teachers in the department for their full timetable allocation may be desirable, in which case increasing the number of roles and responsibilities seems a logical way forward.

Providing accredited awards in PE also has potential value as a marketing tool for influencing the size and nature of intake to a school, and possible enhancement of application for Sportsmark, Sportsmark Gold or Sports College status. Furthermore, examination courses in PE can make a significant contribution to a school's overall examination per centages, which, in a system that has come to rely heavily on league tables, could prove to be a highly commercial product. In this context, PE, coupled with good sporting facilities, a very supportive head teacher and enthusiastic PE staff, can be very influential on parental choice and can, therefore, have a very positive impact on the recruitment of pupils.

Research has also shown that pupils who choose to follow PE at examination level as an option in key stage 4 can expect to receive at least three hours of PE a week in secondary schools. For example, QCA (2002) has shown that the average time allocation for 'core' PE in key stage 4 varies between one and two hours a week but pupils who decide to take GCSE PE receive an additional two lessons. In comparison, pupils who follow 'core' activity programmes may have as little as eighty minutes or 5 per cent of their curriculum time available for PE in a week (Harris 1994, Fairclough and Stratton 1997). The introduction of accredited courses, in this respect, has the potential to ensure that every pupil exceeds the government recommendation of two hours of PE a week (DfEE/QCA 1999: 6) and may, therefore, provide further justification for the inclusion of accredited courses.

It should be acknowledged, however, that the development of intrinsic motives for participation is far more desirable and effective when encouraging participation and retention in physical activity. Participating or competing for the enjoyment of the event, the kinaesthetic feel or the total personal immersion in the activity should not be undermined by the quest for extrinsic and tangible rewards (DeCharms 1968). Theory seems to suggest, therefore, that promulgation of the traditional philosophies of PE are invaluable and at first glance it may be apparent that any form of accreditation may contradict these values. Appreciation of Deci and Ryan's (1985) Cognitive Evaluation Theory may prove decisive in this instance. This theory maintains the importance of autonomy or choice in decision-making. The performer must feel self-determining and not externally controlled if motivation is to be maintained. Consequently it would appear that involving pupils in the decision-making process (that is, whether they strive for accreditation) and its precise nature would foster many benefits. On the basis of this evidence the concept of accreditation being appropriate and productive for all may be inaccurate, as may the provision of a single or limited number of avenues for a particular cohort. The following review is intended as an introduction to the diversity of accredited awards from which an inclusive framework can be formulated, serving the needs and interests of a range of 14- to 16-year-old pupils.

GSCE – Alternative Pathways 14–16

There has, then, been significant growth in formal examinations in PE. Following the inception of the full course GCSE in 1986 there has been a proliferation of subsidiary courses offered by the leading exam boards Assessment and Qualifications Alliance (AQA), Edexcel and Oxford, Cambridge and RSA Examinations (OCR). The first example of diversification came soon after, when the full-course GCSE was also offered as a games-only syllabus catering for pupils with a particular preference and level of attainment in this component of the NCPE. Schools could also select which specification to follow according to the parameters of time and facilities in which they operate. Subsequent alternatives have since been introduced providing a full range of pathways through which pupils entering key stage 4 can gain accreditation for their work. Under inspection these pathways all offer a degree of compatibility with key stage 4 and, therefore, departments are provided with the opportunity of following some specifications in core PE time and the possibility of co-teaching of qualifications. Tables 11.1–11.3 display the increase in pupil entries to PE in alternative pathways at 14–16:

• Short Course GCSE (SC) (Table 11.1)
• Short Course Games GCSE (SCG) (Table 11.2)
• Certificate of Achievement (CoA) (Table 11.3)

Planned for introduction in September 2002, GCSEs in vocational subjects (formerly VGCSE) are intended to replace the existing Part One

Table 11.1 Number of candidates taking the Short Course GCSE (2000–01)

	2000	*2001*
AQA (NEAB/SEG)[a]	137/344	456/434
Edexcel	1,504	1,783
OCR	–	–

Note
a Northern Examinations and Assessment Board (NEAB) and Southern Examining Group (SEG) were amalgamated into AQA. NEAB and SEG published separate figures for Short Course PE in 2000 and 2001.

Table 11.2 Number of candidates taking the Short Course Games GCSE (2000–01)

	2000	*2001*
AQA (NEAB/SEG)	2,289	2,705
Edexcel	2,283	2,949
OCR	1,114	1,320

Table 11.3 Number of candidates taking the Certificate of Achievement (2000–01)

	2000	*2001*
AQA (NEAB/SEG)	1,742	2,784
Edexcel	–	–
OCR	2,011	1,959

GNVQ and this constitutes the next stage in the development of vocational education. Providing an alternative to the traditionally 'academic' GCSE routes, Edexcel (2001) has cited its aims as:

- widening participation in vocational learning
- clarifying the equivalence between GNVQ and GCSE
- raising levels of attainment
- increasing progression routes to post-16 education and training.

Pupils who have an interest in vocational qualifications, prefer on-going continuous assessment to examinations, and are encouraged by working independently would be better suited to this format of assessment. The value of offering alternatives to traditional qualifications at key stage 4 is also of paramount importance when considering the current UK Government's framework for a 14–19 curriculum. This is an issue that will be considered later in this chapter.

British Sports Trust (BST) Leader Awards

Since their inception in 1981 Sports Leader Awards (SLAs) have gathered momentum to the extent that over 50,000 candidates successfully completed one of the four awards in 2001–2002. Their appeal to PE departments derives from the promotion of five core values which displays compatibility with key objectives of core PE at key stage 4 and beyond. The five core values are *personal development and reaching their true potential, a stepping stone for employment, developing leadership, volunteering in communities and reducing youth crime*. In their report on specialist schools, OFSTED (2001) cites that providing access to accredited awards such as the Junior Sports Leader Award (JSLA) has been shown to increase participation across key stage 4. Similarly, some schools have used the JSLA during curriculum time for less enthusiastic, low-attaining and disaffected pupils in order to develop inter-personal and leadership skills (OFSTED 2001). General trends reported by OFSTED (2000) recognised the increase in the provision of awards such as the SLAs and their importance for raising participation and esteem of pupils. Particular reference was given to disaffection shown by girls towards PE and the proactive role that JSLA can have.

The SLAs are progressive over three tiers, building from the JSLA up to the Higher Sports Leader Award (HSLA), all working toward the five core values:

- JSLA   Designed as the starting point for pupils aged 14 and over, containing generic leadership development as well as supporting the personal and social development of the candidate.

- Community Sports Leader Award (CSLA)   For pupils of 16 and over; provides candidates with the opportunity to lead, organise and take sole responsibility for groups of performers.
- Higher Sports Leader Award (HSLA)   Formerly known as the Hanson Award the HSLA was rewritten in 2000. Candidates must be 18 years of age on completion. The course is recognised nationally as an excellent introduction for employment in the leisure, coaching and management industry. Centres have the opportunity to take a module in NGB awards whereby candidates may achieve an additional form of accreditation. Higher education institutions also recognise the value of the award, as a display of valuable skills and experience when enrolling on Initial Teacher Training (ITT) courses.
- Basic Expedition Leader Award (BELA)   A more specialised and progressive course for candidates aged 18 and over wishing to gain a foundation in the leading of outdoor pursuits and outdoor and adventurous activities, which are known to be the least taught National Curriculum activity areas in schools and the activity areas trainee teachers have least experience of whilst on school-based placements (Clay 1999, Stidder and Hayes 2002).

Sports Leader Awards – The success story

Recognition of the value of accreditation and in particular the SLAs can be evidenced by the growth of support from institutions and candidates (Tables 11.4 and 11.5). The evidence presented reiterates the trends observed by OFSTED (2001) that more and more institutions are seeing alternatives to the standard core PE as a functional means of elevating participation in PE at key stage 4 and beyond. Further support can be

Table 11.4 Number of candidates taking SLAs (2000–02)

SLA	2000–01	2001–02
JSLA	19,949	25,573
CSLA	24,989	27,253
HSLA	1,856	1,847
BELA	2,735	2,549

Table 11.5 Number of institutions accrediting SLAs (1997–2002)

SLA	1997–98	1998–99	1999–2000	2000–01	2001–02
JSLA	269	421	581	638	819
CSLA	1,333	1,535	1,681	1,502	1,606
HSLA	131	138	162	132	135
BELA	248	251	279	224	230

drawn from the naturally progressive nature of the SLAs which dovetail with the government vision of a 14–19 curriculum, that is, progressing from JSLA at age 14 to the HSLA up to age 19. Whilst no quantitative data are available to assess their effects upon personal and social growth, participation rates and encouraging functional behaviour, a growing number of practitioners are speaking with one collective voice of the value of the SLA qualifications.

National governing body awards

Within the context of this chapter, the recurrent themes of promoting inclusive practice, raising esteem in physical activity and increasing the likelihood of retention in education post-16 are again pivotal when considering National Governing Body (NGB) accreditation. Flexibility within the NCPE at key stage 4 may allow the delivery of accredited awards parallel to the standard curriculum provision. An appealing feature of NGB frameworks includes the progressive nature of the qualifications, providing further incentive for pupils to continue with formal education. Similarly, the range of attributes that may be accredited, namely leadership, coaching, officiating or practical proficiency promotes yet another inclusive characteristic of NGB awards.

The examples provided below are taken from the activity areas within the breadth of study in the NCPE (2000), with the exception of dance activities, and are intended to promote consideration of best practice according to the parameters in which departments operate. NGBs have been selected at random, with the only criteria being that activities may be commonplace in many institutions.

Athletics activities (UK Athletics)

- The Working with Children in Athletics course allows candidates to achieve level one Assistant Coach status. This course is available after 14 years of age.
- The Assistant Official award is again open to pupils of 14.
- The Norwich Union Shine Awards are proficiency awards available to all pupils up to the age of 16. Candidates can attempt to achieve eight progressive coloured awards up to the prestigious gold award.

Net games (Badminton Association of England)

- The Badminton into Schools Initiative (BISI) includes proficiency awards divided into key stages 1, 2, 3 and 4.
- The Young Officials Scheme includes progressive awards from level one at year 10 up to level four in year 13.
- Leadership and coaching awards commence post-16.

Invasion games (English Basketball Association)

• Basketball apprentice refereeing and table official can be taken at key stage 4.
• Level one coaching can be taken in year 11 and accredited at 16 years of age.

Striking and fielding games (English Cricket Board)

• Level one coaching can be taken during key stage 4 but candidates must work under supervision until 18 years of age.

Gymnastics activities (British Gymnastics)

• Assistant Club Coach can be taken at age 14 and accredited at 15. Progression on to the Club Coach award can be immediate but not awarded until 17 years of age.

Swimming activities and water safety (Amateur Swimming Association, Royal Life Saving Society)

• The Poolside Helper Award from year 10 onwards can be arranged through the ASA. An in-house accreditation also exists called the Youth Swimmer Award, which encompasses a range of leadership, organisational and performance criteria.
• The Bronze Medallion and Life Support level one are open to all pupils and organised externally through the Royal Life Saving Society (RLSS).

Outdoor and adventurous activities

• Opportunities for accreditation in outdoor and adventurous activities may be limited to proficiency due to issues relating to health and safety. For example, the English Ski Council operates a system of accreditation for alpine ski performance and for freestyle skiing but instructors' qualifications are restricted to pupils of a minimum age of 17. Likewise, the British Orienteering Federation offers a leader's certificate course for individuals over the age of 17 who wish to teach orienteering within the confines of a safe, controlled site such as school grounds.

Exemplar approaches to key stage 4 – Specialist sports colleges 'leading the way'

Another contributor to this book (Keech 2003) has shown how Specialist Sports Colleges have facilitated the involvement of pupils in leadership roles within their communities, and in primary schools, through the organisation of local sports festivals. In this respect the establishment of Specialist

Sports Colleges has also had a significant impact on the development of accredited courses for all pupils in PE, such as the JSLA. Pupils are able to spend part of this course working with primary feeder schools as part of the accreditation process, and with 250 sports colleges planned for 2005 (Beckwith 2002) this may indicate the future direction that PE will follow at key stage 4.

In response to the disaffection shown by some pupils in PE, many sports colleges now offer these types of accredited awards during core PE time. This approach has raised achievement levels in key stage 4 compared with the activity choices traditionally offered to pupils (OFSTED/YST 2000). Many more young people now have the opportunity to gain leadership qualifications and accredited awards, for example, as all pupils at these colleges must follow an accredited course in PE at key stage 4 suited to their individual needs (OFSTED/YST 2000). Some of the initiatives include the TOP link programme and Millennium Volunteers Programme (MVP) in which older pupils gain certification for organising sporting events for younger pupils and which provides a natural progression from the JSLA. An example of this was during the 2002 Manchester Commonwealth Games in which 3,000 young leaders organised mini-games festivals for up to 75,000 primary pupils as part of the Department for Education and Skills (DfES) 'Spirit of Friendship Festival' (Beckwith 2002). In addition, one of the nine key principles that the MVP initiative embraces is inclusiveness and, therefore, has the potential to encourage all young people to develop skills and interests through the medium of sport.

Moreover, the majority of Specialist Sports Colleges offer additional opportunities for pupils to obtain awards such as the Duke of Edinburgh Award and national sports governing body awards and have provided more appropriate experiences for pupils across a full range of educational needs (OFSTED 2001). Accredited courses and packages of alternative PE qualifications based on pupil ability and needs arguably give much greater motivation to pupils at key stage 4 and therefore 'should allow all pupils to gain the qualifications that are best suited to their ability' (OFSTED 2000b: 22). Below are two examples of how Specialist Sports Colleges involved in 'partnership' training have introduced a range of accredited course for pupils in key stage 4.

At the Hayesbrook Sports College in Kent, the PE department has developed the key stage 4 and post-16 PE programmes by moving towards wholesale accreditation for all pupils aged between 14–19. By 2003, every pupil in years 10 and 11 will achieve an accredited award in PE. These awards will range from traditional academic qualifications such as GCSE and A level, to coaching awards, leadership awards and basic skill development awards. This includes the JSLA and CSLA, as well as coaching and umpiring courses in conjunction with Active Sports and the Golf Foundation and in partnership with local sports development officers and the local borough council.

Its recent designation as a Specialist Sports College has also further enhanced teaching and learning and increased GCSE PE examination grades. In 2002, 75 per cent of pupils achieved a grade A–C, with a third of pupils achieving an A* or A grade. In this respect, Hayesbrook has also responded to the NCPE requirement for pupils to 'exchange and share information, both directly and through electronic media' (DfEE/QCA 1999: 38). The use of information and communications technology (ICT) in PE, particularly in examination work at key stage 4, has been an effective teaching aid that has enhanced pupils' learning and understanding.

In some schools, the use of ICT is not given sufficient consideration by most PE departments and very few PE teachers have the opportunity to apply ICT skills in a PE context (OFSTED 2000). The use of ICT within the GCSE programme at Hayesbrook is one example of how pupils have developed key skills in PE examination courses through the use of computer-based material. This has enabled the school to introduce other worldwide technologies, such as interactive white boards, computerised video analysis, heart rate monitoring equipment, digital cameras and video conferencing, and further develop an interactive 'classroom of the future'.

A similar picture is apparent at William Parker Sports College in East Sussex, where GCSE PE is regarded as a core subject, with the delivery of all components of the course to all pupils. Since September 2000 pupils have been divided into full course and short course candidates at least four months before the examination period. This division is made according to attendance, fulfilment of practical requirements and intended progression route. Estimation is that within this period 85 per cent of pupils have been entered for the full GCSE and 15 per cent have been entered onto the short course alternative. Whilst it is regarded as appealing at this particular institution that all pupils achieve tangible recognition for their efforts in PE it is also recognised that the needs and interests of all pupils may not be currently addressed. An approach, piloted in September 2002, saw the inception of fast tracking thirty pupils (eventually sixty per year group), who completed their GCSE in one year. This approach will provide one year for further accreditation in the form of AS level modules, vocational GCSE, CSLA or National Governing Body Awards. By 2004 the intention is to offer a flexible range of these alternative forms of accreditation during core PE with a choice of courses open to every pupil.

Whilst these examples of small-scale case studies show a commitment to accreditation, both institutions were keen to point towards the importance of the mode of delivery of course material. In each case the Director of Sport and the Head of Department were aware of the dangers of merely delivering a prescriptive syllabus and creating a 'production line' of qualifications with no adherence to the reinforcement of the essential qualities of PE.

These two institutions are also working models of Deci and Ryans' (1985) Cognitive Evaluation Theory in that students are provided with the autonomy to choose appropriate directions for themselves from a range of accredited opportunities. Both departments have recognised the importance of choice in the roles that students decide to take in their move towards accreditation. This policy is also in keeping with the requirements of the NCPE at key stage 4 where pupils are taught to 'make informed choices about what role they want to take in each activity' (DfEE/QCA 1999 :23). Of equal importance to accreditation is the quality of the teaching and learning process. As a result, a process of monitoring and moderation of delivery in lessons leading to certification is being piloted in 2003, in order to ensure that important values and essential qualities are upheld.

In summary, a number of challenges common to all specialist schools has been identified, one of which is 'to continue the drive to raise standards, tackle under-achievement and extend opportunities for all pupils, maintaining a sharp focus on inclusion' (OFSTED 2001: 48). There are increasing opportunities for sports colleges to respond to this particular challenge and address the design of the PE curriculum at key stage 4. Some of the examples that we have highlighted have great potential in raising pupils' achievements and may serve to inform other schools in this respect.

The qualifications framework and the emerging vision for 14–19: Extending opportunities, raising standards

Traditionally, pupils of English schools are divided at the age of 16 into those who choose to continue with their education and those who don't. The Department for Education and Skills (DfES) is clear about the consequences of poor retention in education:

> For young people the price of disengagement from learning now is often serious problems and persistent failure for the rest of their lives. Low motivation, truancy, behaviour problems and exclusion damage our communities and burden our economy.
>
> (DfES 2001: 1)

The DfES Green Paper *14–19: Extending Opportunities, Raising Standards* (2002) was the first of a series of steps made by the DfES in increasing the numbers of individuals who elect to continue their education and training past the compulsory school years. The vision promoted by the paper was to provide a coherent framework through which individuals could progress using the existing GCSE qualifications as an ongoing progress check at the midpoint of the phase rather than as the culmination of their education. Based upon consultation and extensive responses to this initial publication a second follow-up or next steps document was released in February 2003, *14–19: Opportunity and Excellence*, which builds upon the proposals set out in the initial Green Paper.

It is very evident that the current line of thought is in keeping with the European trend of grouped or collective qualifications, such as the French *baccalauréat* or German *Abitur*, where students are assessed and accredited on the basis of their overall portfolio at the end of the phase. In the overall context of this chapter and indeed the entire book, the DfES (2003a) presents a compelling rationale for the shift towards a collective qualification. Such systems are seen to share:

- common curriculum for all students in the lower secondary ages
- expectations that students will retain a broad range of subjects in the upper secondary ages
- vocational opportunities leading to HE or employment
- inclusive measures for disadvantaged and disaffected students.

In contrast the current UK system is considered to have:

> Firstly, a weak vocational offer. Second, a narrow academic track, narrow in who is on it and narrow in terms of what is studied. The result is a system marked by barriers to learning rather than support for learning.
>
> (DfES 2003b)

It is envisaged that the 14–19 framework will display three logical phases. At the beginning, 14 years of age in the majority of cases, individuals will be provided with a review whereby they will be assisted in identifying long-term goals, selection of study for the 14–16 period and an action plan to assist in the pursuit of goals. The second phase allows students to follow a progressive pathway, which is tailored to their own needs, aspirations and the goals that they have set. According to the Green Paper, 'the phase as a whole should give young people access to a range of general, mixed and vocational options with clear progression routes' (DfES 2002: 9). Further emphasis is placed on the element of choice or autonomy by the School Standards Minister, David Miliband, who agreed that 'To motivate the learner they need to share a sense of ownership of and commitment to the studies in which they are engaged' (ibid.: 4). A particular emphasis in relation to these comments is to enhance the vocational or specialist opportunities that can be pursued by students throughout the 14–19 phase, and the power that students can exert in both their subject content and mode of learning. The final stage would be the overall accreditation. Initial proposals following the 2002 Green Paper were to incorporate all existing accredited awards into a Matriculation Diploma. The diploma would be presented to pupils who continue their education after 16 years of age and would provide recognition of all of the achievements made in all forms of study and in wider contexts outside of the curriculum.

With the DfES aims for reform clearly stated earlier in this section, the presence of two tiers of national qualifications signalling the end of two distinct phases of education is not considered conducive to the new, desirable perspective of one continuous phase. For this reason arguably the most far-reaching reform since the Education Act 1944 is likely to signal the end for GCSE and A level qualifications, to be replaced by an overall graduation certificate, affectionately termed the 'English Bac' for the time being. Decisions regarding the rationale, structure, name and composition of the new qualifications, for projected inception in 2010, have been charged to a Working Group on 14–19 Reform, chaired by Mike Tomlinson, the former Chief Inspector of Schools. An interim report of the group is expected for the end of 2003, with a final report being published in the summer of 2005. At the time of writing the precise form of the award for the 14–19 phase was yet to be decided. It may be expected, however, that the increased emphasis on choice, diversity, vocational experiences and citizenship highlighted in this chapter will be valuable inclusions.

In the context of this chapter the development of a 14–19 curriculum further substantiates the need for diversity at key stage 4. Having alternative pathways available at the review stage will assist in ensuring that individuals are accessing the appropriate qualification and mode of study whether it is predominantly vocational or academic. The provision and piloting of GCSEs in vocational subjects can help bridge the gap that has historically existed between level two and level three courses. Allowing individuals the opportunity to embark upon Sports Leader Awards or National Governing Body qualifications of the nature previously discussed possesses a dual significance when considering the 14–19 curriculum, both of which may be considered to influence esteem, attainment and likely retention. Primarily the qualifications are nationally recognised and are progressive, often with basic levels from the age of 14 into advanced coaching and officiating in adulthood. Second, the recognition of such qualifications in the 'English Bac' adds credibility to the status of the awards and adds weight to the rationale for delivering within a PE curriculum.

HEI response – the new breed of PE teacher

Many new entrants to the PE profession have responded to these pedagogical developments and have accepted that the teaching of examination courses, in particular, now encompasses a significant part of their role and responsibility (Nutt and Clarke 2002). Equally, accredited courses have made a significant contribution to the contemporary PE teacher's repertoire through increased experiences gained during school-based placements and university-based professional training (Stidder and Hayes 2002). In keeping with curriculum developments at key stage 4 and the UK government plan for sport (DCMS 2001), our own data have shown that many schools are now offering these types of courses. Many PE trainees are also gaining pedagogical experience of teaching examination courses and leadership awards to pupils in key stage 4 and contributing to the implementation of the 'Step into Sport' leadership and volunteering project outlined by DCMS (2002).

Preliminary data was collected from a questionnaire survey of year 4 PE qualified teacher status (QTS) trainees at the University of Brighton, to which nineteen students responded. The questionnaire contained eight closed questions regarding experiences of delivery of sports leadership course and NGB awards during their school-based teaching placements. Trainees were asked to consider only their final fifteen-week placement from which they had recently returned. The main findings from the returns were as follows:

- fifteen out of nineteen schools taught sports leadership awards
- thirteen out of nineteen schools taught alternative qualifications including NGB and Duke of Edinburgh
- fourteen out of nineteen trainees were given the opportunity to observe these courses being taught
- ten out of nineteen trainees were given the opportunity to teach on one or more of the courses.

Whilst our findings indicate the presence of evolving expectations upon trainee teachers, we recognise the low number of participants in this small-scale research project and cannot at present make judgements of the national picture. Our data suggest that the repertoire of skills that many new entrants to the profession must now possess include the ability to deliver examination courses and other accredited awards in PE. These experiences are not only reflective of current practice in schools, but are also a requirement within the revised standards for qualified teacher status (DfES 2002). With regards to teaching examination courses, other surveys have shown how partnership training in schools has changed, with most trainees gaining observational and teaching experience in GCSE PE both in a practical and classroom setting. Experiences such as these can contribute to the professional development of trainees as they can develop pedagogical skills associated with classroom-based work, provide opportunities for reflective practice and can potentially increase their employability.

Summary and conclusion

This chapter has outlined the potential that accredited awards can have on pupils' learning in PE within the established 14–16 age range. Whilst we do not profess to have all the answers for an inclusive 14–16 PE curriculum, we do recognise the need for innovation and change from more conventional programmes of PE in schools. It is our contention that a range of accredited awards in PE can provide opportunities for all young people to engage in worthwhile lifetime activities whilst gaining relevant and appropriate qualifications that are applicable within the world of sport and leisure as well as within local communities. Equally, our suggestions are a response to the changing nature of teachers' work in schools and the evolution of the role of the contemporary PE professional. In addition, the likely inception of the 'English Bac' will afford the possible inclusion of all nationally recognised forms of accreditation, further enhancing the portfolio that pupils may present following the completion of this phase of their education. For this reason PE may be considered at the forefront of education in the vision for the 14–19 curriculum. The diverse range of accredited awards that can be introduced is ideally suited, maybe more so than many other subjects, to the intended nature of the collective graduation certificate.

Our purpose throughout this chapter has not been to advocate radical or immediate change to the key stage 4 PE curriculum through a wholesale move towards accredited courses. Rather, our purpose is to raise professional awareness and stimulate discussion regarding the future direction of PE. We hope that our suggestions will activate an agenda amongst teachers and trainees and contribute to the wider educational debates associated with PE and inclusion at key stage 4. This may help in considering alternative approaches to PE that address pupils' individual needs and interests whilst at the same time providing formal recognition of their efforts. Learning and teaching in PE must be the rationale behind curriculum change and it is possible that a choice of accredited awards could provide stimulus, incentive and motivation to all pupils across the ability spectrum. Externally accredited awards, such as those mentioned in this chapter, and the formal recognition of pupil achievement may have the benefits of raising pupil esteem, participation and retention of physical activity. Given that raising standards is a shared aspiration within the profession these factors may present themselves as potential mediators in the achievement of this goal.

Reflective questions

1   Can examination courses in PE increase the academic performance and achievement of all pupils in key stage 4?
2   Can leadership courses in PE address the requirements of the NCPE (2000) and meet the aims for social inclusion?
3   Are leadership courses in PE, as opposed to 'core' PE, better suited for meeting the needs and interests of a wider range of pupils?
4   Are vocational courses in PE more appropriate for particular pupils?
5   Is there still a place for 'core' PE programmes of physical activity during key stage 4?

6 Can accredited forms of PE be taught in such a way as to maintain the essential humanistic values of PE?

7 Is further assessment for accredited courses at the end of key stage 4 an unnecessary burden upon pupils and teachers?

8 What is your vision for an all-inclusive PE curriculum at key stage 4 and what might this look like in the year 2010?

References

Alderson, J. (1988) 'Examination Syllabuses and Curriculum Developments in PE', *The British Journal of Physical Education* 19, 6: 214–16.

Almond, L. (1997) 'The Context of Physical Education', in L. Almond (ed.), *Physical Education in Schools*, Second Edition, London: Kogan Page: 21–33.

Aylett, S. (1990) 'Is GCSE the Cross Roads for Physical Education?', *The British Journal of Physical Education* 21, 3: 333–7.

Beckwith, J. (2002) 'Message from our Chairman: Dynamic Partnerships are Transforming the Development of PE and School Sport', in Youth Sport Trust, *Building a Brighter Future for Young People Through Sport: Annual Review 2001/2002*, Loughborough: Youth Sport Trust: 3.

Capel, S. (1997) *Learning to Teach Physical Education in the Secondary School: A Companion to School Experience*, London: Routledge.

Carroll, R. (1990), 'Examinations and Assessment in Physical Education', in N. Armstrong, *New Directions in Physical Education*, Leeds: Human Kinetics.

Carroll, R. (1998) 'The Emergence and Growth of Examinations in Physical Education', in K. Green and K. Hardman (eds), *Physical Education: A Reader*, Aachen: Meyer and Meyer, 335–52.

Casbon, C. (1988) 'Examinations in PE – A Path to Curriculum Development', *The British Journal of Physical Education* 19, 6: 217–19.

Clay, G. (1999) 'Outdoor and Adventurous Activities: An OFSTED Survey', *The British Journal of Physical Education* 30, 2: 13–15.

DeCharms, R. (1968) *Personal Causations*, New York: Academic Press.

Deci, E. L. and Ryan, R. M. (1985) *Intrinsic Motivation and Self-Determination in Human Behaviour*, New York: Plenum.

DCMS (Department for Culture, Media and Sport) (2002) *'Step into Sport: Leadership and Volunteering'*, London: DCMS.

DfEE/QCA (Department for Education and Employment/Qualifications and Curriculum Authority) (1999) *Physical Education: The National Curriculum for England*, London: HMSO.

DfES (Department for Education and Skills) (2001) Online, available HTTP <http://www.dfes.gov.uk/14–19greenpaper> accessed 7 July 2002.

DfES (Department for Education and Skills) (2002), *14–19: Extending Opportunities, Raising Standards*, London: HMSO.

DfES (Department for Education and Skills) (2003a), *14–19: Opportunity and Excellence*, London: HMSO.

DfES (Department for Education and Skills) (2003b) Online, available HTTP <http://www.dfes.gov.uk/14–19/ourvision.html> accessed 14 February 2003.

Dickenson, B. (1989) 'Accreditation: A Different Dimension for Physical Education', in L. Almond (ed.), *The Place of Physical Education in Schools*, London: Kogan Page: 147–58.

Dickenson, B. (1997) 'Revisiting the Key Stage 4 Curriculum', in L. Almond (ed.), *Physical Education in Schools*, Second Edition, London: Kogan Page: 141–8.

Edexcel (2001) 'Leisure and Tourism Vocational GCSE PE', Edexcel.

Fairclough, S. and Stratton, G. (1997) 'Physical Education Curriculum and Extra-Curriculum Time: A Survey of Secondary Schools in the North-West of England', *The British Journal of Physical Education* 28, 3: 21–4.

Fisher, S. (1997) 'Vocational Curriculum Developments in Key stage 4 Physical Education', *The British Journal of Physical Education* 28, 2: 10–13.

Harris, J. (1994) 'Physical Education in The National Curriculum: Is There Enough Time To Be Effective?', *The British Journal of Physical Education* 25: 34–8.

Hodgson, B. (2001) 'GCSE Physical Education 2001 – All Change or All the Same!' *The British Journal of Physical Education* 27, 2: 30–2.

Hoey, K. (2001) 'The Prince Philip Lecture', *The British Journal of Teaching Physical Education* 32, 1: 20–3.

JCGQ (Joint Council for General Qualifications) (2000) *National Provisional GCSE Results (Full Course, Short Course, Certificate of Achievement)*, June 2000 (All UK Candidates), online, available HTTP: <http://www.aqa.co.uk> accessed 8 November 2002.

Keech, M. (2003) ' "Sport through Education?" Issues for Schools and Sports Development', in S. Hayes and G. Stidder (eds), *Equity and Inclusion in Physical Education and Sport*, London: Routledge.

Miliband, D. (2003) *14–19: Opportunity and Excellence*, speech to AOC/NAHT/SHA conference, 21 January, London.

Nutt, G. and Clarke, G. (2002) 'The Hidden Curriculum and the Changing Nature of Teachers' Work', in A. Laker (ed.), *The Sociology of Sport and Physical Education*, London: Falmer Routledge: 148–66.

OFSTED (Office for Standards in Education) (1995) *Physical Education: A Review of Inspection Findings 1993/1994*, London: HMSO.

OFSTED (Office for Standards in Education) (1998) *Secondary Education 1993–1997: A Review of Secondary Schools in England*, London: HMSO.

OFSTED (Office for Standards in Education) (1999a) *GCSE/GNVQ and GCSE A/AS Level and Advance GNVQ Examination Results 1998/99 England*, Statistical Bulletin.

OFSTED (Office for Standards in Education) (1999b) *The Annual Report of Her Majesty's Chief Inspector of Schools: Standards and Quality in Education 1998/1999*, London: HMSO.

OFSTED (Office for Standards in Education) (2000) *OFSTED Subject Reports 1999 – 2000 – Secondary Physical Education (PE)*, London: HMSO, online, available HTTP: <http://www.ofsted.gov.uk/public/index.htm> accessed 30 July 2002.

OFSTED (Office for Standards in Education) (2001) *Specialist Schools: An Evaluation of Progress, A Report from the Office of Her Majesty's Chief Inspector of Schools*, London: HMSO.

OFSTED (Office for Standards in Education) (2002), *OFSTED Conference: Planning and Assessment in Physical Education*, online, available HTTP: <http://www.ofsted.gov.uk/public/Docs02/subjectsconference> accessed 1 August 2002.

OFSTED.YST (Office for Standards in Education/Youth Sport Trust) (2000) *Sports Colleges: The First Two Years*, London: HMSO.

PEA UK (Physical Education Association UK) (2000) *Physical Education Assessment, Recording and Reporting at Key Stages 1 to 4: Guidance for Teachers*, PEA UK.

QCA (Qualifications and Curriculum Authority) (2002) 'PE in Schools Today', *The British Journal of Teaching Physical Education* 33, 4: 6–8.

Reilly, C. (2002), *Inclusion*, online, available <http://www.sportsteacher.co.uk/features/editorial/inclusion> accessed 5 March 2001.

Scott, T. (1997) 'Key Stage 4 GCSE in PE – One School's Approach', *The British Journal of Physical Education* 28, 2: 14–16.

Stidder, G. (2001a) 'Who's for Exams?' *The British Journal of Teaching Physical Education* 32, 3: 46–8.

Stidder, G. (2001b) 'Who's for Exams? (Part Two)', *The British Journal of Teaching Physical Education* 32, 4: 38–40.

Stidder, G. and Hayes, S. (2002) 'A Survey of Physical Education Trainees' Experiences on School Placements in the South-East of England 1997–2002, *The British Journal of Teaching Physical Education* 33, 2: 43–8.

The Leader (20) 'National Governing Bodies of Sport Need Young Leaders', *The Leader (The Magazine of the Sports Leader Awards)*, Spring, 11: 5.

Theodoulides, A. and Armour, K. M. (2001) 'Personal, Social and Moral Development Through Team Games: Some Critical Questions', *European Physical Education Review* 7, 1: 5–23.

Tulley, R. (1990) 'PE and Sport in the Community: Alternative Qualifications to GCSE and "A" Level PE', *The British Journal of Physical Education* 21, 2: 289.

Van Dalen, D. and Bennett, B. (1971) *World History of Physical Education*, New Jersey: Prentice Hall.

Walters, D. (1991) 'A Theoretical Analysis of GCSE Physical Education Practical Assessment Criteria', *The British Journal of Physical Education* 22, 2: 23–6.

Useful websites

Amateur Swimming Association www.britishswimming.org
Assessment and Qualifications Alliance www.aqa.org.uk
Badminton Association of England www.bafoe.co.uk
British Amateur Gymnastics Association www.baga.co.uk
British Canoe Union www.bcu.org.uk
British Schools Orienteering Association www.bsoa.org
British Sports Trust www.bst.org.uk
Department for Education and Skills www.dfs.gov.uk
Edexcel www.edexcel.org.uk
England Basketball www.englandbasketball.co.uk
English Cricket Board www.ecb.co.uk
English Ski Council www.englishski.org
Oxford, Cambridge and Royal Society of Arts Examinations www.ocr.org.uk
Royal Yachting Association www.rya.org.uk
Sport England www.sportengland.org
Sports Teacher www.sportsteacher.co.uk
UK Athletics www.ukathletics.net

Games became a nightmare: gone were the athletics and team sports and in came cross-country running and star jumps. She was the star jump teacher from hell: Star jumps for warm ups; star jumps for talking while she was talking; star jumps for refusing to do star jumps; and star jumps for forgetting your gym skirt and remembering your shorts instead. Star jumps, star jumps! No amount of complaining could stop her.

B. Mistry (2002) 'Why I Hated School PE',
PE and Sport Today 9: 56.

12 'Sport through education?'
Issues for schools and sports development

Marc Keech

Personal reflections

Applied policy analysis is often seen to be of little relevance to practitioners, whether they are teachers or sport development professionals. What counts, apparently, is whether or not the individual is able to do 'their job'. Agreed – but only in part! Many of those who work in Physical Education, physical activity or sport development often became involved through their enjoyment of sport and/or activity, but now fail to realise that they work within a highly politicised environment. Within ongoing debates about professional development, it is proposed that until practitioners develop a greater strategic awareness of the complex policy context within which they operate, they will not be fully able to realise why policy doesn't always work in practice and therefore lobby more effectively for the resources required to fulfil their responsibilities and do 'their job'. What follows is an overview of some of the current concerns for PE and school sport. It merely scratches the surface of an increasingly complex policy arena but will hopefully provoke further consideration of the position of Physical Education, physical activity and school sport in the contemporary political climate.

Introduction

Bearing in mind the more specific issues relating to inclusive Physical Education (PE) examined previously, this chapter reviews the recent developments in PE and sport policy in England with particular reference to PE and sport as elements of broader social policy concerns. The centrality of schools to the development of young people's sporting opportunities in the local community has meant that schools have begun to reflect, with varying degrees of success, on how to extend and link their provision with the support of, and to, local agencies. The chapter considers issues that schools must reflect upon if they are to demonstrate that they are socially inclusive in the provision of sporting opportunities as well as able to structure an inclusive curriculum that meets the needs of all their pupils. At the heart of recent changes has been the establishment of Specialist Sports Colleges (SSCs) and School Sport Co-ordinators (SSCos) and the initial success of these has also raised a series of problems which must be understood in developing future sporting opportunities for young people. Whilst school–community links and partnerships are the central mechanism for extending opportunities for young people, it is also clear that a more politically aware PE profession would benefit schools that attempt to extend participation for young people and local communities across the social spectrum.

PE and sport policy: one and the same?

Central government sport and PE policy in England under 'New' Labour is still characterised by the traditional dichotomy of increasing the number of medals and titles won at prestigious international sports events, whilst establishing a complex policy network through which to decrease the number of young people in a position of, or at risk from, social disadvantage (Houlihan and White 2002). In pursuing both of these concerns, Sport England, as the key agency for sport development nationally, has targeted young people and, as a consequence, placed a strong, strategic emphasis on school PE and sport. Continuing the trends of the previous government, 'New' Labour has continued to develop the prominence of PE and sport in schools, and also the development of links between schools and local communities. To support this, the government has reaffirmed its 'aspiration' (as opposed to 'commitment') to ensure that all young people aged 5–16 receive their weekly entitlement of two hours of high quality PE and sport in schools, and that the standards of PE and sport in schools will be raised. The mechanisms for this are an intensified focus on training and development for PE teachers, an increased number of coaches in schools (DCMS 2002a), an increased number of young people joining local sports clubs and 'a national infrastructure of Specialist Sports Colleges and School Sport Co-ordinators linked to every primary, special and secondary school in the country' (DCMS 2002b: 1). To augment this, in the four years leading up to 2006 the government has committed an extra £581 million to PE and school sport in England through the New Opportunities Fund for PE and Sport and £130 million through the Space for Sports and the Arts programmes.

Although there are pronounced differences between what constitutes PE and sport (Capel 2000) it is also clear that these historically discrete policy arenas have, in the minds of many politicians and much of the media, been integrated and, therefore, are perceived as synonymous. A crude distinction would be that school sport is the extended curriculum, as PE is more concerned with the education of the physical and the more that sport is prioritised the less educative the activity. So if the current thrust is on sport then the educational value of activities and opportunities has to be questioned. Whilst they are clearly not the same, PE and sport have become integrated into an increasingly significant but complex and 'over-crowded' (Houlihan 2000) policy network in which PE has become the initial focus of engaging young people in PE, physical activity and sport for socially inclusive concerns. As the Government declared in its most recent strategy for sport:

> Wherever possible, new investment in grass-roots facilities should be targeted on schools . . . to create modern sporting facilities for use by schools during the daytime, designed so that they can easily be opened up and made available to the wider community out of school hours. This takes a step further the government's commitment to place the school at the heart of community life.
>
> (DCMS 2000:12)

Increasingly, the government is encouraging those working in sport, along with those working in policy arenas such as health, to consider schools as 'hub sites' for partnership working and policy development and implementation. Figure 12.1 provides a diagrammatic representation of the complexity of joined up policy making which includes PE and school sport and locates the school at the centre of a number of policy initiatives.

The diagram demonstrates that policy is often difficult to understand and implement because of 'initiative overload'; that is, there are too many initiatives within which agents, in this example schools, have to play a role. Partnership working, however, is clearly a non-negotiable element in current public sector working and prioritisation must occur, based on local need. Health, especially of young people, will become a more promi-nent concern in the medium term, particularly with the government's desire to use PE and sport to foster healthier lifestyles. What is also clear from the diagram is that schools are key agents in social inclusion and commu-nity development policies. It is not necessary for those in PE and sport development to know the intricate details of these policies, but it is apparent that both professions must increase their awareness of the issues so that they are able to play a part in whichever direction local decisions take schools and then focus more incisively on demonstrating the contri-bution that PE and school sport can make in order to acquire improved funding to sustain and develop opportunities for young people.

Recent initiatives such as Specialist Sports Colleges, School Sport Co-ordinators and the New Opportunities Funds for PE and Sport may also reinforce the public perception of the similarities between PE and sport. Regardless, the school and its sport facilities are now the strategic focus of development be it in identifying and nurturing able youngsters in a

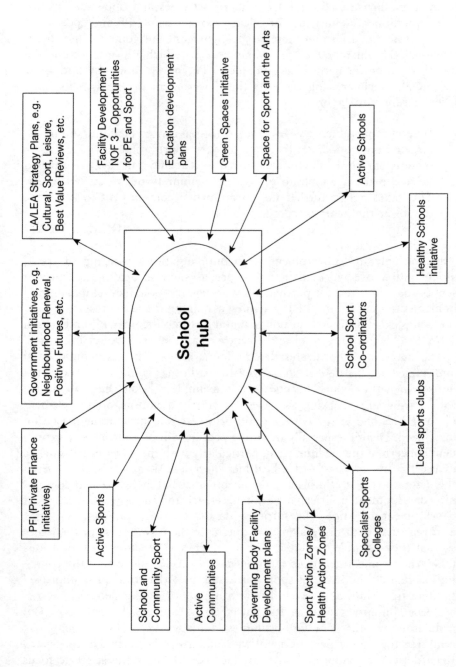

Figure 12.1 Schools as the 'hub site' for joined up policy making involving PE and school sport

talent development scheme, or in engaging disadvantaged and disaffected young people through sport in partnership with community agencies. Within this shift, partnership working is presented as the most effective delivery mechanism. This is a development that has had profound implications for the Physical Education profession, because it is not just extra-curricular sport that is affected, but curricular sport and Physical Education are also implicated in these policy initiatives.

Houlihan (2000: 180) notes that in such densely packed policy spaces the actual position will be one of intense policy competition, where a number of interests are forced to adopt a reactionary stance in relation to policy initiatives and where policy is determined by the balance of exogenous interests. Recent developments have centred PE at the axis of an integrated approach to the provision of sporting opportunities which, in turn, are now driven by broader social policy concerns. Whilst sport policy and development has long since embraced partnership working, both domestically and internationally, partnerships in PE are increasingly being advocated as the way forward (van Deventer 2002) although the composition of these arrangements is of concern to many in the PE profession (Kirk 2002). Partnership in PE and sport can only be successful within a broader and more coherent framework for young people, sport and physical activity (Waring and Warburton 2000: 162). For this to happen the PE profession must first demonstrate a much broader awareness of how sport policy in local areas is being driven by social policy concerns and second more vociferously articulate the potential contribution that PE can make to young people's development.

Making the connection – PE, school sport and social inclusion policies

A Sporting Future for All and its subsequent Action Plan (DCMS 2000, 2001) set out the vision for how education would contribute to the development of young people's sporting opportunities. There are mixed messages regarding the state of PE and school sport. A substantial weight of evidence in recent years contradicts the public perception that PE and sport in schools are in decline (Mason 1995, Roberts 1996, Rowe and Champion 2000). Ironically, the perceived lack of quantity and quality of PE and sport in schools has increased the level of central government attention given to PE and sport. The Labour Government, however, openly contradicted its focus on PE and school sport through the suspension of requirements to deliver the PE curriculum in primary schools in favour of ensuring numeracy and literacy targets could be met. Simply stated, this has meant that time allocated to PE and school sport has often been reduced and the less time young people are exposed to such opportunities, the less likely they are to participate, either in school or elsewhere. PE and school sport, especially in primary schools, currently requires substantial support in order to develop the habitual participation of young people in sport, but those charged with achieving this have not been given the resources to do so. This also brings into stark focus the fact that many young people do not receive their entitlement because schools choose not to provide it and exposes a deep contradiction in current PE and sport policies. This is especially relevant in primary schools where, for the reasons outlined above, opportunities and levels of participation in PE and school sport have significantly declined during that latter part of the 1990s (Rowe and Champion 2000, Warburton 2000). Even so, it is difficult to find primary or secondary schools where there is not some form of extra-curricular activity (Bass and Cale 1999). Despite the attention that extra-curricular activities have received in recent years, they are often limited in scope (Penney and Harris 1997) and only seized upon by or made available to a maximum of one-third of students (Cale 2000). This is of immense concern for current policy and indicates how difficult it is for PE and school sport to meet the social policy agenda. To be socially included an individual must participate, and cannot do so if the access to, or nature of, the opportunity is prohibitive.

Nevertheless, it is possible for schools to play an important role in meeting the competing policy agendas designated to the education profession. Both within and outside of formal curriculum time, a majority of activities have traditionally taken the form of school sport rather than having educational value, with a focus on isolated skill development and representative competition. The drive to a more inclusive curriculum, which incorporates elements of extra-curricular provision, also means that the interrelated concerns of PE and school sport are the initial focus for policies designed to tackle the four key areas of social exclusion, health, crime, education and employment. *A Sporting Future for All* confirms that PE and school sport is an integral component of current sport policy and Prime Minister Tony Blair notes in his foreword to the strategy that this is because 'it is in school where children first get to try sport' (DCMS 2000: 2). The focus on PE and school sport provides a strong message to PE teachers. As Baroness Ashton, Minister for Early Years and School Standards, noted:

> If we can get it right in schools the benefit will be enormous. The positive effects of PE and sport on pupil behaviour and motivation not only reduce the damaging effects of social exclusion but in the long term improve the health of the nation.
>
> (QCA 2001, online)

The Qualifications and Curriculum Authority's (QCA) research into PE and school sport found that regular participation can lead to reduced levels of truancy and improved behaviour (QCA 2001). But once beyond the school gates, opportunities for young people are uneven. Sporting provision takes place within the socio-economic and demographic fabric of the local community and is predominantly dependent on the traditional structures of the voluntary sector that exist within the community. It is important, therefore, that policy makers, especially from traditionally discrete policy arenas, identify the specific elements of PE and school sport's contribution to social inclusion more precisely. Many in PE would like to claim that they teach knowledge, skills and understanding which can be transformed and reproduced beyond the school gate, but this would reflect an unhealthy concern with an attempt to measure the unmeasure-able. Nevertheless, schools must recognise first that their provision can be socially inclusive both through the curriculum and through out-of-school-hours programmes, with little or no extra effort, and second that they are likely to have the initial evidence to demonstrate this. It is important to clarify why this latter point should be the case.

Blair's comment in the front of *A Sporting Future for All* (DCMS 2000) has meant that people who have traditionally not seen the value and future potential PE and school sport have now sat up and realised that the latter has much to offer other policy agendas. The problem is that these same people now think that if their policies aren't working then sport can do the job. Health is potentially the policy area to which PE and school sport can make the best contribution, by engendering life-long participation in sport and physical activity. But it is very difficult for sport to make claims in any policy area if it doesn't have the evidence – and presently that evidence base is limited, despite recent expansion. Calls have been made for sport policies to 'prove' their worth, and that they 'work' (DCMS 1999, Coalter *et al.* 2000, Coalter 2001, Long and Sanderson 2001) in order to ensure that recent injections of funding do not disappear in the future. Recent studies have focused on identifying relevant literature from a range of projects as an evidence base (Coalter 2001) and examining the efficacy of interventionist projects (Leisure Futures 2002, Centre for Leisure Research 2002, Sport England 2002a). Given the directions of 'sport through education' in *A Sporting Future for All*, PE has become the initial focus of sport's social policy remit and it is interesting to note that PE may actually be able to demonstrate its contribution more readily than other sporting agencies. One example of how is presented below.

Previously, schools that have applied for Specialist Sports College status have been able to use the application process to begin to raise standards of provision, initially through an audit that forms the basis of future strategic planning. Specialist schools are raising standards at nearly double the rate of comprehensive schools (Youth Sport Trust 2002), although the precise nature of how standards are being raised and the measure-ment of them requires more explicit clarification. The accountability required of schools with accredited status has ensured that more focus on standards of achievement has taken place. The accreditation required through the Activemark and Sportsmark initiatives would enable similar developments to take place. The Sportsmark/Sportsmark Gold initiative was introduced by Sport England (then the English Sports Council) in 1997 and was followed three years later by Activemark and Activemark Gold. The initiative rewards schools that demonstrate achieved standards in the provision of PE and sport and which recognise community involvement. To achieve the Gold award, all schools must provide two hours of PE in the curriculum, in line with the government statement that young people are entitled to that amount of provision. It is expected that schools involved in applying for the third tranche of New Opportunities Funding (NOF 3) will have carried out audits to provide the requisite data to local education authorities. Furthermore, progression to Gold awards recognises the ongoing development of the provision of opportunities. The initiative also demonstrates the school's performance regarding the nature and extent of the curriculum and extra-curricular activities, competition opportunities for young people, coaching qualifications of teachers and adults other than teachers (AOTTs) and links with local sports clubs. For some, the awards should enable greater communication and improved co-ordination of opportunities in schools and local communities (Waring and Warburton 2000).

Further research could then develop monitoring of key issues which have been associated with raising standards, such as investment in staff development, the use of pupil leaders for younger pupil support, citizenship through volunteering and leadership awards in PE and sport, curriculum enrichment and improved out-of-school-hours provision. Such a focus would enable analysis of the ongoing commitment of schools to, first, raising standards, second, their contribution to sport in the community and third, the continued involvement of key stakeholders in the organisation of the previous two points. Through the acquisition of accreditation, schools are then able to demonstrate how they have raised standards (supporting the entitlement of two hours of high quality PE and sport each week, within and beyond the curriculum). Furthermore, they can demonstrate how they have achieved higher standards across the whole school and in the community through PE, sport and other forms of structured activity (as set out in their development plans). More links are needed between the work of Sport England and community development work in local authorities in order to extend opportunities for young people beyond the school gate into communities. It is highly debatable as to whether sports development officers (SDOs) see community development as part of their job, but if schools can demonstrate a strategic approach to evaluating the progress of PE and sport they may force local agencies into providing more sustainable opportunities. To get young people (re)engaged is immensely challenging. But many communities are not aware of the resources they have and there is a need for a greater degree of sport literacy, a responsibility that SDOs are either unable or unwilling to take on. SDOs don't have as strong an appreciation for Physical Education as they could have and this requires PE departments to be proactive in demonstrating their achievements within and beyond the curriculum. It only requires the head teacher to be unenthusiastic about sport – because they favour the arts or technology, for example – for the potential to ensure that young people receive their entitlement of two hours of high quality PE and sport per week to be immediately hijacked.

These developments can hardly be called a 'hidden agenda' but if PE is to fulfil the social policy remit ascribed to it, those working in the profession must be increasingly aware of and make connections with other policy developments. Social inclusion through PE and sport can be achieved in a number of ways. PE and sport have the potential to increase individual confidence and self-esteem but they can also contribute to the development of local social networks through the development of new volunteer initiatives or sports leadership awards, designed to complement the Community and Junior Sports Leader Awards (CSLA/JSLA), which have been prominent in recent years. Notwithstanding arguments that question whether this is within the remit of schools, such developments can only be achieved if schools adopt an approach that proactively engages with the local community and solicits something similar in return. It is this engagement that provides the material basis for the development of partnerships, be that in the Specialist Sports Colleges, in non-specialist schools involved with sporting and community agencies or in local authorities, now increasingly required to use the school as a central focus for community sport development. Given the much sharper focus on PE and school sport under 'New' Labour, there is a question over whether the PE profession is ready to accept the widening brief of the physical educationalist in return for the increased funding for PE and school sport that is available. Inevitably, change is not a homogenous process and tends to depend on the individuals involved at local levels of provision.

Specialist Sports Colleges and School Sport Co-ordinators: Partnerships toward social inclusion?

Perhaps the best summary of the current relationship between PE and sport is encapsulated in the phrase favoured by the British Association of Advisors and Lecturers in Physical Education (BAALPE) – 'Quality PE produces quality sports-people'. In light of the BAALPE phrase, it is worth considering the emergence of SSCs, which can be considered exemplars of the government's thinking on the need for partnerships in current policy. Located at the hub of a family of feeder primary and secondary schools SSCs are the:

regional focal points for excellence in physical education and community sport, extending links between families of schools, sports bodies and communities, sharing resources and developing and spreading good practice, helping to provide a structure through which young people can progress to careers in PE and sport.

(OFSTED/YST 2000: vii)

Schools are rushing headlong into acquiring specialist status, with 20 per cent of all schools now advertising themselves as a Specialist School (Hackett 2001). For many, the incentive of acquiring specialist status is the additional funding that accompanies it, and for SSCs the funding has to support a number of broad aims. Houlihan (2000: 185) has identified the operation of SSCs in which individual schools accept that they are obliged to expand opportunities for community use of school facilities and also target under-represented participation groups. In addition, schools have been prompted to formalise links with local authorities and governing bodies of sport, increase the range and quality of sports coaching, improve the quantity and quality of competition and develop community sport.

Whilst SSCs have enthusiastically embraced the need to develop local networks in communities and with other schools (Houlihan 2000, OFSTED/YST 2000), partnership working in PE and school sport has also been the source of conflict, tension and frustration. In contrast to local authority and sport specific development officers, PE teachers have traditionally been less favourably disposed to accepting multi-agency working, often because workloads can easily spiral out of control and demoralisation sets in, because of imposition of policies over which they have little control. More pragmatically, it is not possible for some SSCs to work with all of their feeder schools. An example is the SSC located in a rural area, which has seventeen feeder primary schools, some of which have particularly under-developed PE provision. In this area, the physical barriers presented by the local infrastructure threaten the move toward socially inclusive PE and school sport. Having entered into this arrangement, the SSC has not been able to share the resources in a mutually beneficial way with all its stakeholders, which has inevitably created underlying tensions due to the lack of obvious outcomes for some partners.

Where partnerships have been developed carefully and co-operatively, however, considerable benefits have accrued and the range of opportunities for young people has expanded. It is also important to contextualise these developments within the overall remit of Specialist School – the raising of school standards. Furthermore, Sports Colleges are responsible to the Department for Education and Skills (DfES), and not to sporting agencies. Notwithstanding these concerns, SSCs are at the nexus of three policy sectors: talent identification and development, education and the requirement to raise standards in the whole family of schools, and the development of school/community sport (Houlihan 2000: 183–4). This inevitably leads to tension and conflict between individuals representing each of the sectors, and requires prioritisation. Where this occurs, there are numerous examples of good practice (Youth Sport Trust 2002) although it is in the area of community development (and by association, meeting social inclusion agendas) that SSCs seem least able to demonstrate what it is they have actually impacted upon. The management of priorities has become the responsibility of heads of PE, directors of sport and, in terms of addressing social exclusion, School Sport Co-ordinators

The aim of the SSCo scheme is to increase sports opportunities for young people through co-ordinated PE, school sport and out-of-hours learning activities that effectively link with local community sport facilities and development programmes, particularly in deprived areas. The six areas of work for SSCos are strategic planning, primary liaison, school–community links, out-of-school-hours learning, coaching and leadership, and raising standards. Co-ordinators are experienced PE teachers, released by funding from the Sport England Lottery Fund. The basis for the work of co-ordinators is the preferred partnership model (Figure 12.2).

The preferred partnership model can be summarised in three parts: first, the local education authority (LEA) identifies an experienced teacher, preferably within a Specialist Sports College, to act as the Partnership Development Manager (PDM) to support and manage the development of the local school partnership. This teacher is taken off the teaching timetable for approximately two days a week. Each PDM is charged with working with four to six partner secondary schools (depending on local circumstances) and within each of these the SSCo, also released for about two days per week, co-ordinates the development in the school and the associated family of primary schools. Third, each SSCo would work with up to five primary schools in which the Primary Link Teacher (PLT), normally the PE curriculum co-ordinator, ensures that the programmes are delivered within their own school and that appropriate links are developed with other schools. Each of these teachers would be taken off the teaching timetable for about twelve days a year (Sport England 2001). A critical issue for the future is the extent to which PDMs will be able lead local partnerships. PDMs are to be full-time officers in the near future, which possibly indicates that as the scheme rolls out nationwide by 2007, there will be a need for larger clusters, incorporating as many as eight secondary and forty primary schools.

A significant factor in the scheme is whether those involved are able to develop the model locally. It was quickly apparent to LEAs that the rigid implementation of the model was not possible, based as it is on the assumption that co-ordinator schemes will predominantly take place in deprived areas, and this has been latterly acknowledged by funding partners. 'The model must be seen as the starting point only, not a prescriptive template' (Sport England 2002b: 4). In itself, this presents a problem which policy makers, not just LEAs, must deal with in order to support

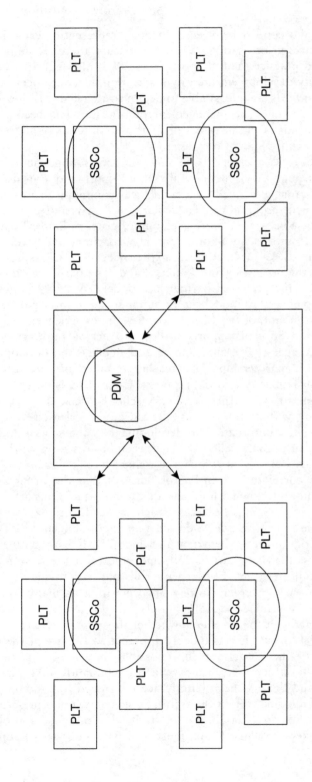

Figure 12.2 Preferred partnership model

Source: Youth Sport Trust 2000: section 1.3.

Key: PDM – Partnership Development Manager; SSCo – School Sports Co-ordinator; PLT – Primary Link Teacher.

the deliverers. In areas where, for example, there have initially been fewer SSCs designated (such as Hampshire) or where there are many more primary schools than on the preferred model, prioritisation takes place and it is unclear to many what are the criteria that define allocation of resources. Despite exhortations to 'engage all the schools involved' (Sport England 2002b: 5), the initial implementation of the scheme has struggled to come to terms with the envisaged holistic planning and management structures required to meet the aims of the programme. Some schools are unwilling to get involved, fearing increased workloads for little immediate return, and there is lack of understanding regarding the programme at senior management level, particularly in primary schools where head teachers are more concerned with resourcing work toward numeracy and literacy targets. Despite this, it is claimed that:

> It is impossible not to conclude that the SSCO [work] has made giant leaps in its first year and there are many lessons that can be passed on to future Partnerships and to the PE and sport system in general.
> (Sport England 2002b: 4)

Quite what these 'leaps' have been is open to debate given that many of the exemplars of good practice often have caveats of caution attached to them. More prudently, the 'lessons' learnt are not new ones – rather they are long-term issues in partnership working, contextualised in PE rather than sport or even business, which could have been avoided with more careful planning and greater education and training for those involved. The lesson of 'engaging [all] the schools' demonstrates the need to set out clearly roles and responsibilities, to involve all partners at every level of decision-making, to share good practice and inform people of developments (Sport England 2002b: 5). There is little here that would shock local authority SDOs. Co-ordinators have taken on a strategic role, enabling provision to take place, yet training has followed in an (often locally initiated) ad-hoc mode rather than having been proactively planned. The need for greater support in writing development plans is identified as one element of future lessons in enabling co-ordinators to 'make the transition'. LEAs have stepped in to fill the gaps recently but it was interesting to note that how to obtain and plan the administrative and training support required was not on the agenda at the 2002 National Conference for Co-ordinators.

Whilst highly laudable, the scheme and its implementation have been hindered first by the short-sightedness of policy makers responsible for the scheme. The management and provision of training programmes has been neglected at the expense of the rush to implement the scheme. Furthermore, the scheme has been hindered by shortages of teachers, despite claims to the contrary (Sport England 2002b: 7), in some areas making the goal of supporting the delivery of PE through the scheme somewhat redundant. In addition, the use of part-time members of staff, supply teachers and specialist coaches as replacements for experienced teachers, viewed as an example of good practice in the national evaluation summary (Sport England 2002b: 7–8), has brought into question the ability of some schools to demonstrate continuity in the delivery of their curriculum. The employment of Specialist Link teachers has attempted to nullify these concerns and provides added value to many schools involved, in that the former can help to train and develop colleagues, manage new projects and enhance the curriculum through their specialist role. With the funding of these posts limited at the time of writing to a maximum of three years, the sustainability of their contribution remains in doubt. The solution to these issues is for the Department for Education and Skills to provide Standards Funding for the schemes as quickly as possible. Quite how willing they are to take on this commitment is open to question.

David Moffett, Chief Executive of Sport England from January until December 2002, was enthused by the scheme, particularly its potential to link schools into broader sports development programmes, and he promised a co-ordinator in every secondary school in England (Moffett 2002). Whether Moffett's successor, Roger Draper, will support his predecessor's views remains an open question. Three factors will determine the long-term success of the scheme. First, the ability of co-ordinators to strategically plan inter- and intra-school competition will inevitably favour some at the expense of others. How this is negotiated, managed and implemented will determine the extent to which partner schools view the benefits as positive and, consequently, remain involved. Second, local sporting infrastructures do not offer remotely homogenous exit routes into all the sports and the creation of new local clubs is dependent on the traditional backbone of sport, the volunteers in local communities. This is not the direct responsibility of schools, which must concentrate on building upon existing networks within their schools and seek to maximise opportunities with local clubs; rather it requires the solicited engagement of relevant local agencies. Third, and much more pertinent to everyday PE and school sport, whether sufficient financial or human resources are available to implement the scheme nationwide remains to be seen. This issue has also recently been compounded. The government spending review in the summer of 2002 committed increased funding for the scheme, but allocated it to the Department for Education and Skills for two years starting in April 2004. It was not clear whether Sport England will get any funding from April 2003 for the scheme. Prevarication on funding issues has resulted in discontent and uncertainty for many of those initially involved. If future funding is the responsibility of the DfES then a sensible timescale is required which phases out Sport England's involvement. All schemes starting in 2004 thereafter will then become the responsibility of the DfES.

Notwithstanding the fumbling of senior policy makers, the co-ordinator scheme is worthy of reflection as it can be identified along with SSCs as being at the forefront of addressing social exclusion through PE and school sport. At a superficial level the provision of opportunities develops methods to permit participation by a greater number of young people and the potential for the scheme is strong. But, as Sue Campbell, the advisor to the DCMS and DfES has noted with Malcolm Tungatt, there are many more considerations:

> There needs to be a clear goal to work towards in order to prioritise effectively. This is development work. Making certain schools work together is not always easy. With extra funding and flexibility it is possible to employ more staff to help release teachers and share certain roles. However, the increased success brought increased pressures, as more schools wanted to join the partnership. It is important to keep the partnerships to a realistic and manageable size in order to maximise their efforts. Each individual must learn to prioritise and to say no when they need to or they risk jeopardising the work of the entire partnership. Partnerships are not easy to manage. They require collaboration, understanding, patience and vision. Schools and their school sport co-ordinators should sit at the heart of their communities.
>
> (Campbell and Tungatt 2002)

If partnerships are to become successful and schools to become the focal points of local communities, then it is essential that local authorities and voluntary sector sporting agencies are aware of their work. Whether localities possess the capabilities to make the connections is doubtful unless they are properly resourced. One model has been advocated which may facilitate improved local connections and increased sustainability for local sporting opportunities. It is to that model that the chapter now turns.

Socially inclusive PE and sport – 'sport (through) education'?

If PE and school sport are to be inclusive they must be managed in such a way as to make connections in the curriculum with other sporting organisations or agencies. Penney and Chandler (2000a, 2000b) recognise the need to proactively shape policy developments and advocate four strands of an alternative National Curriculum for PE: first, movement and physical literacy; second, physical activity, health and fitness; third, competition and co-operation; and fourth, to make activities a challenge. These strands have a much greater degree of relevance than current practice for the sport/social policy axis and would engender a greater degree of relevance for PE's potential contribution within it. Although this may prove difficult in areas with poorer sporting infrastructures, local communities provide much of the materials through which schools can enhance their provision. Irrespective of this, a more flexible approach to the PE curriculum has potential. Currently, the SSCO scheme is advocating primary school festivals as a way of developing connections within the curriculum and into community development:

A strategically planned festival will offer:

- continuity/sustainability in a school and community context
- have links with other partners – that will take time to develop/ negotiate
- the opportunity to deliver more than one SSCO programme outcome

(Arnold and Wolsey 2002)

The worth of festivals can be seen if they are integrated into more connected curriculum activities. Research in the UK has focused on whether the model of Sport Education may be a more appropriate way through which to implement the present National Curriculum (Almond 1997, Kinchin *et al.* 2001, MacPhail *et al.* 2002). Sport Education, a pedagogical model/framework designed by Daryl Siedentop during the 1980s and early 1990s, has been advocated as a model which can meet the challenge of PE set out at the 1999 World Summit on Physical Education:

Quality physical education ... (is) the most effective and inclusive means of providing all children, whatever their ability/disability, sex, age, cultural race/ethnicity, religious or social background, with the skills, attitudes, knowledge and understanding for life long participation in sport and physical activity.

(cited by Penney et al. 2002: 71)

Penney *et al.* (2002) anticipate that Sport Education will be of interest to many outside the Physical Education community but accept that further development of the model is required. It might also be suggested that promoting the efficacy of the model to other policy communities is the greatest challenge if the connections between PE and sport advocated by government are to be achieved. Briefly, Sport Education offers an alternative to current methods of teaching PE employed in the UK. It utilises a seasonal format for units of work, the formulation of teams for each unit with pupils adopting a variety of roles, teaching and learning directed to formal sporting engagement, a culminating event, such as a festival, record keeping by the team as a basis for feedback and a celebration of the festive nature of sport (Siedentop 1994). As Penney *et al.* (2002: 57) note, the model exhibits commonalities in both the way in which curriculum experiences are designed to correspond with experiences in the contexts of institutionalised sport, and in the ways in which experiences have been designed to be different from institutionalised sport.

At first glance, Sport Education offers a range of opportunities to those in PE and other policy communities concerned with the role of PE and school sport in the sports development process. With a focus that goes beyond the current concerns of skill development and competition, the model has the potential to engender more positive lifelong attitudes to health and physical activity. Elements such as celebrating the festive nature of sport can be linked with citizenship or Personal and Social Education (PSE) lessons, focusing on increasing the knowledge of young people about the rules and values of sport and thereby also enhancing cross-curricula developments. Facilitating the development of young people in roles of coaches, officials or administrators can enhance linkages, in the first instance, with current sports leadership awards, and potentially sports coaching qualifications. Overall, the model has the potential to engage pupils of all ages and offers the chance to facilitate the development of enthusiastic, competent and literate sports people who can carry their knowledge and understanding with them into their communities and later life.

Notwithstanding the promise that Sport Education holds, it is important to be realistic about the capacity of PE and sport to affect society more generally. Penney *et al.* (2002: 60) assert that the model could only offer students 'temporary' inclusion. This is particularly the case if the model is developed within current PE and sport structures in the UK. Whilst Sport Education offers improved benefits within the school environment (Kinchin *et al.* 2001, MacPhail *et al.* 2002) the transition from school to club or community sport is often the point at which young people experience disengagement from the potential benefits of participation or performance and leads to drop-out. In reviewing the evidence Penney *et al.* (2002: 62) comment that there is very little evidence to suggest that advocates of Sport Education have considered the mismatch between the dominating values and interests within the school and the actual practice of community sport. If this is related to current policy, the majority of SSCOs are currently located in areas of social or sporting deprivation. Young people may often be provided with opportunities in schools that are unsustainable beyond the school gates. It is too early to comment on whether the potential of Sport Education can challenge the conventions of PE in the UK, although it holds far greater potential than the current curriculum and has the potential to challenge the values and methods through which PE teachers are currently educated. If Sport Education is to challenge the conventions governing sport, however, there is a need to engage on a variety of levels with policy makers from sport and areas of social policy. One would question the ability of Sport Education to make the connections in its local communities, especially as in many localities the structures to support the work in schools are not in place or, if they are, often lack sustainability. At the very least, in areas in which Sport Education is being developed, the relevant sporting agencies in the community, in particular sports development officers and local junior clubs, must have some form of knowledge and/or involvement in order for them to understand their role in extending the Sport Education experience into non-school contexts. Whether those working in sport policy and development are willing to support the developments in schools is perhaps the defining factor in whether Sport Education can make the connections required in the current sports strategy.

Conclusion

PE and school sport is now located at the nexus of a complex and overcrowded policy arena. Competing sectoral concerns often overwhelm PE departments, whose provision becomes less effective with regard to meeting broader policy remits, and whose members become increasingly demoralised as a result. The profession faces immense challenges but has the potential to become more active and vocal in what it can contribute to and achieve, particularly in other policy arenas, with little or no extra effort. The biggest problem is to convince key policy makers of the wider benefits of PE and school sport. There is not nearly enough funding to meet the agendas of competing sectoral interests, although developments outlined in this chapter indicated that some change has occurred. It is important to show how all the initiatives outlined are benefiting the schools and communities. This is necessary in order to gain more funding and make PE and school sport a greater priority within government policy. Schools are more able to contribute to this than they think and it us up to policy makers to design strategies and support networks to enable them to realise their potential.

The further expansion of the SSC programme and the SSCo scheme will inevitably lead to increased partnership working and it is debatable as to whether the profession can, or indeed, wishes to, change its working practices sufficiently, in order to take advantage of the resources that are available to develop local opportunities. Irrespective of the difficulties this presents, the support of local agencies can enhance the curriculum within schools. If this, in turn, presents problems and challenges PE teachers, one may point to the benefits of a more politically aware profession, able to manage the opportunities that increased support and funding will present, and better able to demonstrate the value of what they do to the competing policy arenas. The variety of data produced by schools to achieve accreditation can be used by partner agencies to demonstrate the value of engagement in PE and school sport. Sport Education has been identified as the model with the greatest potential to provide sustained evidence of the socially inclusive nature of PE and school sport. Despite the reservations identified in this chapter and elsewhere, it's time to consider whether local sports development networks can support Sport Education, if sport is to really sustain socially inclusive polices for young people. More broadly, the PE profession must be challenged to demonstrate a much greater political and strategic awareness of sport and social policy, for if it fails to do so it also risks failing to provide young people with the greater range of opportunities that could become available to them.

Acknowledgement

I am very grateful to Steve Padfield of Sport England's Active Schools team for his perceptive comments on an earlier draft of this chapter and for the use of Figure 12.1.

Reflective questions

1 How are the differences between PE and sport articulated within your PE department and are these differences reflected in your practice?
2 Is it necessary for the members of the PE profession to develop knowledge of other policy areas such as health or social policy?
3 What is the nature and extent of support for PE and school sport from your school management? What are the reasons for your answer?
4 Consider how the profile of, and support to, PE and school sport could be enhanced by partnerships with other schools and local agencies.
5 Too many initiatives? What can be done to streamline and simplify the support available to PE and school sport?
6 What are the likely barriers to more schools implementing Sport Education?

References

Almond, L. (1997) *Physical Education in Schools, Second Edition*, London: Kogan Page.
Bass, D. and Cale, L. (1999) 'Promoting Physical Activity Through the Extra-curricular Programme', *European Journal of Physical Education* 4: 45–64.
Cale, L. (2000) 'A Whole School Approach to Physical Activity Promotion', *European Physical Education Review* 6: 71–90.
Campbell, S. and Tungatt, M. (2002) 'Transformation', in Sport England workshop presented at the School Sport Co-ordinators Conference, East Midlands Conference Centre, 14 March.
Capel, S. (2000) 'Physical Education and Sport', in S. Capel and S. Piotrowski (eds.), *Issues in Physical Education*, London: Routledge: 131–43.
Centre for Leisure Research (2002) *Count Me In: The Dimensions of Social Inclusion Through Culture and Sport: A Report for the Department of Culture, Media and Sport*, Leeds Metropolitan University, online, available HTTP: <http://www.lmu.ac.uk/ces/lss/research/countmein.pdf> accessed 7 June 2002.
Coalter, F. with Taylor, J. and Allison, M. (2000) *The Role of Sport in Regenerating Deprived Urban Areas*, Edinburgh: Scottish Executive Central Research Unit.
Coalter, F. (2001) *Realising the Potential of Cultural Services: The Case for Sport*, Research Briefing 12.3, online, available HTTP: <http://www.lganet.gov.uk/index.htm> accessed 18 January 2002.

DCMS (Department for Culture, Media and Sport) (1999) *PAT 10: Report to the Social Exclusion Unit – The Contribution Arts and Sport can make to Social Inclusion*, London: HMSO.

DCMS (Department for Culture, Media and Sport) (2000) *A Sporting Future for All*, London: DCMS.

DCMS (Department for Culture, Media and Sport) (2001) *A Sporting Future for All, the Government's Plan for Sport*, London: DCMS.

DCMS (Department for Culture, Media and Sport) (2002a) *The Coaching Task Force: Final Report*, London: DCMS.

DCMS (Department for Culture, Media and Sport) (2002b) *A Sporting Future for All: The Government's Plan for Sport: Annual Report 2001–2*, London: DCMS.

Hackett, G. (2001) 'The Schools with Something Special', *The Sunday Times*, 25 November: 11.

Houlihan, B. (2000) 'Sporting Excellence, Schools and Sports Development: The Politics of Crowded Policy Spaces', *European Physical Education Review* 6, 2: 171–93.

Houlihan, B. and White, A. (2002) *The Politics of Sports Development: Development of Sport or Development Through Sport?* London: Routledge.

Kinchin, G., Penney, D. and Clarke, G. (2001) 'Teaching the National Curriculum Physical Education: Try Sport Education', *British Journal of Teaching Physical Education* 32, 2: 41–4.

Kirk, D. (2002) 'Quality Physical Education through Partnerships: A Response to Karel van Deventer', Paper presented at the 12th Commonwealth International Sport Conference, 19–23 July, Manchester, UK.

Leisure Futures (2002) *Positive Futures: A Review of Impact and Good Practice*, London: Sport England.

Long, J. and Sanderson, I. (2001) 'The Social Benefits of Sport: Where's the Proof?' in C. Gratton and I. Henry (eds), *Sport in the City: The Role of Sport in Economic and Social Regeneration*, London: Routledge.

MacPhail, A., Kirk, D. and Kinchin, G. (2002) 'Promoting Sport Education through Team Affiliation', Paper presented at the 12th Commonwealth International Sport Conference, 19–23 July, Manchester, UK.

Mason, V. (1995) *Young People and Sport National Survey, 1994*, London: Sports Council.

Moffett, D. (2002) 'The Business of Sports Development', Closing Address to the 11th Annual Sports Development Seminar, Nottingham, 3–5 April, 2002.

OFSTED/YST (Office for Standards in Education/Youth Sports Trust) (2000) *Sports Colleges: The First Two Years*, London: The Stationery Office.

Penney, D. and Harris, J. (1997) 'Extra-curricular Physical Education: More of the Same for the More Able', *Sport, Education and Society* 2: 41–54.

Penney, D. and Chandler, T. (2000a) 'A Curriculum with Connections?' *British Journal of Teaching Physical Education* 31, 2: 37–40.

Penney, D. and Chandler, T. (2000b) 'Physical Education: What Future(s)?' *Sport, Education and Society* 5: 71–87.

Penney, D., Clarke, G. and Kinchin, G. (2002) 'Developing Physical Education as a Connective Specialism: Is Sport Education the Answer?' *Sport, Education and Society* 7: 55–64.

QCA (Qualifications and Curriculum Authority) (2001) 'PE and School Sport Project', online, available HTTP: <http://www.qca.org.uk/ca/subjects/pe/pess.asp> accessed 14 March 2002.

Roberts, K. (1996) 'Young People, Schools, Sport and Government Policy', *Sport, Education and Society* 1: 47–57.

Rowe, N. and Champion, R (2000) *Young People and Sport National Survey, 1999*, London: Sport England.

Siedentop, D. (1994) *Sport Education: Quality PE through Positive Sport Experiences*, Champaign, Ill.: Human Kinetics.

Sport England (2001) *School Sport Co-ordinators Report: Consultation Report on the National Placement Strategy, August 2001*, London: Sport England.

Sport England (2002a) *Active Communities Projects: A Review of Impact and Good Practice*, London: Sport England.

Sport England (2002b) *School Sport Co-ordinators: Making the Difference: Initial Summary of Phase 1 Projects*, online, available HTTP: <www.sportengland.org> accessed May 2002.

van Deventer, K. (2002) 'Quality Physical Education through Partnerships', Paper presented at the 12th Commonwealth International Sport Conference, 19–23 July, Manchester, UK.

Warburton, P. (2000) 'Initial Teacher Training: The Preparation of Primary School Teachers in Physical Education', *British Journal of Teaching Physical Education* 4: 6–8.

Waring, M. and Warburton, P. (2000) 'Working with the Community: A Necessary Evil or a Positive Change of Direction', in S. Capel and S. Piotrowski (eds), *Issues in Physical Education*, London: Routledge, 159–69.

Youth Sport Trust (2000) *Guidelines for School Sport Co-ordinators*, Loughborough, Youth Sport Trust.

Youth Sport Trust (2002) *Best Practice in Sports Colleges: A Guide to School Improvement*, Loughborough, Youth Sport Trust.

Index

References for figures and tables are in *italics*; those for notes are followed by n